Witness

A History of Oak Hill College 1932–2000

Witness to the Word

A History of Oak Hill College 1932–2000

Rudolf Heinze & David Wheaton

First published in 2002 by Paternoster Press

08 07 06 05 04 03 02 7 6 5 4 3 2 1

Paternoster Press is an imprint of Authentic Media,
P.O. Box 300, Carlisle, Cumbria, CA3 0QS, UK
and
P.O. Box 1047, Waynesboro, GA 30830-2047, USA

Website: www.paternoster-publishing.com

British Library Cataloguing in Publication Data
A catalogue record for this book is available from the British Library

ISBN 1-84227-163-6

Cover Design by FourNineZero
Typeset by WestKey Ltd, Falmouth, Cornwall
Printed in Great Britain by Cox & Wyman, Reading

Contents

Foreword

The four years I spent as full-time lecturer at Oak Hill College from 1966–70 were among the most formative of my life and ministry. At the age of thirty-one I was younger than at least one-third of the students and was therefore able to enjoy both the pleasures of the football field and the responsibilities of the staff room. I blush when I remember that I used to attend the Monday staff meetings in a tracksuit with my football boots by my side, waiting impatiently for the meeting to end so I could run out to train with the students! Prebendary Maurice Wood, the principal, later to become Bishop of Norwich, was very patient with me. Along with countless 'Old Oaks' I am so grateful for the role that Oak Hill has played in my personal and theological formation as well as my spiritual development.

Rudi Heinze and David Wheaton have produced a thorough, well-written history of Oak Hill, offering a valuable description of its life and ministry over the years. Serious historians of the Church of England will be very grateful for their labours. In particular, this book will be a great resource to those who wish to deepen their understanding of the crucial contribution of evangelicalism to the Church of England over recent decades.

As with other theological colleges, Oak Hill has had to withstand many challenges. I remember some ten years ago, when the synod came within a whisker of taking accreditation away from the college, how Oak Hill fought bravely and fiercely to correct the impression that its ministry was finished and prove that its distinctive contribution could strengthen the church. With the strong support of its parent body, the Kingham Hill Trust, and its many supporters, Oak Hill recovered from that shaking and is the stronger for it.

Over the years Oak Hill has clearly and proudly maintained its identity as an evangelical college, providing solid ministerial training with a steadfast commitment to the authority of Scripture. At the same time its teaching staff have been and are committed to the historic Anglican tradition, enabling Oak Hill to make a major contribution to the wider church.

The college has a wonderful motto: 'For we do not preach ourselves, but Jesus Christ as Lord, and ourselves as your servants for Jesus' sake' (2 Cor. 4:5). It is my fervent prayer and expectation that God will richly bless Oak Hill as it continues to live up to its motto in its work of preparing men and women to serve God as devoted pastors and effective preachers of the gospel of Jesus Christ.

The Most Revd and Rt Hon. Dr George Carey,
Archbishop of Canterbury
February 2002

Introduction

In his 1922 New Year letter to the prayer union of Kingham Hill School Charles Baring Young, the founder of Oak Hill College, wrote:

> It is possible, doubtless, to play the part of a guide and teacher of others, and to lead them in the ways of wisdom and knowledge to a considerable extent by the torchlight of our own learning and accomplishments; but this is not what is meant by the apostolic injunction to shine as lights in the world. The light within us comes from above, and is not to be displayed for any purpose of self-glorification, but as witnesses for Him whose name we bear.[1]

Although he wrote this a decade before Oak Hill was established, at a time when he had no thought of founding a theological college, the college that was to emerge as the result of his vision has throughout its history sought to be a witness for the Word made flesh. Its motto has long been 2 Corinthians 4:5: 'For we do not preach ourselves, but Jesus Christ as Lord, and ourselves as your servants for Jesus' sake.' The college was established to train effective witnesses to the Word and in order to do so it has sought to be a witness in teaching, community life and outreach.

---

[1] A.F. Jarvis, *Charles Baring Young of Daylesford 1850–1928: His Life and Work*, p. 126.

Oak Hill was founded at a time when great changes were taking place in British church and society. Throughout its existence the college has had to adjust to rapid and often radical changes in the environment in which it has sought to carry out its mission. It has also had to adjust to changes in educational philosophies and methods as well as administrative changes in the agencies that supervised and validated theological education in church and state. Its theological position has been challenged by new scholarship and changing cultural values. It has been misrepresented, misunderstood and often unfairly attacked from the outside. For many people the label 'conservative evangelical' means unthinking, non-academic, bigoted, closed-minded and un-Anglican. As is clearly documented in this study these epithets certainly do not apply to Oak Hill, yet misrepresentation has led to some very serious threats to its continued existence, which it has survived only by the grace of God.

Oak Hill has also been confronted with internal divisions and has had to adjust to a growing diversity within the evangelical tradition. At times it seemed unlikely to survive, so the fact that it is about to celebrate its seventieth birthday is a testimony to God's provision for his people, an important part being the able and dedicated leaders whose particular gifts were precisely what the college needed at each stage in its history. Although they differed significantly in their personalities and gifts, each made a vital contribution that was essential at the time they were called to lead.

After initial chapters dealing with Charles Baring Young and his world, as well as the four-year history of the 'test school' that preceded the establishment of the college in 1932, a chapter has been devoted to the administration of each of the six principals who have led Oak Hill in the past seven decades. We have also included 'personality profiles' to illustrate how the college has sought to fulfil its mandate, and ask the understanding of the many other faithful witnesses to the Word from among the 2,000 who have entered the college during its first seventy years whose stories we should love to tell, but which space prevents. Since the history of Oak Hill is inextricably intertwined with what was happening in the wider world during the twentieth century, throughout the book we shall be commenting on the changes that were taking place in church and society, how they affected the college, and how it responded. Our narrative ends by seeking to isolate the ongoing themes of the college's history and the potential for the future. We do so with the realization that just as the past was filled with surprises, the future is equally unpredictable. However, we are confident that in so far as the college continues to be a witness to the Word in the sense in which the founder understood the dominical injunction, it will be able to meet each of the challenges of the future as it has those of the past.

We cannot conclude this introduction without expressing our gratitude to those who have been unstinting in their help while we have been compiling this history. The Kingham Hill trustees and college council have granted free access to their records, and many present and former members of the staff and student body have given us interviews and provided information. Others have taken the trouble to read through the first draft of the book and have made helpful suggestions, which we have attempted to incorporate. To mention individuals would be invidious, but when those concerned read these words we trust they will know how much they have our gratitude. We also hope that those mentioned by surname only after their first introduction will understand that we have had to do this in the interests of economy. The only exception we must make is to thank Wendy Bell, Librarian, and Peter Wood, Development Officer, at Oak Hill for their unfailing assistance and encouragement, and Margaret Gingell, without whose painstaking labours the typescript would never have left the word processor.

1

The Founder and his World (1850–1928)

> There is a deep stirring of men's minds at the present time in connection with problems, scientific and religious; yet with all this there is a lamentable spirit of indifference with regard to practical religion ... In politics and industry there are serious matters of dispute, and men of evil will whose avowed object is to stir up strife. In the religious world men's minds are upset with increasing force by the assaults of superstition and unbelief ... You may live to see some revolutionary changes in the existing order of things.[1]

Charles Baring Young wrote these words the year before he died, also the year before the so-called test school that preceded the establishment of Oak Hill College was opened at Bohun Lodge. His comments on church and society at the end of his life reveal how much change had occurred during his lifetime. The faith that had motivated his life's work and to which he was devoted seemed under serious threat, and the society he had known during much of his life had changed radically and in ways that he could not possibly have approved. As he looked to the future there was every reason to believe that the potential 'revolutionary changes in the existing order of things', which he suggested the old boys of Kingham Hill might experience in their lifetime, would further undermine the values of the world he had known. The country was entering a new era and the new college was to be established

---

[1] Ibid., pp. 133–4.

in an environment that differed radically from that which had existed when Baring Young was born.

The year after Baring Young's birth a religious census revealed that approximately sixty-one per cent of the population of England and Wales attended a worship service on the census Sunday. Although the compiler of the census expressed dismay over the large numbers of people who did not attend, the census provides evidence of the strength of Christianity in the mid-nineteenth century.[2] The Christian faith permeated society to such a degree that Adrian Hastings has described England 'in the mid-Victorian age' as 'possibly one of the most consciously religious societies that ever existed'.[3] The age was in many ways dominated by the Christian tradition with which the Baring Young family identified. The nineteenth century has been labelled 'the evangelical century'[4] and at the time Baring Young was born the evangelical movement was 'the strongest force in British life'.[5] The Baring Young family belonged to that branch of the evangelical movement known as Anglican evangelicals, because they had remained within the established church when the Methodists left to form a new denomination after the death of John Wesley.

From the beginning the movement attracted wealthy and well-connected laymen whose commitment to the Christian faith led them to campaign vigorously for reform in church and society. They also gave generously of their personal fortunes to provide for the dispossessed and the victims of injustice in their society. The

---

[2] Herbert Schlossberg, *The Silent Revolution and the Making of Victorian England*, p. 287. Schlossberg believes it is probable that even a higher percentage attended and that attendance at worship actually increased in the years following the census.

[3] Adrian Hastings, *A History of English Christianity 1920–1990*, p. 34.

[4] D.W. Bebbington, *Evangelicalism in Modern Britain*, p. 149.

[5] Owen Chadwick, *The Victorian Church*, part 1, p. 5. A more recent study comments: 'In retrospect what is remarkable in urban Britain in the nineteenth century is the extent to which a predominantly evangelical pietism managed to spread its values and preoccupations far beyond the doors of the churches it controlled.' David Hempton, *Religion and Political Culture in Britain and Ireland*, p. 141.

so-called Clapham Sect, which included William Wilberforce, is the best-known example of Christian laymen dedicating their lives and fortunes to the service of others. This tradition of upper-class Christians given to the service of the less fortunate was to be a prominent characteristic of Anglican evangelicalism in the Victorian period. The Baring Youngs were one of those upper-class Victorian families, and Oak Hill College has throughout its history been a beneficiary of that long-standing evangelical tradition.

Charles Edward Baring Young was descended on his father's side from a prominent banking family. His grandmother was the daughter of the founder of the very successful banking house of Baring Brothers. His mother Elizabeth's family had Puritan roots. One of her ancestors was John Winthrop, the first governor of the Massachusetts Bay Colony, and another, Stephen Winthrop, had served as a colonel in Cromwell's army during the Civil War. Charles Baring Young, the founder's father, was a very successful businessman, entering the family banking house and eventually becoming a partner and a director of the Royal Exchange Insurance Company. He married Elizabeth in 1843 at the age of forty-two and Charles Edward was born seven years later, the middle child between an older sister, Margaret Lucia, and a younger brother, Arthur William. A.F. Jarvis describes the family as 'deeply religious', pointing out that 'the evangelical piety which ran so strongly in the family derived from the first Charles Baring of Exeter and from the Puritan Winthrops had a profound influence on the lives of the children'.[6] In typical evangelical manner the family gathered for daily prayer and was committed to a strict observance of the Sabbath. Evangelical children were brought up with many restrictions and prohibitions that led some to rebel and to carry 'a feeling of oppression and bitterness, which lingered long into adulthood'.[7] However many others remembered their childhood with warm memories of the love and encouragement they received from their

---

[6] Jarvis, *Baring Young*, p. 10. Jarvis includes a detailed history of the family and a family tree in his book.

[7] Ian Bradley, *The Call to Seriousness: The Evangelical Impact on the Victorians*, pp. 183, 186.

parents. They also received a rigorous and thorough education and were taught a high degree of self-discipline and self-respect and a strong urge to do good in the world.[8] These are clearly qualities that were exhibited in the life of the founder of Oak Hill College.

Charles Edward grew up in a house overlooking Hyde Park. He was sent at the age of nine to board at the Preparatory School, Blackheath, run by the Revd R. Cowley Powles. Evangelical families took care to send their children to schools that would maintain their values, and it was here that he came into contact with Charles Kingsley, the father of one of his fellow pupils and one of the founders of the Christian Socialist Movement.[9] The exuberant Kingsley clearly made an impression on the boys, who remembered him years later. This early association with Kingsley may have helped Charles Edward to develop the deep concern for the poor that he was to carry with him his entire life.

In May 1863 Charles Edward left Blackheath to go to Eton, where he came under the influence of the evangelical classical scholar, James Leigh Joynes, and one of the older boys, Quintin Hogg, who established a Bible study class, which Charles Edward attended. The year before he went to Eton his father had purchased the estate of Oak Hill, and he spent his vacations at the house that was later to become the college. In 1868 he went to Trinity College, Cambridge, where he again came into contact with Kingsley, and took his BA degree in 1872. For the next four years he seems to have travelled and studied law. In 1876 he received his MA, and was called to the bar at the Inner Temple. However, rather than pursuing a legal career, he devoted the remainder of his life to the service of poor boys like those who had been the subject of Kingsley's novels.

By the time Charles Edward completed his formal education the religious tradition to which he and his family adhered had

---

[8] Bradley, *Call to Seriousness*, p. 189. See pp. 179–93 for a discussion of the strengths and weaknesses of evangelical family life.

[9] For an appreciation of Kingsley see Susan Chitty, *The Beast and the Monk: A Life of Charles Kingsley*, and Brenda Colloms, *Charles Kingsley*.

begun to suffer a gradual decline. The publication of Darwin's *Origin of Species* in 1859 and *Essays and Reviews*[10] two months later presented serious challenges to evangelical beliefs about the Bible. Furthermore, the introduction by Anglo-Catholic clergy of vesture, ornaments and practices taken directly from the Roman church led many members of the Church of England to feel that their Protestant heritage was being abandoned.

While evangelicals struggled, in the long run unsuccessfully, to confront these new challenges, evangelical social work, often carried out by converts to the evangelical faith from the upper and upper–middle classes, continued unabated and even increased. In his *History of the English Church in the Nineteenth Century,* written in 1910, F.W. Cornish commented that evangelicals are 'known to the world, not by their writings, which are forgotten, but by their lives, which never can be forgotten'.[11] Among the vast number of social causes that evangelicals espoused few were more significant than their work among children. In addition to starting children's homes and orphanages and providing education in the 'ragged schools', evangelicals provided housing and recreation for adolescents among the working poor. Teenagers, who were expected to work and take care of themselves, often had trouble finding adequate housing or managing economically on the low wages they received.

Quintin Hogg, whom Charles Edward had known at Eton, and Arthur Kinnaird, another Eton contemporary, became very involved in work among teenagers. They were instrumental in establishing a society known as the Homes for Working Boys in London in 1870 to provide suitable accommodation for boys

---

[10] *Essays and Reviews* contained a series of essays, six of which were written by Anglican clergy, that applied German higher criticism to the Bible. It included an essay by Benjamin Jowett, contending that the Bible should be read 'like any other book'. See Ieuan Ellis, *Seven Against Christ: A Study of 'Essays and Reviews'* for a good analysis of *Essays and Reviews* and its impact.

[11] From Kathleen Heasman, *Evangelicals in Action: An Appraisal of their Social Work*, p. 15.

who had come to London for employment. They opened homes in various areas of London, eventually expanding to seven homes with some four hundred beds.[12] Charles Edward was invited to join the committee that ran the society in 1876 and became its treasurer in 1883, managing to clear the society's debt and more than doubling the income from public subscriptions from just over £3,000 to £8,700. He also made regular visits to the homes, where he would take evening prayers, hold Bible classes and accompany the boys on recreational activities. Every year he took the staff and the boys to Oak Hill for a day's outing. He continued as treasurer until 1890 when he resigned in order to devote the remainder of his life to Kingham Hill School, which he had founded in 1886.

At the same time Baring Young was also pursuing a parliamentary career. His father had hoped that his son would enter Parliament, but he did not do so until after his father died in December 1882, when he inherited the estate of Oak Hill and a considerable fortune, both of which he would devote to the service of others. In September 1883 he purchased the estates of Daylesford and Kingham Hill in the Cotswolds, the latter of which was to become the site of Kingham Hill School. In November 1885 he was elected Conservative MP for Christchurch, being re-elected in the 1886 election with an increased majority and remaining in Parliament until the summer of 1892. This was a time of considerable ferment in British politics, with the defeat of the first Irish Home Rule Bill in 1886 leading to divisions in Gladstone's Liberal Party and a Conservative government under Salisbury.

Baring Young was not often involved in the parliamentary debates, but he was clearly concerned about educational issues. His maiden speech opposed a proposal to establish a national system of Evening Continuation Schools, and expressed his concerns about individual freedom of choice. Although he supported providing additional educational opportunities especially after the age of

---

[12] Heasman, *Evangelicals in Action*, p. 118. A.F. Jarvis, *Fifty Years of Kingham Hill*, p. 29 says there were 8 homes with accommodation for 350 boys.

thirteen, he opposed making this education compulsory. He showed a sincere sense of compassion for working boys who would be forced to attend school whether they wished to or not. It was a courageous speech that expressed a principle that he espoused throughout his life: that of being totally committed to the free enterprise system and clearly very suspicious of state control.[13]

He expressed similar sentiments in 1891 when he seconded an amendment to the government's Elementary Education Bill, designed to protect voluntary and religious schools. Once again he championed the cause of individual choice and responsibility, stating: 'My chief objection to the measure is that is it is a step towards state socialism.' He believed that those who were able to pay for the education of their children but not allowed to do so might lose control of their education. The amendment was defeated 318–10. Baring Young was one of the ten in opposition, showing that he was a man of principle even when it came to opposing his party.[14] A year later Baring Young gave up his parliamentary career and retired to Daylesford to spend the remainder of his life in providing the type of education that accorded with the principles he had espoused in those speeches.

He purchased the Kingham Hill estate in order to provide homes for poor boys in a healthy environment where they would be educated and receive training. A central part of their training was spiritual instruction. Durham House, the first home, was completed in 1886 with twelve boys in residence. When Baring Young announced that he planned to build another house, his mother, still hopeful for her son's political career, tried to dissuade him, enlisting the help of a friend, who replied: 'Charles is the most obstinate of men, nothing can stop him when once he has made up his mind.' Mrs Young admired Charles's courage and faith and thereafter often drove over to Kingham Hill to view the progress of the work.[15]

---

[13] A portion of the speech is quoted in Jarvis, *Baring Young*, p. 26.
[14] Ibid., p. 27.
[15] Ibid., p. 36.

By the close of the century there were five houses with approximately two hundred boys in residence. Baring Young spared no expense in providing what was needed to carry on the mission of Kingham Hill. Classrooms, a library, a gymnasium and workshops were built and in 1894 he opened Latimer House in Fitzroy Square in London to provide a home for boys when they left Kingham to work in the capital. In addition he started two industries, an engineering firm and a piano factory, to provide training and work for the boys. He also purchased a house and farm in Canada and encouraged boys to emigrate there at his expense. He made visits to Canada in 1904, 1909 and 1914 to see how the boys were managing in their new homeland. Baring Young provided for the work to continue after his death by establishing the Kingham Hill Trust in December 1912. The original trustees included his brother Arthur, himself, and two friends who had been closely associated with the school.

While Baring Young was devoting his energies and fortune to Kingham and the other homes he established major changes were taking place in society. New scientific discoveries, an improvement in standards of living and a growing optimism about the future and man's potential made much of Christian teaching seem outdated. Even the middle classes were beginning to question the faith. An astute contemporary observer noted in the years preceding World War I that 'it is the middle class which is losing its religion ... Among the middle classes – the centre and historical support of England's Protestant creed – the drift away is acknowledged by all to be conspicuous.'[16] Heavily influenced by science and a belief in progress, the 'new man' of the twentieth century 'was fast casting off every garment which traditional and classical religion had taught him to wear'.[17]

In order to communicate the faith some Christian theologians revised its teachings to accord with the new world view. Christian teaching, they argued, must be translated into modern thought

---

[16] C.F.G. Masterman, *The Condition of England*, pp. 14, 268, from Hastings, *History of English Christianity*, p. 41.

[17] Roger Lloyd, *The Church of England 1900–1965*, p. 61.

forms and vocabulary. This involved a willingness to question anything that did not appear 'scientific', especially miraculous events such as the virgin birth and the resurrection. It meant de-emphasising sin and the need for redemption and stressing human potential and progress. The moral teachings of the Christian faith, the brotherhood of man and the fatherhood of God became the central teachings of what was labelled English modernism. This was clearly a very different theology from that taught by Victorian evangelicals and held by Baring Young.

In addition to the challenge from the new theology, Anglican evangelicals found themselves losing the struggle with the heirs of the Oxford Movement. While Roger Lloyd's unequivocal declaration of victory for Anglo-Catholicism may be a bit overstated,[18] efforts to control ritualism had failed. In 1903 the new Archbishop of Canterbury, Randall Davidson, received a delegation of a hundred MPs urging more effective action against ritualism. He responded by appointing a Royal Commission on Ecclesiastical Discipline, which, after two years of study, reported that 'the law of public worship in the Church of England is too narrow for the religious life of the present generation' and that 'the machinery for discipline has broken down. The means for enforcing the law ... are defective and in some respects unsuitable.'[19] Thus began the process of Prayer Book revision that would culminate in the presentation of a revised *Book of Common Prayer* to Parliament in 1927. Baring Young was troubled by these challenges to his beliefs and wrote in a prayer letter, 'How shall we act in the face of these dangers? ... How shall we distinguish between the true and the false?' His solution was typical of his approach to problems in general: 'First, search the Scriptures; second, pray for the guidance of the Holy Spirit; third, obey – this is the test of faith – and remain steadfast to the end.'[20]

---

[18] 'The Anglo-Catholics had won, and in 1899 it was evident that they had won. They had out-thought, out-lived and out-suffered all their opponents.' Lloyd, *Church of England*, p. 121.

[19] Alec Vidler, *The Church in an Age of Revolution*, p. 163.

[20] Talbot Mohan, *History of Oak Hill College*, p. 10.

In August 1914 Europe went to war and for four years the divisions in church and society became a secondary matter as the nation rallied against a common enemy. The war was viewed as a great moral crusade, a holy war against an evil foe. Not surprisingly, Baring Young gave it his full support. His house at Oak Hill was given to the government for use as a hospital and Latimer House was used partly to house refugees and partly as a hospital. Three houses at Kingham Hill were closed because of the drop in the number of boys. At least sixty-three old boys from Kingham died in the war. When the war ended on 11 November 1918 Baring Young wrote:

> Victory has crowned our arms! ... Let us in the first place lift up our hearts to Almighty God, the Giver of all victory, who has led us all the way hitherto, and has crowned our efforts in this long struggle with such magnificent success! ... The fighting is over; and so we are able to keep the festival of Christmas, the festival of the Prince of Peace, with glad hearts once again and with joy unclouded by anxiety – yet subdued, as it must be, by the thought of all we have gone through during these years of gloom ... When the Lord turned again the captivity of Zion, we were like them that dream. The Lord hath done great things for us, whereof we are glad.[21]

Although the terrible cost of the war undermined the confidence of the previous age and its optimism about human nature, the most publicized statement of Christian belief in the immediate post-war period continued to proclaim the very beliefs that the war had shown to be shallow and simplistic. In 1921 English modernists held a conference at Girton College, Cambridge. The consequence was a massive debate and a huge outcry, because the published conference papers called into question fundamental Christian beliefs and articulated in uncompromising terms the English modernist's belief in the glory of man.

---

[21] Jarvis, *Baring Young*, pp. 72–3.

In the same year as the Girton conference Baring Young published his own hymnbook, entitled *Hymns of Prayer and Praise*.[22] The book of 1,240 hymns included 'the best and most popular hymns and tunes, together with some which are not so well known, and others again which have fallen out of general use, but which have much to recommend them'.[23] It also included a hymn written by Baring Young, first used in the evening service at Kingham on Trinity Sunday, 22 May 1921. The words of the hymn reveal a radically different theology to that of English modernism. Baring Young's theology gave the glory to God and emphasized human dependence on God's mercy and grace in a fallen and broken world:

> From the land of darkness freed,
> When the depths their foes had swallowed;
> Lord, Thy people Thou didst feed,
> Living streams their footsteps followed:
> We are filled with heavenly bread
> From the treasures of Thy grace;
> Through the desert as we tread,
> Streams abound in every place.[24]

After the war life returned to normal at Kingham Hill. The houses that had been closed were reopened, pre-war activities were restored, 'and something like normality returned to the Hill'.[25] However, the world around Kingham changed radically in the post-war years. The motor car and the aeroplane revolutionized transport, while the founding of the BBC in 1922 introduced a new form of mass communication. In addition, women received the right to vote, Southern Ireland received its independence and the Labour Party replaced the Liberal Party as the major opposition.

---

22 C.E.B.Young (ed.), *Hymns of Prayer and Praise with Tunes*.
23 Ibid., p. iii
24 Ibid., p. 623, no. 611.
25 Jarvis, *Baring Young*, p. 75.

In 1922 Baring Young reached his seventy-second birthday. Despite an accident in December 1918 in which he broke his collarbone, he continued to be active and his commitment to evangelism remained unceasing. In his 1922 prayer letter he commented on the changes that were occurring in society:

> In spite of all the vaunted progress of the age there are multitudes who are in spiritual darkness; it is given to us, if we will, in some measure, however small, to help dispel that darkness; and a blessed privilege it is to bear witness to that Lord and Saviour who has done everything for us.[26]

In the remaining six years of his life, Baring Young would make a major contribution to continuing the work of 'bearing witness to that Lord and Saviour who has done everything for us' as he took the initial steps that would lead to the founding of Oak Hill College. These years were difficult for the evangelical movement in the Church of England as more and more divisions arose among them. At the same time, the *Book of Common Prayer* was being revised in a way that some evangelicals felt posed a threat to the gospel. Although such divisions were not new, those that developed in the 1920s were far more serious than the earlier ones:

> The unity of evangelicalism was broken during the 1920s. The movement had always been marked by variety in doctrine, attitude and social composition, but in the years after the First World War it became so sharply divided that some members of one party did not recognise the other as evangelical – or even, sometimes, as Christian.[27]

The divisions were the result of differing views of Scripture and a readiness on the part of some evangelicals to accept aspects of liberal theology and church ritual that more conservative evangelicals felt were contrary to the teaching of Scripture and the heritage

---

[26] Ibid., p. 127.

[27] Bebbington, *Evangelicalism in Modern Britain*, p. 181.

of the Reformation. Those who would be called liberal evangelicals felt they were not betraying the gospel or the teachings of Scripture. They believed they could maintain those doctrines that were essential to the faith while showing flexibility on peripheral issues. While rejecting the most radical conclusions of biblical critics, they sincerely believed that such criticism provided a way of coming to a better understanding of Scripture. They also believed that other parties in the church had something to teach them and decried the party spirit that had created divisions in the Church of England.

The tensions in evangelicalism and the divisions in the church were manifested in a graphic way when the effort to revise the *Book of Common Prayer* failed to win the approval of Parliament in 1927 and again in 1928. The proposed new Prayer Book had emerged after over a decade of debate, revision and counter-revision. The New Prayer Book Measure was, after much debate, passed by large majorities in the Convocations and the Church Assembly. It was then presented to the House of Lords and passed by a margin of 241–88; however it was rejected by the Commons 238–205. It was again presented to the Commons in a modified form, which included closer restrictions on the provision for a reserved sacrament. However the Commons again rejected it by an even larger margin.

Although evangelicals successfully prevented a revision of the *Book of Common Prayer*, which they believed would have compromised their doctrinal position, it was a pyrrhic victory. They had won by appealing to a secular assembly in opposition to overwhelming majorities in the Church Assembly. As a result evangelicals were pictured as narrow, bigoted obstructionists who stood in the way of progress, and who were willing to use unprincipled means to achieve their objectives. In addition the divisions between evangelicals were exacerbated. Although all evangelicals were opposed to changes that would compromise doctrine, liberal evangelicals were willing to be flexible. Once the new Prayer Book was accepted by the church, liberal evangelicals were prepared to come to terms with it and they opposed the campaign to have Parliament overturn the decision of the church. Conservative evangelicals on the other hand felt betrayed by those who had initially expressed the same concerns they had. The fact that none of the opponents of the revised Prayer Book was elevated to the episcopal bench in the years following its defeat, but a number of liberal evangelicals did achieve high office, led to additional grievances.[28]

Among those who had led the fight against the revised Prayer Book was the Revd Herbert William Hinde, vicar of St Mary's, Islington from 1921–32. Hinde served as chairman of the Islington Clerical Conference during the years when the controversy was at its height. Although he gained a reputation as one of its most strident opponents, his speeches on the topic do not fit the caricature of conservative evangelicals as being unyielding, unthinking obscurantists. He was quite willing to acknowledge the legitimacy of differing opinions among evangelicals. In his address to the Islington Clerical Conference in 1925 he conceded that among evangelicals 'some diversity must be expected and allowed. We are all entitled to our convictions, and privileged to profess them. And the right we claim for ourselves we acknowledge for others.' He also pointed out that the strength of evangelicalism was 'in union not in uniformity, our union being based upon our great evangelical principles'.[29] In addition he expressed concern that the divisions in the church were undermining its 'work and witness ... at a time when her whole strength and her whole energy are required for the task before her'. While expressing his own great desire for unity he reiterated the position on which, he maintained, all evangelicals agreed – that unity could not be achieved at the expense of truth:

> We would all like to heal the breach in our own Church, aye, and the breaches in the real and true Catholic Church so that with undivided strength and unhindered energy she might lay hold of the world for her Lord and Master. But such unity may be too dearly bought. Not

---

[28] Bebbington, *Evangelicalism in Modern Britain*, p. 205. There is good discussion of the Prayer Book revision struggle in Vidler, *Church in an Age of Revolution*, pp. 162ff and Hylson-Smith, *Evangelicals in the Church of England*, pp. 233ff.

[29] *Islington Clerical Conference Reports*, 1925, pp. 39–40.

> every form of unity is profitable or desirable ... we are not prepared to compromise the truth of God for the sake of unity.[30]

Hinde also pointed out that evangelicals were not averse to changes in the Prayer Book that would make it possible to communicate more effectively to the modern world: 'We evangelicals yield to none in our desire to forward the true corporate interest of the Church and sympathetically to consider and co-operate in an attempt to make our Prayer Book more effective in these modern days.' But, he asserted, these changes could not be achieved at the expense of doctrinal compromise.[31]

Hinde was promoting another cause at the same time as he was engaged in the Prayer Book controversy. In the second decade of the twentieth century concern was being expressed in many quarters about the growing shortage of clergy, already becoming evident at the end of the nineteenth century, when there was a drop in the number of clergy just when the population was increasing.[32] The concerned Church Assembly set up a commission to study the problem of staffing parishes. The commission reported in 1930 that, although there had been an increase in the number or ordinations at the end of the decade, 438 ordinations a year were needed to maintain the present number of clergy and 588 a year were needed to make up the deficit in numbers. The Central Advisory Council of Training for the Ministry (CACTM), the body that supervised theological education, pointed out that the commission warned that there would soon be 'a grave shortage of clergy' unless more men could be encouraged to study for ministry. In order to achieve this it was necessary to find more adequate means of financing theological education for qualified candidates. In its report CACTM concluded that: 'if it could be made known that funds were available for those who

---

30 Ibid., pp. 7, 9.

31 Ibid., p. 40.

32 There were 2,324 ordinations between 1886 and 1888. Ten years later there were only 1,994. In those ten years the population had increased by three million. Lloyd, *Church of England*, p. 75.

hesitate to offer themselves owing to the financial difficulties, but are unable to meet the whole cost of training, an increasing number of men would come forward'.[33]

The problem of finance was a serious one. The cost of theological education was substantial. According to Lloyd:

> Those who came from poor homes had the scales very heavily weighted against them, and the figures show that a lamentably high proportion of those who had a genuine vocation for the ministry, and who were, or could have become, sufficient for it, must have been denied the chance to answer their call simply for lack of means ... If the parent of a boy in the Church of England had £1000 to spare, he could be sent to Oxford or Cambridge, and be ordained in due course. Another boy would find the door to the sanctuary locked, bolted and barred, just because his parents had not £1000 to spare for his education and could not afford to dispense with the weekly wage he was bringing into the home.[34]

Anglo-Catholics had already addressed the problem. Their theological colleges at Mirfield and Kelham could provide the means for poorer candidates to study for ordination.[35] At the 1925 Islington Clerical Conference, Prebendary Sharpe, the vicar and rural dean of Paddington, stressed the need for increasing the number of evangelical ordinands. He first commented on the general shortage of ministerial candidates, attributing the drop in numbers to 'the general attitude towards institutional religion ...

---

[33] Church Assembly Publications vol. X, p. 3. No. 336 report of CACTM (October 1930).

[34] Lloyd, *Church of England*, pp. 149–50.

[35] Mirfield did not require payment during training but after ordination each student was asked to pay half the cost of training at a rate of £50 a year, spread over a period of five or six years: see F.W.B. Bullock, *A History of Training for the Ministry of the Church of England in England and Wales from 1875 to 1974*, pp. 76–7. Kelham had a provision that those who were unable to pay would have their expenses excused.

the lack of discipline in the church, and ... financial difficulty'. He then described the specific problem facing evangelicals:

> The most serious shortage of clergy is to be found with us evangelicals. Our six theological colleges are not all full, while Kelham and Mirfield are full up for some time to come. The principals of all our colleges tell us that if only they had more bursaries to give to needy students many more places would be filled. An evangelical Mirfield, well endowed, where men are taken at a young age is badly needed, and I believe would be more than filled if it could be obtained.[36]

He urged action 'to see what can be done to foster vocation to ministry' and 'to help financially in all suitable cases', stressing the need 'to act with as little delay as possible'.[37]

Hinde included a similar appeal in his speeches as he travelled the country in the campaign against the revised Prayer Book. He pointed out that many were not entering the ministry because they could not afford the cost of training and 'because there was no suitable college' where they could study. 'What was needed', he said, 'was a place where the genuinely converted, who knew they were called of God, could be given a thorough training which was thoroughly Bible-based.' Hinde received a letter quite out of the blue one day from an address in the West End of London, asking him to go and see its writer. According to Hinde's account, when he went to see this person, he was told quite abruptly, 'I want you to go and see a house. A house in Southgate. Here's the address. When you've been, come back and tell me what you think of it.'[38] The man who spoke those words was Baring Young.

However, according to another account that appears also to have come from Hinde,[39] at one of the meetings he mentioned the

---

[36] *Islington Clerical Conference Reports*, 1925, pp. 35–36.

[37] Ibid., p. 36.

[38] Letter from the Revd David E. Gardner to David Wheaton in January 1975 recalling a talk given by Hinde to students on the foundation of the college.

[39] A memo in the Oak Hill archives, possibly in the hand of former bursar R.C. Stredder, attributes the story to Hinde.

programme at Mirfield, and spoke of his visions for a test school where boys from evangelical homes could be provided with a year of subsidized study and where they could test their vocation. After his speech a stranger came up to him and bluntly asked him what it would cost to provide such a school. The stranger was, of course, Baring Young, and he invited Hinde to visit him in London. At their meeting Baring Young accepted Hinde's plans for a test school.[40] We do not know precisely when the meeting took place, but it may well have been in early March 1928. On 21 February Hinde wrote to John Kinahan, an assistant secretary of the Church Pastoral Aid Society (CPAS), describing in detail his plans for a test school. In that letter there was no mention of the Baring Young offer;[41] however, a letter written to a Mr A.B. Keith on 13 March begins by stating that 'a certain gentleman hitherto unknown to me, even by name, has laid upon me a very great responsibility. He owns two large houses standing in their own grounds; he is prepared to put either of them to the purpose of a test school for ordination candidates.' Hinde continued by describing Baring Young's offer, pointing out that he would provide the house, and would pay the rates and taxes. He added: 'The bargain is, however, that those who direct the school as governing body shall be of conservative evangelical views and appointed by a board of trustees whom he will nominate in the first place for that and other things.'[42]

---

[40] Mohan, *History of Oak Hill College*, pp. 11–12. Jarvis does not mention Hinde's role in suggesting the idea for the test school. He seemingly attributes the idea to Baring Young, who, he says, had 'for some time past ... pondered much on the recruitment to the ministry of the church': Jarvis, *Baring Young*, p. 82. This accords with Hinde's account in the same book where he states that Baring Young 'proposed the institution at Barnet of a prematriculate test school for men who felt a call to Holy Orders, could not afford the cost of training, and whose ability might be doubted until tested': Ibid., p. 119. However, Hinde may simply have been hesitant to give himself credit for the idea in what was intended as a eulogy for Baring Young.

[41] Letter from Hinde to Kinahan, 21 February 1928.

[42] Letter from Hinde to Keith, 13 March 1928.

Although he was rapidly declining in health, Baring Young devoted a good deal of time in the last months of his life to his new project without neglecting his beloved Kingham Hill. In June 1928 the Kingham Hill trustees met, with Baring Young in the chair, to agree on specific arrangements for the test school. Baring Young had invited Hinde to suggest a suitable first principal, and Hinde had suggested the Revd A.W. Habershon, at that time vicar of St John's, Blackheath. Habershon visited Baring Young in the late summer, and described encountering 'a tall, quiet, grey-haired gentleman in black coat and striped trousers' whose 'whole atmosphere spoke of a man of self-discipline and spartan habits'. During the meeting Baring Young described his vision for the test school and the future. Habershon describes how:

> In a business-like way, but with a voice of tender friendship, he explained his intentions: revealing how he had founded the school and home at Kingham for boys from poor homes, who had little opportunity in life, and no money with which to make a start; how he had started a farm in Canada to which many of the boys had emigrated and where they had successfully established themselves for life; how he wanted, in his deep desire to uphold and spread the evangelical faith in a world and church spiritually dead, to found a college, based on bible truths and evangelical churchmanship, to which men might go who could not afford the fees of existing training centres, and there be prepared for ordination to the ministry of the Church of England. His intention, he explained, was to carry out his scheme in two stages: first, to found a test school, where men could be prepared for matriculation, if necessary, and tested as to their vocation to ministry, and, second, at a later date to found a permanent college for full theological training if the first scheme developed satisfactorily.[43]

In the last month of his life Baring Young even attempted to recruit one of the Kingham Hill old boys for his new test school.

---

[43] 'Memoir of the Revd A.W. Habershon's meeting with the founder', in the college archives.

On 18 August 1928 he wrote to R.D. Fryer, describing the new school and suggesting that he might be interested in joining the first class:

> We are just starting a college, to be called the 'Oak Hill College', for the training of candidates for the ministry. In the first place it is with the object of giving a year's preliminary training leading on to further preparation at some more advanced hall or college. You told me some time ago that you had a desire to be ordained. Are you in the same mind still? If so, I should be so glad to welcome you as one of the earliest perhaps the very first student in this college.[44]

The effort to recruit Fryer succeeded. Even though he was not 'the very first student', he is included in the 1931 photograph of students at the test school, and he was part of the first intake at Oak Hill College in the following year, subsequently spending a lifetime of service in the ordained ministry.

During the last months of his life Baring Young continued to be involved at Kingham Hill. In June he gave his final address at Sunday evening chapel, in August he attended the annual reunion and preached from the chapel porch. On 19 August he attended his last chapel service and three days later visited Kingham Hill for the last time. Shortly afterwards he was confined to bed. Three days before he died some of the boys from the Hill came over to sing hymns in front of the house. When asked if he wanted them to stop he responded 'No, no! Let them sing on. I could listen for hours.' When the hymn singing ended the Revd William Mitchell-Carruthers, a close friend and the school chaplain, who was at his bedside, read Psalm 27 to him. Baring Young then asked that he read the first fourteen verses of John 14. Afterwards he asked that verse 27 of that chapter be read: 'Peace I leave with you, my peace I give unto you: not as the world giveth, give I unto you. Let not your heart be troubled, neither let it be afraid' (KJB). On 22 September he died, 'peacefully and painlessly'.[45] At the memorial

44 Jarvis, *Baring Young*, p. 83.
45 Ibid., pp. 85–6.

service in Kingham Hill chapel the chaplain paid a fitting tribute to this man who had given so unselfishly of himself and his resources to the service of others:

> He was one of the most humble and unassuming of men I have ever known – ready at all times, so to speak, to take a back seat, when from every point of view he had a right to a prominent place. Another trait in his character was his utter unselfishness. He was always thinking of others – never of himself ... Another outstanding trait in his character was his fidelity to duty ... His religious principles were absolutely and entirely based upon the Word of God. He never swerved a hair's breadth to the right or to the left. Compromise was a word he detested. I am sure he would have walked to the stake, with head erect, rather than yield in the matter of Protestant Principles or Reformation Truth. Above all, he was deeply spiritual. This was the undercurrent of his life. The love of Christ was the dominating influence in all he did.[46]

The first principal of Oak Hill College, Hinde, wrote a tribute to Baring Young for Jarvis's biography that spoke of the founder's dedication to the service of God and his unselfishness. However, in addition, Hinde commented briefly on another aspect of Baring Young's character that for many was not so attractive. 'It was said he was something of an autocrat and it was said in terms which suggested he was in fact very autocratic. And no doubt to us in these democratic days that was a justifiable statement.' He then commented on the founder's theological position, which was stated in the trust deed of Oak Hill College:

> In the Christian Church he was himself a member of the Church of England, and therein his views, held with firm conviction and great clearness, were 'distinctly and definitely Protestant and Evangelical in the strictest sense of the terms'. On the basis of the Thirty-nine Articles and the Book of Common Prayer, he adjudged this to be the position

---

[46] Ibid., pp. 114–15, and 'In Memoriam Charles Baring Young' *The Record*, 18 October 1928.

> of the Church of England. He was not unaware that other teaching was also heard in the Church of England but by use of the aforesaid phrase he made clear what he considered to be the true doctrine according to Holy Scripture.[47]

When, at the end of his life, Baring Young wrote in his prayer letter that 'in the religious world men's minds are upset with increasing force by the assaults of superstition and unbelief' he was not exaggerating, at least from his theological perspective. Evangelicalism was weak and Anglo-Catholicism had become 'the central moving force within the church, reshaping its ethos and symbolism'.[48] Conservative evangelicals found themselves 'hemmed in on every side' as ritualism, liberalism and the divisions among evangelicals all presented serious threats.[49] At the same time the church was losing the intellectual struggle in the wider society. Hastings maintains that 'the principal intellectual ... orthodoxy of England in the 1920s was no longer Protestantism, nor was it Catholicism or any other form of Christianity. It was a confident agnosticism'.[50] In their effort to maintain the theological tradition to which the founder was so deeply committed, those who taught and studied at the college would often find themselves in radical opposition to the dominant beliefs of the culture. Although the college came into existence at a particularly challenging time for the tradition it represented and sought to perpetuate, those who led the new venture could find reassurance in the founder's words to the old boys of Kingham Hill in his final prayer letter: 'See that ye be not troubled; if your heart be fixed, trusting in Christ you have nothing to fear; He is yours and you are His, and you can face the future with good hope and courage, whatever it may bring.'[51]

---

[47] Ibid., pp. 118–19.
[48] Hastings, *History of English Christianity*, p. 195.
[49] Ibid., pp. 200–201.
[50] Ibid., p. 221.
[51] Jarvis, *Baring Young*, p. 134.

2

The Foundation: 'A Test School' (1928–1937)

> Preb. Hinde, after prayer, explained his proposals which were that Bohun Lodge should be a College for 'preliminary year' and a Test School, accommodating about 22 students; that the Trustees should appoint a Governing Council who should appoint a Principal and Tutor, but that in the first instance for the sake of time for Mr. Young to appoint the first Principal; that the Council should be free to advise these men as to where to go at the end of the year, though normally it may be expected that they would go to St. John's Hall. The goodwill of the Governors of St. John's Hall was assured, and should this College open in October, they will forthwith cease to take 'preliminary year' men.[1]

The above record has been preserved only because of the foresight of Mr John Kinahan, who wrote to Prebendary Hinde on the day following the meeting at which the above took place, suggesting that it would 'be well to have some record of our meeting yesterday' and sent him 'a rough draft' for him to correct.[2] The draft was returned by Hinde and then sent on to Baring Young. It contained a record of the meeting of the Kingham Hill trustees on 19 June 1928, at which Hinde's proposal to open a 'test school' was accepted by the trust. The test school was designed to provide

[1] Minutes of Kingham Hill trustees, 19 June 1928.
[2] Letter from Kinahan to Hinde, 20 June 1928.

a place where men could undertake a year of preliminary study before beginning theological college and where those who felt called to the ordained ministry could test that call. At the meeting Baring Young offered Bohun Lodge, the house he had recently purchased adjoining his family home at Oak Hill, as a site for the school. He also agreed 'on behalf of the trust to defray expenses of altering and furnishing, annual rent, rates and taxes and such running expenses as might be necessary'. Students would be charged a fee of £90 a year. If, however, students could not raise this amount of money the Kingham Hill Trust was authorized to provide the necessary assistance.

Hinde suggested names for the college council, and it was agreed that 'a Trust Deed or Memorandum ... be drawn up, possibly on the lines of St. John's, Highbury, to regulate the proceedings and powers of the directors'.[3] Shortly afterwards, the meeting between Habershon and Baring Young described in the previous chapter took place. At that meeting Habershon heard the founder's proposal both for a test school and, if that proved successful, 'to found a permanent college for full theological training'. Habershon was then invited to become the first principal of the test school, and after prayer asked Baring Young 'If I accept this position, what will be your method regarding expenditure and financial decisions?' Baring Young responded 'I shall leave you a free hand. You will make your own decisions and spend as freely as you think necessary. I have offered you the position. I shall trust you.'[4]

The idea of an ordination test school did not originate with Hinde. It had first arisen at the end of the World War I to meet the needs of young men whose experience of the war's horrors had led them to think of the Christian ministry as a better way of serving their fellows. Until the war it had been assumed that leadership rested with the traditional middle and upper classes, but experience in battle had proved that there were men of

---

[3] Ibid.
[4] Memoir of the Revd A.W. Habershon's meeting with the founder.

humbler origins who possessed leadership qualities and who had been sent for officer training. Now the church also came to recognize that those without the background of formal educational qualifications could have a genuine call to the ministry. To help them, an ordination test school was set up at Le Touquet in France as early as December 1918, and later transferred to a disused prison and subsequently a private house in Knutsford. Such was the demand for the courses that it is recorded that in January 1920 there were 287 candidates in the school.[5]

The test school was opened at Bohun Lodge in October 1928, less than a month after the founder died. It would endure for almost a decade during an especially turbulent period in British history. In order to understand the challenges the new college faced as it sought to prepare men for an evangelical ministry it is important to review briefly the environment in which the college was established, the prospects for the Christian faith in that environment, and the particular problems confronting conservative evangelicals.

On 24 October 1929, one year after the test school opened, the New York stock market collapsed. This sparked a world-wide depression that affected Britain in a particularly serious way. By the summer of 1931 nearly three million were unemployed. During the depression years the divisions in British society became even deeper. Although the industrial north, Wales, Clydeside and Northern Ireland were hit hard by the depression, the south-east continued to prosper. There were two separate Britains in the 1930s. In some villages in the north of England and south Wales practically the entire population was out of work, while unemployment rates remained very low in the south. In some areas there was little or no hope of finding work. Many intellectuals became convinced that capitalism had failed and some found their answers in communism.

The depression also led to the triumph of Adolf Hitler in Germany. During the years that the test school was in existence

---

[5] Bullock, *History of Training*, p. 80.

Hitler began to expand the Nazi empire, eventually leading to World War II. In many parts of Europe democracies founded after World War I collapsed and many people turned either to a godless communism or totalitarian fascism as the hope for the future. Economic problems, combined with the new popular social and political ideologies, posed a challenge to a church that continued to lose its hold and influence on a society that often found its escape from the problems confronting it in the new and increasingly popular world of the cinema.[6] However, at the same time as there were significant declines in numbers of baptisms and confirmations as well as in the number of children attending Anglican Sunday schools, a revival of orthodox belief began among intellectuals, which would result in Christianity again becoming intellectually respectable.[7]

In spite of their apparent victory in preventing Prayer Book revision, conservative evangelicals had not actually blocked the use of the 1928 Prayer Book. Despite the opposition by them and others who felt the church should abide by the decision of Parliament,[8] the bishops issued a statement proclaiming the church's right to determine its form of worship. They also allowed ministers to use the changes introduced in the 1928 Prayer Book during 'the present emergency', an 'emergency' that lasted for four decades during which time very little was done to control even the most radical deviations from the official liturgy.[9] Conservative

---

[6] 'Weekly attendance at the parish church might be crumbling ominously, but weekly attendance at the Odeon or the Ritz was almost de rigueur for 1930s men.' Hastings, *History of English Christianity*, p. 245.

[7] Hylson-Smith, *Evangelicals in the Church of England*, p. 270.

[8] This included the Church Pastoral Aid Society, 'which normally avoided controversial matters' but which 'openly expressed its conviction that the church should accept and abide by the decision of Parliament.' K. Hylson-Smith, *The Churches in England from Elizabeth I to Elizabeth II*, vol. 3, p. 188.

[9] Ibid. Hylson-Smith speaks of 'liturgical confusion within the church' and a 'crisis in church-state relations'.

evangelicals also found themselves in 'an isolated position' within the church, as many resented the tactics they used in the Prayer Book controversy. They were, in Manwaring's words, 'made to feel out on a limb, even discredited in Anglicanism'.[10] Although evangelicals remained strong in the parish and evangelical churches were full, their influence in the wider church continued to decline. A number of liberal evangelical bishops were appointed in the 1930s, but 'no strictly conservative evangelical' was appointed to the episcopate.[11] Evangelicals also isolated themselves from the wider church. According to Barclay, they 'behaved as if they were in a congregational church, ignoring the authorities as far as possible', and 'feeling marginalized by others, evangelical churches had developed a defensiveness and often a traditionalism about them. If they were to keep the faith, it seemed necessary to do it as their forebears had done'.[12] Barclay's description of evangelicals at the time the test school was founded may help us to understand better that first generation of Oak Hill students:

> There was generally among conservative evangelicals something of an intellectual inferiority complex and a negative attitude to contemporary 'high' culture. This helped to produce an anti-intellectualism that was fed by seeing some promising people turned away from old paths by wider interests. The older leaders often advised people (including myself) not to read theology because it never seemed to do anyone any good unless they positively needed it for the ministry. When, as a first-year science student, I mentioned my interest in current poetry

---

[10] Randle Manwaring, *From Controversy to Co-existence: Evangelicals in the Church of England 1914–1980*, p. 36. 'The detractors of Evangelicalism, numerous as ever, were quick to write off the victors as "Low-Church controversialists" ... All in all and reviewing the years which followed, it must be conceded that the triumph was rather hollow and produced something of a stalemate for Evangelicals.' Ibid., p. 39.

[11] Ibid., p. 43.

[12] O.R. Barclay, *Evangelicalism in Britain 1935–1995*, pp. 23, 25.

> (T.S. Eliot and W.H. Auden), I was told that it would be best not to broadcast it or I would be thought by some to be 'unsound'.[13]

Habershon was thus faced with more than his share of problems as he sought to build a new college and to attract students who would minister effectively in this challenging environment. It would be difficult to overestimate the responsibility laid on the shoulders of the still relatively young principal even in the initial stages of establishing the new college. Between the time of the trustees giving the final approval for the test school on 19 June and its opening in early October an overwhelming number of things needed to be done. Habershon had to arrange publicity for this new venture, interview and recruit staff as well as students, and supervise the adaptation of the property from a country gentleman's mansion into premises suitable for a college. At the same time he still had responsibilities in his parish on the other side of London. However he managed to do all that needed to be done so that, when the college opened its doors on 5 October 1928, there were fifteen students and three staff in residence. Three weeks later the Habershons hosted an 'at home' to enable friends of the new college to inspect the premises. In addressing the assembled company the principal explained what the college hoped to achieve and how this would be done. He pointed out that the normal period of training at the college would be one year. During that period students would be prepared for the matriculation examination of the theological college or university of their choice. In addition, preliminary doctrinal and devotional training would be given.

The training took place in a lovely setting. Photographs in the early prospectus show how the spacious ballroom (but without its built-in organ) had been transformed into a large study room with individual tables partitioned by bookshelves, while the main entrance led into a large hall and billiard room. A recess under the staircase was at first used for a chapel until a larger room with

---

[13] Ibid., p. 26.

splendid views over the lawns became the permanent chapel. There was also a dining room and a library with a magnificent carpet given by Mr Arthur Young, the brother of the founder. Young also gave an initial donation of £120 for the purchase of books 'which will help men to know, believe and preach the Word of God'.[14] The first floor of the 200-year-old property had been adapted for living accommodation. A corridor ran the length of the house: at one end was the principal's flat, and at the other end were the rooms for the students, with the principal's study in-between. From the house there were views of terraces and lawns, with azaleas, rhododendrons, and many trees, including a tulip tree, and the rustic bridge over the lower lake, all backed by the ancient oaks of the old Enfield Chase deer forest. The grounds had a football pitch, two tennis courts and a fives court. There were also vegetable gardens and a greenhouse, cared for over many years by the very helpful Mr Burke, who had been head gardener when the property was still a private house: 'We had so wondered what would happen to the old place. I am so glad you are coming down to open it as a college. I will do all I can to help you.'[15]

In his first report to the college council on 3 April 1929 the principal spoke of the initial problems of the building work not having been completed in time for the beginning of term. Workmen were still busy for the first six weeks of the first term. For a fortnight there was no hot water, and for three weeks no central heating. Despite the hardship the principal reported that 'the men however took it all very well and the term opened with a good spirit'.[16]

At the end of the first academic year the principal wrote a report on the work of the college, possibly for the Kingham Hill trustees. He set out what he perceived as the fundamental spiritual need of a society experiencing the turmoil described earlier in this chapter:

---

[14] From a memoir by the Revd A.W. Habershon in the college archives.
[15] Ibid.
[16] Principal's report, 4 March 1929.

> 'Sir, we would see Jesus' was the cry long ago of men of thoughtful character and longing heart as they came in search to the disciple of Him Who alone could satisfy the deepest yearnings of their souls. The cry is being repeated today by countless hundreds of men and women in our cities and villages, in our churches, schools and colleges. Men and women who feel the need of 'something' in their lives are realising that 'none but Christ can satisfy' and they are demanding (though often in unspoken accents) of Christian men and women, clergy and laity, – 'We would see Jesus'.[17]

Habershon went on to state that 'the aim of the evangelical is to reveal Jesus by himself first entering into a life of personal consecration and surrender to the Saviour'. Then, having experienced the reality 'of sins forgiven and power imparted', he can 'go out with a living message to save souls from a life of sin unto that life of liberty in Christ which he himself has already tasted'. His message must always be based on Scripture, 'believing that the claims from God in that Word are in every aspect true; and he appeals to sin-caught men and women to accept a God-given free salvation on the authority of "Thus saith the Lord" '. In addition, 'he teaches that such a life begun in Christ must be maintained daily, and he therefore emphasises the vital need of daily Bible reading and prayer, and the sacrament of the Lord's Supper as a means of grace'. This will 'lead him to the continuance of a life on fire for God, and to the perfecting of that faith in Christ which gained him his salvation, and without which all else has little meaning or power'.[18] It is in the context of this statement that he continued later in that same report to define the purpose of the infant college:

> The purpose of the college is to bring men up to the required matriculation standard of the university or theological college to which they ultimately intend to go, and also to give such doctrinal and spiritual

---

[17] Principal's report, 3 April 1929.
[18] Ibid.

> instruction as shall lead them to see clearly the demands of the Lord Jesus upon their lives and to enter more deeply into an experience of His love and power; and lead them also into a definite 'reason for the hope that is within them'. For this it is necessary to maintain the 'personal touch' with the men, and every effort is made to make the atmosphere of the college one of trust, friendship and 'home'.[19]

In the last part of this aim the principal was ably supported by Mrs Habershon, and the students, all of whom were single, and few of whom would at that stage have serious friendships with the opposite sex, greatly valued the hospitality afforded them in the Habershons' flat.

The earliest prospectus has the title *Oak Hill College*, and is emblazoned with the coat of arms of the Baring Young family, suggesting that from the first it was known by that name rather than Bohun Lodge Test School. The minutes of a meeting of CACTM held on 23 October 1928 also used that name. In this meeting the chairman reported that 'Oak Hill College, East Barnet' had recently been opened as a preliminary test school for candidates for ordination. At a meeting of the same body on 11 June 1929 the chairman stated that he had had a letter from the principal of 'Oak Hill College, East Barnet'. The question arose at that meeting whether the college should be included in the official list of colleges in the pamphlet 'Training for the Ministry',[20] and whether it should be informally inspected for this purpose. The principal of St John's Hall, Highbury, informed the council that there were about fifteen men in residence at Oak Hill, that it was administered in connection with St John's Hall and that it was primarily for men taking the St John's Hall preliminary year. It was, however, agreed that the college should be visited.[21]

---

[19] Principal's report on the work of Bohun Lodge 1928–9.

[20] This pamphlet was produced every year or two to inform candidates recommended for training for the ministry as to their options for places at which to train.

[21] CACTM Minutes, 1923–33, pp. 276, 314–15.

Unfortunately there is no record of this visit in the college archives, possibly because of its informal nature.

In addition to using the name Oak Hill College the test school also used the crest and the motto of the later college. In his principal's report of 6 June 1929 Habershon referred to the fact that Arthur Young had granted permission for the Young family's coat of arms to be hung over the front door and the dining room mantelpiece. He also permitted the family crest to become the college crest, to be used on all books and so on, and to be worn on blazers. The family motto, 'Be right and persist', became with their crest the motto and crest of Oak Hill College and is still displayed in the college dining hall. Although the message it conveys is serious and viewed in the proper perspective reflects much of what the college has stood for throughout its history, it also has been the object of a good deal of humour over the years. Students often decorated the crest and even the principal was not averse to using the college motto to make a humorous point. On one occasion before the students were setting off home for the holidays, they were reminded of the perils of the roads and urged to 'Keep left and survive'!

Oak Hill College began with three staff members. The principal shared the teaching load with a resident tutor, the Revd N. Ashby, who taught Latin, Greek, and English and Greek Testament, and a non-resident tutor, L.C. Rolleston, Esq., who taught Logic and Mathematics at a salary of 7/6d per lecture! Habershon retained responsibility for teaching Old and New Testament, English History, Church History, Christian Evidence (apologetics?) and the Acts of the Apostles according to examination requirements. In addition he taught doctrine as a part of the compulsory curriculum of all students. Fortunately, he had a good academic background to enable him to do justice to this heavy and varied teaching load. He also had the advantage of parish experience. After military service during World War I he had gone to Oriel College, Oxford, where he had taken a degree in modern history. In subsequent studies at Wycliffe Hall he gained a distinction in the diploma in theology, and had served a curacy at the parish church of St Nicholas, Sevenoaks, prior to his incumbency at Blackheath. He also combined his academic and spiritual interests with physical activity, taking full advantage of the recreational facilities afforded by his new premises. It is recorded that the well-kept hard tennis court became renowned for the fierce and strenuous battles waged there between the principal and the Revd S. Roberts (vicar of Christ Church, Barnet), and the latter's two churchwardens, Messrs Waymouth and Short.

By the end of the first year the number of students had risen to eighteen. Two others had left after the first term. One had decided that the he could not accept the evangelical content of the teaching, and transferred to Salisbury Theological College. The other had decided to approach his bishop with a view to taking a shorter course of theological training than the three or four years envisaged. The college's records do not tell us how that request was received! At the end of the year nine candidates had been successful in meeting the entrance requirements for St John's Hall, plus two for Durham and one for Cambridge. Of the remaining six, two were not due to sit examinations until the following year. One student, who had failed the entrance requirements for St John's Hall, returned for a further attempt. Two others who had failed for St John's Hall and one who had failed for Edinburgh did not return. It is interesting to note that with only eighteen students in the first year the infant college coped with the syllabi for no fewer than four different sets of entrance requirements. This potential weakness drew comment from the bishops' inspectors when they visited the college once it had opened as a fully-fledged theological college.

These opening years also saw regular changes of staff. E.D. Dawson-Walker, who was himself later to be ordained after training at Ripon Hall, joined the staff in the second academic year. When the Revd Ashby left in 1929 the principal asked if it were vitally necessary that tutors who were not teaching religious subjects needed to be members of the Church of England, provided they were in sympathy with that church and were prepared to enter into all the college activities. The employment of lay staff, some of whom were subsequently ordained, was a practice that has been repeated at various times during the college's history. Mr Dawson-Walker continued on the staff during the following academic year, when he was joined by one W.J. Rolfe, who again continued for a further year, when Dawson-Walker was replaced by Mr A.H. Cooke.

The failures of some students can hardly have been due to lack of opportunity to study. In the report on the work of Bohun Lodge quoted above the principal listed the following daily timetable:

8.00 a.m.	Breakfast (after breakfast, prayers for the domestic staff and quiet throughout the college)
8.45 a.m.	Chapel service concluding with a five-minute devotional 'thought' on the Greek Testament
9.30 a.m.–12.45 p.m.	Compulsory work hours or lectures
1.00 p.m.	Lunch
5.00 p.m.–6.45 p.m.	Compulsory work hours or lectures
7.00 p.m.	Evening meal
8.00 p.m.–9.30 p.m.	Compulsory work hours or lectures
9.30 p.m.	Evening chapel, except on Wednesdays when there was Evening Prayer and sermon at 6.00 p.m.
	Quiet was to be observed after 10.00 p.m.
	Saturday was a free day after 1.00 p.m. until chapel at 9.30 p.m.

Surprisingly, Holy Communion was not initially celebrated in the college, although by the end of the Easter term 1930 the principal was asking the trustees for a better chapel 'where we can have our own communion services', the present one being quite insufficient![22] Until this was provided members of the college attended Christ Church, Cockfosters, for communion on Sundays and saints' days, and for the rest of Sunday they

---

[22] Extract from the principal's report for the October 1929 and January 1930 terms.

were free to attend where they pleased. The most popular churches were said to be Cockfosters, St Paul's, Hadley Wood, St Mary's, East Barnet (in whose parish the college is situated), and St James's, New Barnet. It is interesting that there was a link with Cockfosters, which at that stage was not regarded as an evangelical church, but had a well-respected pacifist vicar in Prebendary B.C. Hopson, who drew a large congregation from a wide area by his preaching. There does not appear to have been any scheme for practical training, but that may have been due to the fact that in those days the Church of England was far stricter about who might conduct services and preach. It may also not have been thought desirable to encourage hopes that might not be realized among the students. The college's purpose was to enable its students to pass their entrance requirements, and other areas of training could come later, though the prospectus does state that 'every applicant is expected to undertake, as directed by the principal, some kind of church work during the term'.[23]

As mentioned earlier college fees were fixed at £30 per term (£90 per annum), and the trust was committed to providing assistance for students who were unable to raise payment. In addition at the opening 'at home' in October 1928 the principal took the opportunity to appeal for bursaries to enable him to offer places to students who were not in a position to afford those fees. At the end of the first year he was able to report that the fund stood at £441-1-0d. At a time when there were serious economic problems in the wider society it was an especially impressive achievement to raise that amount of money in such a short period.

The college required that every applicant be a bona fide candidate for holy orders. At this time there were no selection conferences such as there are today, so those applying would have had to obtain sponsorship from a bishop prepared to ordain them at the end of their training. This system placed an extra responsibility on the principal. He had to discern whether those applying

---

[23] College prospectus.

to the college would not only benefit from the academic level of the teaching, but also were of the right spiritual calibre and had leadership potential for ministry in the church.

A statement in the principal's report at the end of the Easter term 1930 reads: 'Two other men will be leaving – one who was studying for Highbury, but who has been thought in agreement with his father to be unsuitable at his present stage for the ministry.'[24] The reference to paternal consultation gives an interesting sidelight as to how radically different the student body was in those early days from what it would later become. It also reflects that at this time the age of attaining majority was twenty-one years, and so students who had not yet attained that age would have been very much *in statu pupillari.* One also wonders whether the man in question was, in common with a number of his peers, a son of the vicarage.

That the test school met a real need can be evidenced from the way in which the numbers of students grew to twenty-five in the second year, twenty-nine in the third year and twenty-eight in the fourth year. Its success can be measured not only in the number who went on to university and theological college courses, but also in those it helped to discern that they did not have a vocation!

Perhaps the most fitting summary of what was achieved in those early days at Bohun Lodge comes in the words of a student who was one of the first to proceed to the fledgling Oak Hill College. Brian Woodhams, who concluded his ministry as Archdeacon of Newark, wrote of his days at the test school: 'It will ever be of precious memory to me and many others because of the inspired bible teaching of the then principal, the Revd A.W. Habershon, who gave many of us our love for the Word of God, and implanted in us a longing to study it.'[25] Woodhams's recollections of the test school over half a century after he studied there is a testimony to the success of the school in achieving its objectives.

---

[24] Principal's report, 1930.

[25] Letter from Woodhams to David Wheaton.

He and many others who were to have lengthy and fruitful ministries laid their foundations there. The test school clearly succeeded in achieving the objectives Hinde and Baring Young had in mind when the institution was founded. By 1932 the time was ripe to launch the second part of Baring Young's vision – the foundation of 'a permanent college for full theological training'.

3

Establishing the College and the War Years (1932–1945)

> From my conversation with Mr. Charles Baring Young I understand that his great aim in his Trust was the 'physical and spiritual welfare of the lads and youths of England' (I think that was the actual phrase that he used) and also the securing of clergymen of the right type for our Church of England ... I want to suggest to you and the other Trustees that the original Oak Hill house should be turned into a Post-Graduate Theological College, and conducted on Conservative Evangelical and Protestant lines, such as Mr. Baring Young intended Oak Hill should be.[1]

Two years after the founding of the test school Hinde wrote to Arthur Young, who was now the chairman of the trustees, suggesting that a permanent college be established. In his meeting with Habershon shortly before his death, Baring Young had suggested that this might be the second stage, 'if the first scheme proved satisfactory'.[2] Hinde now began to pursue this possibility. In May 1929 he wrote to Mr Kinahan of the Kingham Hill Trust pointing out the need for a new theological college. His argument was based on the fact that both the test school and St John's Hall were likely to be full in the coming year and there would be insufficient places for evangelical ordinands. He pointed out:

---

[1] Letter from Hinde to Arthur Young, October 1930.
[2] Memoir of A.W. Habershon's meeting with the founder.

> Gilbert [the principal of St. John's] believes there is room for a College such as St. John's in addition to St. John's, and for full courses. St. John's Hall governors are always saying that they think Gilbert takes too many and that the advantage of personal contact with the men is jeopardised. I anticipate that very soon they will put a definite limit to his numbers. Gilbert says that if they do so this year it will be very serious for many men. It is also clear that the supply of funds for ordination candidates is not being maintained at present. This will necessitate something very shortly.[3]

The letter to Arthur Young in October 1930 cited above followed. In it Hinde pointed out that the trustees were 'at present ... not spending all their income' and he suggested two ways in which it might be used. The first was a proposal for grants to be made to evangelical organizations that aimed at the physical and spiritual well-being of poor boys. The second was the proposal for founding a new theological college. He defended the second proposal by pointing out that there was a 'dearth of accommodation in evangelical theological colleges for graduates' and that 'all our evangelical theological colleges (of varying theological points of view) are full, and this seems especially true of those of the conservative views'. In addition, he pointed out, 'this is more serious as the Anglo-Catholics are building extensively and putting into the ministry a large number of men'.[4] Expressing his confidence that 'these are days of a rising tide of evangelicalism', the letter went on to state:

---

[3] Letter from Hinde to Arthur Young, October 1930.

[4] It was not only among the evangelical section of the Church of England that the shortage of men for the ministry was being felt. In the Introduction to the 1930 *Church of England Year Book* it was stated that 'the shrinking of the numbers of the clergy continues apace. In spite of the fact that the number of ordinations in 1929 exceeded by 54 the number in 1928, it seems sufficiently well-established that the annual supply is not sufficient in each year to repair the wastage by death or resignation of that year.' *Church of England Year Book* 1930, p. v.

> This would involve I fear an outlay of not less than the amount spent on Oak Hill College, even though greater care might be exercised in that expenditure, but I do not think it need be so great a charge on current funds. We might expect more from the students. I know that other people think it would be a very good thing to have some such College in London as Ridley at Cambridge, and Wycliffe at Oxford, and I am of opinion after much thought that Oak Hill could not be better used, nor more in accordance with what I conceive to be the mind of Mr Young.[5]

Within the week a reply was received from Arthur Young expressing his enthusiastic support for the proposal. He stated that 'Oak Hill house with its adjoining buildings, such as the laundry, would accommodate fifty young men at least, so that it would be a grand addition to the work of training candidates for Holy Orders.' He called a meeting of the trust on 6 November to consider the proposal.[6]

The pressure on places at the evangelical colleges may reflect an answer to the prayers and efforts of men like Hinde at a time when evangelicalism was at a low point in its influence on the Church of England. It laid the foundations for the growth in numbers of evangelical clergy in the succeeding generations. It would appear that the trustees responded positively to the proposal, as later in 1930 there was correspondence between Hinde and the trustees' solicitors seeking clarification as to whether the trustees had the necessary powers to run a theological college. As a result a supplemental trust deed was published on 10 July 1932, granting the trustees:

> POWER (1) To found and endow control and carry on or permit to be carried on upon any convenient part or parts of the landed property of the Trust in England Theological Training Schools or Theological Training Colleges for the purpose of training youths (up to but not

---

[5] Letter from Hinde to Arthur Young, 23 October 1930.
[6] Letter from Arthur Young to Hinde, 30 October 1930.

> beyond the age of 25 years) who are desirous of obtaining ordination in the Church of England and are without adequate means of paying the expenses of their training.
> POWER (2) To make annual or other grants to or for the purposes of any such Schools or Colleges and their maintenance equipment and upkeep.
> POWER (3) From time to time to make rescind and alter the Rules and Regulations for the control conduct and administration of such Schools or Colleges in such manner as will in the opinion of the Trustees best promote the efficiency thereof and so far as convenient (but without prejudice to the powers aforesaid) to delegate the administration of any such School or College to a Council or other Governing Body.[7]

While the project was not legalized until July 1932, the trustees had already made an approach to the central authorities of the Church of England in March of that year. The minutes of CACTM record that on 18 March 1932 the Inspections Committee had also 'considered the proposed foundation of new Theological Colleges at Barnet and Clifton. The Governing Body of the former would be identical with that of Oak Hill College, East Barnet, and the Bishop of Norwich had consented to be the Visitor, subject to the goodwill of the two Diocesans concerned, London and St. Albans.' The same minutes record:

> That subject to proper safeguards with regard to the Trust Deed (if any), to Statutes, to the Visitor, the nature of the responsibility entrusted to the Principal, and inspectors, this Council advises the Bishops that Oak Hill Theological College may be regarded as a place of training from which candidates for Holy Orders may be received.[8]

Final confirmation was provided on 27 July 1932, when the same body reported in its minutes that the bishops had accepted the

---

[7] Supplementary Trust Deed Extending Powers of Kingham Hill Trust, 10 May 1932.
[8] CACTM Minutes, 1923–32, pp. 280, 282.

resolution sent forward by CACTM in connection with the new colleges at Clifton and Barnet.

The above reference to the trust deed raises an issue that was to pose problems for the college in later years. When Francis Close, then rector of Cheltenham, a protégé of Charles Simeon and subsequently Dean of Carlisle, founded the Church of England Colleges of St Paul and St Mary for the training of teachers, he included a statement in their trust deed of 1848 that was intended to ensure that these colleges' theological position would continue to be based on the historic Anglican formularies. This required that 'the religious education to be conveyed in

> ... the Colleges shall always be strictly SCRIPTURAL EVANGELICAL AND PROTESTANT and in strict accordance with the ARTICLES and LITURGY of the CHURCH OF ENGLAND AS NOW BY LAW ESTABLISHED in their literal and Grammatical Sense and that those principles should forever be preserved as a most sacred trust at any sacrifice of pecuniary loss or temporal interests AND this will and purpose is hereby recorded and affirmed in dependence on the aid and blessing of Almighty God and in sole reliance upon the teaching of the Holy Ghost through the only Lord and Saviour Jesus Christ.[9]

The Revd Alfred Peache, who founded St John's Hall, was a friend of Close, so it is not surprising that in the foundation of that college he incorporated a similar clause, with which Hinde, as secretary of their council, would have been familiar. It may have been at Hinde's suggestion that when the test school was established, the trustees specifically proposed that 'a Trust Deed or Memorandum ... be drawn up possibly on the lines of St. John's Highbury to regulate the proceedings and powers of the directors'.[10] The Kingham Hill trust deed had originally been drawn up in 1912, and it is also quite likely that those responsible for

---

[9] Trust Deed of the Church of England Foundation of St Paul and St Mary in Cheltenham dated 12 April 1848.

[10] Minutes of Kingham Hill trust, 28 June 1928.

its drafting had used the earlier documents as a source for their stipulations. It is a strange feature of the developments within the Church of England in the nineteenth and twentieth centuries that such stipulations should have been necessary, as in a sense the position laid down in these documents is no more than that to which clergy of the Church of England are expected to give their assent at ordination and any subsequent appointment. However, since the 1830s the tractarians had been maintaining that the Anglican formularies could be interpreted in a more Catholic way, and that is why men like Close spelt out their requirements so clearly. Interestingly, those who inspected the college in 1955 wrote in their report that 'it is evident that the Trust Deed is free from tiresome clauses'.[11]

At the Islington Clerical Conference in January 1932 Hinde announced the trustees' decision to open Oak Hill as a new theological college, and stated that he would be intimately associated with it as chairman of its governing body. It is also a reflection of the times of the Depression that he went on to say that 'the cost of a university under the circumstances of today is far too great for many a boy and perhaps for that reason other vocations are set before him'. He also devoted the main part of his address to emphasizing the importance of the supply and support of a Protestant ministry. He stated that by this term he meant a ministry that is 'unashamedly Protestant and therefore does not seek to explain away the term or try to make out that it is obsolete, but will fearlessly proclaim the Gospel and base all its teaching on Holy Scripture'.[12]

While the negotiations with the lawyers and the church authorities were being conducted, the trustees had been considering who should be the first principal of the new foundation. In the light of all he had contributed to the founding of the college it is hardly surprising that they selected Hinde. In April Hinde circulated an announcement that the trustees had appointed him to the post, reporting:

---

[11] 1955 CACTM Inspection Report.
[12] *The Record*, 15 January 1932.

> The present Oak Hill College was established in 1928 by the late Mr Charles Edward Baring Young. He made the proposal of the gift to me and laid upon me the responsibility of being chairman of its council. As I announced at the last Islington Conference the Kingham Hill Trustees, in whom the property is vested, have decided to open the other mansion on the estate as a full course theological college for non-graduates, and to amalgamate the two places as 'Oak Hill College'. They have invited me to be principal. By the terms of the trust the college must be for non-graduates (but men may graduate while at the college) who will be ordained at not later than 25 years of age and who cannot afford a residential career at a University. It is to be conducted on Evangelical Church of England lines. The fees will be £90 per annum, inclusive of all except laundry and books, and there are bursaries of £30 per annum. The course will be one of three years from matriculation.[13]

When the time came for Hinde to leave St Mary's, Islington, he told the congregation at his farewell that he had twice refused the offer of the principalship, but then felt a call had come from God to accept it.[14] As a token of their love and affection the congregation presented him and Mrs Hinde with a magnificent communion service consisting of two large solid silver chalices and a flagon together with two patens in a substantial, specially made box. This communion plate is still in current use in the college.

It had been a fairly simple matter to adapt Bohun Lodge from a country mansion to a college catering for some twenty or so students and a relatively small staff. However, more major works were needed to make the neighbouring property at Oak Hill suitable for the needs of some fifty students and a proportionately larger staff. While there is little information in the archives about the history of Bohun Lodge, much has been discovered about the history of Oak Hill. The house is described in the following manner in a draft text submitted to the college authorities by Bridget Cherry:

---

[13] Printed letter from Hinde at Islington vicarage in college archives.

[14] *The Record*, 8 July 1932.

> A long white mansion overlooking ample grounds with some fine trees, sloping down to Pymmes Brook. The core of the present building is a neat C18 villa which replaced an older house on the Monkfryth estate (so called from its early ownership by St Alban's abbey). The house was called 'newly erected' in 1790 when it was bought by John Kingston M.P. A drawing of c.1800 by Oldfield (Herts Record Office) shows an E entrance front with two story centre of three bays recessed between lower three bay wings, all over a service basement, and a longer W front. The present E front, flush with the wings, and with a Diocletian window over a central pedimented Ionic porch, is probably part of a substantial remodelling by Sir Simon Haughton Clarke (+1832), a wealthy man who had married the heiress of a Jamaican planter and bought the house in 1810. He appears also to have added the large, plain extension to the S (now containing the library),[15] perhaps for his picture collection (it has a dentilled cornice, like the centre of the E front) and the conservatory to the N. Both are shown on the Tithe Map of 1840.[16]

During the nineteenth century the house was leased out to various tenants. In the 1850s Lord Feversham took over the estate, and it was from him that the Baring Young family bought it. An unusual feature of the house, reflecting the architectural period, is the fact that there are no visible staircases in the main entrance hall or corridors. The main staircase is an attractive stone cantilevered spiral one, concealed behind a door to the left of the main entrance.

At the time of the conversion of Oak Hill for the purposes of the college the Kingham Hill trustees owned the whole of the land between what is now Cat Hill and Osidge Lane, and from Chase Side to Church Hill Road in East Barnet. The area nearest to Osidge Lane still bore the name of Monkfryth, and had been up

---

[15] In 2000 the library was moved to its new location in the Academic Centre.

[16] College archives: Bridget Cherry's draft for inclusion in *The Buildings of England: London 4, North*, sent to the college by the author.

for sale. Hearing that William Booth, the founder of the Salvation Army, was hoping to purchase the property for the work of his organization, Baring Young is reputed to have bought it in order to keep him out. Keen Christian as he was, it did not appear that his ecumenism went to the extent of being able to cope with the enthusiasms and brass bands of the Salvation Army on his doorstep!

While the main reception rooms on the ground floor were adequate to house classes of the size the proposed college was likely to need, and the upper floor could be adapted for flats for the principal and another member of the academic staff, there was insufficient room for student accommodation. Therefore the laundry (to which in their heyday the Baring Youngs had sent their weekly washing from the house in Hyde Park Terrace to dry in the purer air of Southgate), together with the stables and groom's cottage, were demolished and a wing added to provide each of the envisaged fifty students with a ground-floor study and a bedroom above. As neither of the Baring Young brothers had spent much time at Oak Hill, there was neither electric lighting nor an adequate drainage system. The extent of all this work shows that the suggestion to Arthur Young that conversion would require no less expenditure than was laid out for Bohun Lodge was true.

Although the work with pre-matriculates ('pre-matrics') at Bohun Lodge was to continue on those premises for another five years, it was decided that the person in charge there should act as deputy to the principal of the new foundation, so Habershon was asked to seek another post. This was an unfortunate ending to the splendid work he had done in establishing the college in its early years, inaugurating the bursary fund, and making the work and its needs known to the wider Christian public. He returned to parochial ministry and for the next thirty and more years exercised an influential evangelical ministry in Cheltenham, New Malden, Chislehurst and Tunbridge Wells.

Archbishop Marcus Loane gives an interesting picture of the man who became the first principal of Oak Hill, describing him as 'tall and spare in figure, an aristocrat in bearing and autocratic in outlook, decisive in conviction and courageous in churchmanship'.[17] This is reflected in his portrait that hangs in the college. He was, however, not the stiff, unyielding Victorian of popular mythology, pompous and arrogant in the proclamation of his faith, being aware, in fact, that conservative evangelicals sometimes acted in this manner. When describing his experiences as a member of the Christian Union at Cambridge, which he greatly valued, he also warned that there was a danger in such circles of students 'lacking a becoming humility' and possessing a 'certain intolerance'.[18] One of his early students, E.J. Walser, spoke of Hinde as being 'a good principal, who could be very strict at times, and would stand no nonsense, which is no doubt a good thing when dealing with young ordinands. He was very much the schoolmaster, and when he came into the classroom we all had to stop our work and stand while he was present.'[19] Yet behind the stern exterior there was a deeply caring pastoral heart, and both Prebendary and Mrs Hinde sought to continue the family atmosphere established by the Habershons. At the memorial service following Hinde's death in 1955, Bishop Hugh Gough, who had been one of Hinde's curates at Islington, spoke of the enjoyable Sunday evenings spent following the day's services in the Hindes' drawing room, enjoying refreshments and singing hymns round the piano.[20] That practice was maintained for the students in the early days at Oak Hill.

---

[17] M.L. Loane, *These Happy Warriors: Friends and Contemporaries*, p. 4. An interesting picture of Hinde from the perspective of a small boy who grew up in his Islington congregation is found in J.E. Morpurgo, *Master of None* .

[18] F.D. Coggan (ed.), *Christ and the Colleges*, pp. 31–2. Barclay suggests that 'what had looked like arrogance to older people like Hinde was partly a new confidence in biblical doctrine that made the rising young leaders call the bluff of the establishment and so appear cheeky or rude to authorities.' Barclay, *Evangelicalism in Britain*, pp. 27–8.

[19] Letter from the Revd E.J. Walser in college archives.

[20] Reminiscence by David Wheaton, who was present.

The new principal faced an enormous challenge as he led the newly established college through a period of continuing crisis in British history. Fascist dictators in Germany and Italy and an ambitious Japan propelled Europe and the world towards another great conflict. During the 1930s Britain and France responded to aggressive acts by Japan, Italy and Germany by pursuing policies that were later branded as 'appeasement', encouraged by a theology that found it difficulty to appreciate the reality of evil. In 1938 the long-awaited report of the Doctrinal Commission set up in 1922 was published under the title *Doctrine in the Church of England*.[21] It reflected the optimistic beliefs about man's nature that were prevalent in the 1930s. Although the commission that wrote the report was selected to represent different points of view or traditions, the fact that it did not include anybody who truly represented the conservative evangelical position was indicative of their lack of influence in the Church of England.[22] Consequently, it is not surprising that the final report did not adequately reflect their position. Leslie Paul points out that 'the commission indeed found it difficult in that ameliorating climate to believe in sin or evil at all, except as something a pre-arranged evolution would presently eliminate'.[23] The report was out of date almost as soon as it was issued, as Hitler's actions and the outbreak of World War II revealed the reality and power of sin and evil.[24]

---

[21] Archbishops' Commission on Christian Doctrine, *Doctrine in the Church of England*.

[22] G.W.H. Lampe, in the introduction to the 1982 republication of the report, stated that it was 'regrettable' that none of the members of the commission 'was representative of the hard core of conservative biblicism or of the dogmatically self-conscious Evangelicalism which held rigidly to the theology of the Reformers and its formulated expression in the Thirty Nine Articles'. G.W.H. Lampe in *Doctrine in the Church of England*, p. xxxi.

[23] Leslie Paul, *A Church by Daylight*, pp. 100–101, taken from Alan Wilkinson, *Dissent or Conform: War, Peace and the English Churches 1900–1945*, p. 97.

[24] The brutality of the totalitarian dicators was to have a pronounced effect on English Christianity. Hastings points out that 'the secular

Although evangelicalism was still weak and continued to have relatively little influence in the Church of England, during the 1930s the foundations were laid for future growth. Some very creative and successful work among young people was carried out by the Crusaders' Union and the Children's Special Service Mission (CSSM, now known as Scripture Union) in Easter and summer camps. In the year the college was founded Eric Nash, affectionately known as 'Bash', was appointed by CSSM to work among public school boys, whom he regarded the natural leaders of society. Some of the best-known future leaders of Anglican evangelicalism, including John Stott, Dick Lucas, David Sheppard and Michael Green, were converted at these camps.[25] Many other young men who attended the various camps and house parties also entered the ordained ministry. Some helped to make up the first classes at Oak Hill, though, on the whole, Nash preferred his men to go to Ridley Hall at Cambridge, which he felt to be more acceptable in the eyes of the establishment. In 1937 a report on Oak Hill College stated:

> If it were asked what, in general, is the type of man who is to be found at Oak Hill, it would probably be correct to say, 'the Crusader and CSSM type' – one quite easily recognisable. These keen young fellows,

---

[24] (*continued*) vision ... faded as the late 1930s man, agonised by Hitler upon one hand and Stalin upon the other, increasingly frightened by what was just around the corner ... was more and more inclined to look for God instead, to hope for the reassurance, if not of some unforgettable burst of light, at least of the tempered optimism of the crucifix.' Hastings, *History of English Christianity*, p. 289.

[25] 'All the major public schools were reached by the careful, thoughtful and dedicated work of the Iwerne Minister Camps represented by "Bash" and his assistants. Their follow-up work was outwardly very low-key but meticulous and yielded dividends in the number of committed Christians going into Anglican ministry and into the professions.' Manwaring, *From Controversy to Co-existance*, pp. 58–9. See Timothy Dudley-Smith, *John Stott: The Making of a Leader*, pp. 91ff. for a more detailed description of the methods used.

> accustomed to Bible-classes and beach services, to 'squashes' and holiday camps, will make splendid leaders of youth in the parishes to which they pass when they leave college walls and lecture-rooms behind them.[26]

Many Oak Hill students spent their summer vacations working in the various camps.

Another important development was the formation of the Inter-Varsity Fellowship of Evangelical Unions (IVF) in 1928. Hinde, who had been greatly blessed by the fellowship of the Christian Union during his Cambridge days, commented on the importance of IVF in 1934:

> If the Lectures and Teaching of the Universities are to be of true value, there must be on the part of the student the devotional and thoughtful study of the Mind of God revealed in Holy Scripture. But such a disposition on his part will not come naturally; it will need fostering, and will be very much easier where there is true Christian fellowship. Evangelical Unions serve this end, and are the stronger and more effective when linked together in such a way as is provided by Inter-Varsity Fellowship.[27]

Although membership was small in comparison with the Student Christian Movement (SCM) whose leadership was liberal, and conservative evangelicals were at times subjected to a great deal of ridicule at the universities, those who did not bow to the pressure to conform would play a significant role in the future.[28] The publishing programme introduced by the IVF in the 1930s and

---

[26] 'Youngest Anglican Theological College', *The Life of Faith*, 17 November 1937.

[27] Coggan, *Christ and the Colleges*, p. 32.

[28] 'While the SCM had massive official support, the IVF was constantly under fire for its theological position and for being hostile to the rationalist traditions of a university ... It was sometimes said that the CUs were not in sympathy with the spirit of the universities and had no place there.' Barclay, *Evangelicalism in Britain*, p. 21.

subsequently expanded under the Inter-Varsity Press (IVP) would also provide an opportunity for conservative evangelicals to make serious contributions to scholarship.

It was in this changing and challenging environment that Hinde and his staff worked for the first seven years of the college's history. Some of the changes that were taking place made society a good deal more receptive to the type of biblical Christianity that would be taught at Oak Hill. However, new and promising movements like the Oxford Group Movement could easily mislead eager young people committed to evangelism. The deteriorating international situation also confronted Christians with difficult choices. Although with the benefit of hindsight it is clear that appeasement was a disastrous policy, those living at the time, who still had vivid memories of the tragedy of World War I, were understandably anxious to do all they could to avoid war. In addition, even before the college was established, there were movements in the Church of England that threatened the type of theological education to which Oak Hill was committed. In January 1921 a report to the archbishops had included a statement by the chairman and general secretary of CACTM, maintaining that all candidates for ministry should be graduates and that 'the non-graduate colleges would be better abolished'. On 28 October 1930 a Commission on Staffing of Parishes, which had been appointed by the Church Assembly in the previous year, issued a report that included among its thirteen recommendations a provision that 'assent to the xxxix Articles should be no longer required as part of the doctrinal test necessary for admission to Holy Orders'. In February 1931 a CACTM report to the Church Assembly stated that it was 'uneconomic to maintain so many theological colleges when the universities had well-endowed divinity faculties' and it was recommended that 'the church should make more of theological colleges and hostels at the new universities'.[29]

Hinde was the ideal leader to guide the college through the challenges it faced in its initial years. First he set about

---

[29] Bullock, *History of Training*, pp. 83, 89.

attracting students, but with the project getting off the ground at such relatively short notice it is not surprising that the first academic year began with only ten students, although there were five on the academic staff. In addition there were seventeen students at Bohun Lodge. Two of the students had transferred from Bohun Lodge: they were Woodhams and Fryer, to both of whom reference has already been made. The latter had the unique distinction of having been educated at all three of the founder's institutions.

Unfortunately, not all the student records from these early days are preserved, but from those available it would appear that the majority of students were young men who had left school at fourteen or sixteen and been employed in family firms or as junior clerks. One notable exception was Peter Johnston, who became the first person from Oak Hill to be ordained, and later followed Hinde as vicar of Islington and prebendary of St Paul's. He joined the new college at its inauguration, coming from the Royal Navy, where he had held the rank of sub lieutenant.

Hinde was keen to complement his own contribution in the pastoral field and wanted to appoint colleagues with good academic qualifications. He appointed as his vice-principal the Revd G.G. Dawson, who was to gain the degree of Doctor of Divinity while teaching at Oak Hill. Other staff members were the Revd A.A. Gray, Scholar and Carus Prizeman of Jesus College, Cambridge, who had first-class honours in the classical tripos and second-class honours in the theological tripos, and Geoffrey Watkins Grubb, with second-class honours in theology from New College, Oxford. Rolfe continued on the staff at Bohun Lodge. Grubb became the first member to be ordained while on the staff, serving a part-time curacy at the nearby parish of St Paul, Winchmore Hill from 1933–5, and married the principal's daughter, Kathleen.

The year began with great enthusiasm and the type of good humour that was to be an ongoing characteristic of Oak Hill students. A report in *The Record* after the completion of the first term contained this description of life at the college:

> All men have entered into their respective courses with zest, and judging from the high standard at the terminal examination results, the future success is assured. The farm supplies the college with milk and vegetables. The college has a principal's flat, chapel, common room, tutors' studies, library, lecture rooms. Each man has a separate study, simply but satisfactorily furnished. It is intended for fifty men. Lectures have been given during the term on some larger aspects of Church work, Archdeacon Dallimore and Dr. Richardson of the Church Army being amongst the speakers. On November 5th the students held a mock trial, Guy Fawkes being the criminal and the 'rag' was productive of much spontaneous witticism, which provoked the amusement of invited friends. Both colleges form an entity and unite for Sunday and mid-week services. Daily services are held in the respective chapels ... Games are played most afternoons. There are four hard and four grass tennis courts, a fives court, hockey field and indoor showers. A new adventure on such a large scale must in its initial stages give cause for some anxiety, but the fellowship, the inspiration of the common religious and social life and the intellectual enthusiasm provoke grateful thanks to God for His over-ruling love and providence. It is with a mighty 'Laus Deo' that our first and most eventful term has drawn to a close.[30]

A local development was to have considerable effect upon Oak Hill's accessibility. It had been decided in 1932–3 to extend the Piccadilly tube line through Southgate and Oakwood to Cockfosters. The original prospectus of 1928 stated that 'the nearest stations are Oakleigh Park and New Barnet (for luggage). A frequent omnibus service from Finsbury Park and Palmers Green (No. 29 for Cockfosters or 629 for Potters Bar) passes the College Gate.'[31] From Oakleigh Park the walk would have been well over a mile, so the arrival of underground trains at Southgate with the adjacent bus station made the journey to and from London as easy as it is today. About the same time the postal address was changed from East Barnet to the London postal area of N14.

---

[30] *The Record*, 16 December 1932.
[31] College prospectus.

A reporter from *The Record* took that tube journey to attend the spring garden party at the college in 1933. 'Alighting at the recently opened Southgate station on the Piccadilly tube', he wrote, 'a few steps and we are in the open country; we take a deep breath as we become conscious of the fresh health-giving atmosphere scented with the fragrance of recently fallen rain on leaves and pasture land.' Guests, the reporter wrote, were greeted by music provided by the Metropolitan Police Band, and there then follows a full description of the premises.

The timetable followed appears to have been much the same as that established at Bohun Lodge, except that rising was at 6.45 a.m., with chapel at 7.30 a.m. and breakfast at 8.00 a.m. As well as the opportunities for sport in the afternoons there is mention of the ominous fact that in subsequent years led to contention: 'the students are encouraged in gardening'![32]

Two other events that took place in 1933 are of significance for subsequent developments. The first was the college's first visit from 7–9 June by inspectors appointed by CACTM, Canon G.W. Evans and the Revd C. Mayne. Their report was very positive about the facilities offered by the college, and explained how the workload of the two institutions was shared between the tutorial staff. It was noted that the vice-principal was now living at Bohun Lodge and acting as director of studies for the whole college, taking classes for the matriculation students and lecturing in Christian worship and Christian morals for the theological students. The principal gave instruction in pastoralia, but did not otherwise take part in the teaching programme. This last fact was picked up as a weakness, and led to a letter from the Bishop of Manchester (Guy Warman, at that time chairman of CACTM) to Hinde encouraging him to take on some of the doctrinal teaching, and suggesting that his contribution in the fields of church, ministry and sacraments, 'and perhaps not least soteriology', would be valuable. He went on to state a fact that has always been at the heart of the

[32] *The Record*, 2 June 1933.

college's strategy in making staff appointments: 'it is in these departments that the experience of a parish priest who has taught the faith pastorally is of special value'.[33]

The inspectors also noted with approval that the lecturers showed in all cases a good grasp of their subject and a considerable power of expressing important points clearly, without overdoing the dictation of notes. They approved that a Greek Testament class was studying the epistle to the Philippians, which was outside the examination syllabus, and emphasized that 'the students are not merely working to pass an examination but to develop their intellectual life'.[34] The library was also praised for the fact that the selection of books showed no sign of partisanship or narrowness, and that the students were encouraged to read widely. They picked up the point noted earlier that it seemed to complicate the work of Bohun Lodge that the pre-matriculates were working for such a variety of examinations, but it was difficult to see how that could be avoided, since they were wishing to head for different colleges or universities. It was felt to be a disadvantage that the two departments were kept entirely separate for their daily services and especially their communions. While the inspectors spoke warmly of the time set apart for quiet and meditation each morning, they expressed concern that students should receive some help in knowing how to make best use of it. Hinde responded, after consulting with his staff, to each of the points at issue in the bishop's letter, and then concluded with the interesting comment: 'you say you want these men to be open to a considerable amount of freedom of thought. I think I may say they are, and I would like to add (with that cocksureness which marks some of them) that it is to their loss, for I am persuaded that my groove is the best.'[35]

The other event of significance in that year concerned the principal's family. The Hindes had two daughters, and the younger,

---

[33] Letter from the Chairman of CACTM to Hinde, 19 July 1933.

[34] Report of first CACTM inspection of the college, 1933, in the college archives.

[35] Letter of 4 October 1933 from Hinde to the Chairman of CACTM.

Marjorie, was a trained dispenser who had gone out to work as a missionary in Cairo. There she had met a young clergyman, Leonard Hickin, and they had fallen in love. Hickin had been greatly blessed by attending the Keswick Convention in 1924, to which he ascribed his becoming a committed Christian, and had heard Hinde preach. He described his future father-in-law as a true saint, a man whom he greatly admired, though he did not necessarily endorse all his opinions. It was therefore with some trepidation that the couple cabled their parents to let them know of their proposed engagement, and for Hickin to ask Hinde for his daughter's hand. Would Hinde welcome a son-in-law who had somewhat liberal views, and did not see eye to eye with him in all his beliefs? Their fears turned out to be groundless. Apparently Hinde went up to CMS (Church Missionary Society) House (Hickin was serving with that society) to find out from the secretary what sort of a person he was, and then called on Hickin's parents, impressing them both with the prayer he prayed for them all before he left their house. The happy couple were married on 14 September 1933 at Cockfosters Church, and the reception was held in the dining hall and grounds of Oak Hill College – the first of many such happy occasions to follow for various members of the staff as well as students and their families.[36]

The praise given by the 1933 inspection team to the academic staff was justified by the results announced at the following year's garden party. Of the eight students who had sat the General Ordination Examination (GOE) at the end of their first year, seven had passed, obtaining no fewer than five special marks for distinction.[37] Over the first seven years the numbers of students steadily increased, with seventeen ordinands and twenty-six pre-matrics in 1933–4; nineteen ordinands and twenty-six pre-matrics in 1934–5; twenty-three ordinands and fifteen pre-matrics in 1935–6; twenty-three ordinands and fifteen pre-matrics in 1936–7; twenty-five ordinands and fifteen pre-matrics in 1937–8; and

---

[36] For these details the authors are grateful to C.E. Hillas, *Recorded Memories: An Autobiography of Canon Leonard Hickin.*

[37] *The Record*, 8 June 1934.

twenty-seven ordinands and ten pre-matrics in 1938–9. At the outbreak of war in 1939 there were only five pre-matrics with twenty-three ordinands. It speaks well for the principal that in that time there was only one change in the academic staff, when Mr Gray left on being invited to become principal of the CMS training college in Stoke Newington. He became the first member of staff to move on to a principalship: it has been striking to see the number of other staff members who have gained such appointments during the years that have followed.[38]

PERSONALITY PROFILE

John Carter was the second former student of the college to be elevated to the episcopate, the first being Dick Lyth, who was consecrated bishop of Kigezi in Uganda in 1967.

John and his brothers, Bindon and William, grew up in Belfast in the 1920s. When their father, a machinery merchant, died, John was aged ten, and his mother sent the two older boys over to Kingham Hill to be educated. William joined them later.

During the course of preparation for confirmation in 1936 the warden, the Revd Douglas Horsefield, suggested to John that he might consider the possibility of a

[38] These have included Alan Cole (master of Robert Menzies College, Sydney, Australia, 1972–9), J. Stafford Wright (principal of Tyndale Hall, 1951–69), Donald Lynch (principal of the Church Army Training College, 1953–61), Jim Packer (principal of Tyndale Hall, 1969–72 and Trinity College Bristol, 1972–9), David Wheaton (who returned as Oak Hill's principal, 1971–86), Geoffrey Shaw (principal of Wycliffe Hall 1979–88), Christopher Byworth (warden of Cranmer Hall, Durham, 1979–83), George Carey (principal of Trinity College Bristol, 1982–7), Ian Cundy (warden of Cranmer Hall, Durham, 1983–92), Philip Crowe (principal of Salisbury and Wells Theological College 1988–95), John Goldingay (principal of St John's Nottingham 1988–97) and Mike Butterworth (principal of the St Albans and Oxford Ministerial Training Course 1997–present).

call to the ordained ministry. The trustees sponsored him to go to Oak Hill in 1938.

John experienced all the hazards of studying during the Blitz and was evacuated to Kingham Hill. He gained his Intermediate BA (London) in 1941, and then enlisted in the RAF to do his bit in World War II, being sent to South Africa to be trained as a pilot. On his return to Oak Hill the trustees continued their financial support, enabling him to complete his BA finals in 1947. John was then offered a government grant for further theological training, which he took up at Wycliffe Hall, Oxford, and was ordained in 1949 to a curacy at St Mary's, Walthamstow.

After a further curacy at Immanuel, Streatham, John received a call to a parish in Cape Town, and has spent the rest of his life in South Africa. In 1968 he was consecrated as Suffragan Bishop of Johannesburg to the Diocesan, Leslie Stradling, resigning in 1977 and then serving in parish ministries. Having been supported on and off for seventeen years by the trustees, John's verdict is: 'When the Kingham Hill Trust takes on a responsibility, it doesn't give up. I thank God for that!'

In 1936 the last link with the founder's family was severed when Arthur Young died. He had maintained a keen interest in Charles's foundations and chaired the trustees until his death. At this date it was still unclear how the college was governed. While the first prospectus from Bohun Lodge lists the members of a college council as well as the trustees, the principal was the only member to have a place on both bodies. Significantly, the inspection report of 1933 contained a reference to the fact that the principal was one of the trustees, 'and will be also chairman of the council when it is formed'.[39] It is not likely that such an arrangement would have gone unchallenged in later inspections. In more recent times, when much of the General Synod's budget is spent on training for the ministry, sharp questions would have rightly

[39] 1933 CACTM Inspection Report.

been asked about the composition of a governing body, and to whom it is responsible. This was an issue that will continue to attract attention in this history. As late as 1936 the principal was still working on a draft constitution, and it is interesting to see from correspondence in this connection that the secretary of the trustees, A.B. Keith, was urging a membership of six and the majority laymen. This was because there was a fear that clergy would not feel able to oppose their bishops in any confrontation that might arise. In the following year Hinde was still seeking to establish a council, and wrote to a potential member that it was needed in order to give more detailed attention than could be secured from the trustees alone.

In 1937 the trustees took the decision to close Bohun Lodge and concentrate their work on the Oak Hill premises, accommodating the pre-matrics along with the ordinands. In a circular to students they stated that while some 191 men had taken the preliminary course there, numbers for the following year were low, and the property itself was in need of extensive roof repairs. Bohun Lodge and its estate would therefore be put up for sale, but the warning was given that the proceeds would benefit not the college, but the trust, whose first charge was the maintenance and carrying on of the Kingham Hill homes for boys. The same document underlined the fact that determined the trust's policy for many years: that the college was to be the *last* charge upon trust funds![40]

In 1937 Grubb left the college when he was appointed to the living of Cullompton in Devon. In his place Hinde appointed a young man who had just returned from a period of missionary work in the diocese of West China with the China Inland Mission (CIM, later to become the Overseas Missionary Fellowship). This was the Revd Alan Stibbs, who thus began a long and fruitful association with the college – for many people over the years he *was* Oak Hill. He and his family moved into the Farm House and a year later he succeeded Dr Dawson as vice-principal when the

---

[40] Statement circulated to the student body by the principal in 1937, now in college archives.

latter moved to become rector of Kirkheaton in the diocese of Wakefield. Stibbs brought with him two young children, the older of whom, John, became a teacher and was later to help the college in various ways. In recalling the early days after their arrival at Oak Hill, John spoke of the principal appearing an intimidating figure to a young child. He was 'a tall man, always dressed in black', and 'chapel every morning at 7.00 a.m. or soon after, and again in the evenings, was a strict requirement of all students and staff, and everyone was expected to be properly dressed with a jacket and tie. It was said that Hinde would stand near the chapel entrance to check attendance, and to see whether students' shoes were clean.'[41]

Hinde's interests were not confined to the domestic affairs of the college. In the wider church there were constant debates about the nature of training that should be expected of ordinands. It was only in the early years of the century that some bishops were beginning to waive the requirement of a university degree, but it was still expected that candidates should have a knowledge of Latin and Greek as well as a sufficiency of scriptural and theological knowledge to pass the examination of deacons. In spite of this progress there was still some prejudice against the non-graduate clergy, and in 1937 the archbishops set up a Commission on Training for the Ministry. As a contribution to their debate Hinde submitted a paper arguing that, whatever degree they might have obtained, all ordinands should be required to sit for a theological diploma granted by a central church body. Non-graduates taking this course should spend no less than three years at a theological college and take the diploma in three parts, one each year. He recommended that there be at least two viva voce examinations a year:

> to ascertain (a) whether the man thinks; (b) his devotional habits and his devotion and earnestness of purpose; (c) his manner and language i.e. whether he has any provincial accent and whether he has any

[41] Interview with John L. Stibbs, 28 April 1999.

> hesitancy or unease of expression; (d) his reading ability; and (e) what, if any, practical, e.g. parochial, work he is doing.

After suggesting a better correlation of the teaching of church history, Christian doctrine, Christian worship and moral theology with the text of the Old and New Testaments, Hinde went on to plead that 'the Bible papers should deal definitely with the message and content of the whole Bible as we have it now'. Even though he recognized that 'literary historical critical research has done much to help in the understanding of it' he maintained 'it seems necessary that the Bible should be read to see what it has to say for itself: its face value must be appreciated'. He lamented the fact that 'this method of study of the Bible seems to be a thing of the past and its plain message has been obscured. Its revelation to man of the Nature and Being, the Plan and the Purpose of God seem to have no place in the present scheme'. Finally he urged that 'a greater place should be given to the homiletic study of the Bible'.[42] This last point echoes a concern expressed at the Lambeth Conference in 1908, where the bishops had voiced their unhappiness about the character of biblical study taught in the theological colleges. They complained that they wanted 'the young men to hear less of the Bible as a series of literary problems and more of it as God's Word'.[43] Oak Hill clearly sought to put that emphasis into practice. Throughout his ministry on the staff Stibbs gave a 'Bible analysis' to the student body at one of their early-morning chapel services. During Leslie Wilkinson's principalship this was complemented by an a second exposition given by another staff member, often on an Old Testament book to balance Stibbs's focus on the New.

Hinde continued his service to the wider church when he was re-elected to Convocation and therefore to the Church Assembly. Here he continued to represent the position of the founder's trust deed as he constantly called upon the church to remain true to the teaching of the Anglican formularies. In 1936, following

---

[42] H.W. Hinde, *Memorandum to the Archbishops' Commission on Training for the Ministry*, dated 18 March 1937.

[43] Lloyd, *The Church of England*, p. 151.

discussions between delegates of the Church of England and the Romanian (Orthodox) church, proposals were laid before the Church Assembly to set up a relation of inter-communion. In debate Hinde expressed grave doubts as to whether the Romanian church clearly understood what the Anglican Church believed, protesting that the report contained a misrepresentation both of their views and of Church of England doctrine.[44]

Anticipating the publication of *Doctrine in the Church of England* later that year, Hinde addressed the Islington Clerical Conference in 1938 on 'The Bible as the Rule of Faith'. Here he said of the report, 'if it is based on the Bible and does not depart from its teachings we shall welcome it. Otherwise, if it is based on any other authority, we shall resist it as an unwarrantable challenge to divine authority and a misrepresentation of revealed religion.'[45]

Hinde's comments on Geoffrey Fisher's enthronement as Bishop of London in 1939 reveal his continuing commitment to the Prayer Book that he had fought so hard to retain a decade earlier. Although his comments show an irenic and gracious spirit he did not hesitate to criticize aspects of the service that were not in accord with the Prayer Book. He first praised Fisher as one whom he believed 'will reach the hearts of church people generally and win the respect of all men'. He also commended 'the way he did his part in the service which was so natural and so easy, and yet so dignified, so unpretentious and yet so convincing and so masterful that one felt the new bishop of London is the right man for the post at this important period'. However, he also commented:

> I, for one, regretted the omission of the Ten Commandments and the substitution of our Lord's summary of them, because it meant a recognition of the Revised and rejected Prayer Book. Many of us feel tired of everyone being a law to himself and wish we could hark back to what is lawful and right. But, of course, his omission of the

[44] *The Record*, 5 June 1936.
[45] *The Record*, 14 January 1938.

> Decalogue is a small matter compared with two other great deviations from the Book of Common Prayer: the adoption of the Eastward Position and the invisibility of the manual acts (at the Communion). These involve doctrine, and at any rate I personally regretted it. Having made this criticism as is in duty bound and as impelled by conscience, I hasten to say that nevertheless I found the service very helpful.

He then concluded on a positive note: 'In my judgement there is much to encourage us to anticipate in this, and nothing to the contrary.'[46]

The last six years of Hinde's principalship coincided with one of the most destructive wars in British history, in which London itself became a battlefield. The college was not only literally in the battleground, but the supply of students, which had been steadily increasing during the thirties, now began to dry up. Many potential students were called up, and others who would in the normal run of events have been applying to the college felt duty-bound to volunteer for military service and put their calling on hold. Donald Lynch, who had been appointed as a tutor the previous year, wrote of those days in a letter: 'The college term in autumn of 1939 began a few days after the declaration of war. Since an early air attack on London was probable we were all issued with gas masks and tin hats. The college set up a first-aid team and a fire squad to deal with incendiary bombs.' He enclosed a photograph of a group with tin hats, gas masks, stirrup pump and bucket, adding that the last were for 'misuse as well as for use'![47] On 20 October 1939 Hinde issued a message to evangelicals, published in *The Record*. He spoke of the unity of the nation as being magnificent and a great cause for gratitude, and he urged Christian people to show the true unity of the Spirit in the bond of peace. Urging his readers to draw together in true fellowship as 'all one in Christ Jesus' he stated that:

---

[46] Ibid.

[47] Letter dated 23 November 1992, containing photographs from Donald Lynch, to college librarian, and now in college archives.

> Barriers which in the ordinary way separate us must be removed or temporarily set aside. Great issues are at stake and we must stand shoulder to shoulder ... There will be suggestions of compromise both with regard to doctrine and practice. We must seek to our utmost to preserve unity, but we must not deviate one step from the pathway of truth set before us in the Bible. Nothing is to be gained by it. The child of God will find no blessing in contravening the Father's will.[48]

By 1940 numbers had dropped to twenty-five, and members of staff moved on to other posts. Lynch, for example, went to a pioneering job in a large parish in a developing area of London. Although the principal promoted a scheme that allowed those students who, in the early stages of the war were not liable for 'call-up' until they reached twenty years of age, to begin their studies with a view to concluding them after the cessation of hostilities, it does not appear to have been a popular option. In September the *Luftwaffe* was bombing London almost every night, and so in the interests both of study and safety evacuation became desirable. The obvious solution was a move to Kingham Hill, where the school kindly put one of the boarding houses at the college's disposal. Stibbs went with them to assume responsibility for their work, while the Hindes remained at Oak Hill to act as caretakers and keep watch over the property.

Conditions at Kingham were far from ideal. Students not only had to sleep in dormitories but also had to share rooms for study. Food and fuel were at times not easy to obtain. Although compared with those in the London area they enjoyed a peaceful detachment, after two and a half terms at Kingham it was decided that the college should return to Oak Hill, where there was a greatly reduced number of students expected for the following academic year.[49]

The London Blitz was to have a further consequence of great significance for the college. St John's Hall had evacuated at the

---

[48] *The Record*, 20 October 1939.

[49] A fuller account of this period is in a report by Stibbs in the college archives.

beginning of the war to Wadhurst School for Girls in Sussex, where their numbers had steadily dwindled from seventy-five at the outbreak of war to twenty-six in 1942. In November 1940 the Highbury premises were severely damaged when a parachute mine rendered the buildings unusable. The following March their basement had been made available for a stretcher party depot; at the end of June 1942 the whole college (or what remained of the buildings) was requisitioned for use by the National Fire Service. At about the same time St John's suffered a further loss in the death of their principal, Dr Gilbert. In view of the exigencies of the time their council agreed to defer the appointment of a new principal and moved their remaining students to Oak Hill, where Hinde (still secretary of their council) would be their acting principal. An unidentified St John's student wrote a description that is a testimony to the leadership of Hinde and describes the problems faced by the community during the war:

> Prebendary Hinde won the respect of all of us, for he was a man of iron will, but with deep devotion to our Lord. The winter of 1944–5 was bitterly cold. We sat in our studies with cassocks (and often times dressing gowns) on, and tried to study with the temperature well below freezing; the austerity of war made central heating in the building impossible. Those were the days when there were no CACTM grants and fees at the College were £90 per annum. In the grim autumn of 1944 we watched from the terrace in front of the college the flying bombs passing over London.[50]

The war prompted the principal to produce a newsletter, published each term, which became the precursor of *The Oak Leaf* and the subsequent *Oak Hill Newsfax*. The main purpose was to keep in touch with those students now scattered abroad in the forces as well as those who had been ordained and were serving in a variety of situations. Out of nearly fifty who had been ordained since the college had opened for that purpose, at least three were

[50] G.C.B. Davies, *Men for Ministry: The History of the London College of Divinity*, p. 94.

serving in the church overseas, while several others who were serving in the forces as chaplains had found themselves posted abroad. The missionaries included the Darlington brothers (David and Evan, sons of a former CIM missionary) in Upper Burma, ministering to refugees from the Japanese advance, and Malcolm McNicol in northern Nigeria. Copies of surviving letters demonstrate the principal's pastoral concern to keep in touch with them and to encourage them in the Lord.

In 1941 Hinde and his family experienced a terrible loss. Following her marriage to Leonard Hickin in 1933 their daughter Marjorie had gone with him to serve as missionaries with the CMS in northern Nigeria. During a furlough in 1941 they were delighted to find that Marjorie was pregnant, and so it was agreed that she should stay at home with her parents while her husband return to Nigeria. At midday on 14 October he received a cable from his father-in-law: both his wife and the baby had died during childbirth. She was buried in the churchyard at Cockfosters, where they had been married. By 1943 Hickin had decided that his days of service in Nigeria would not continue after his next furlough that year. Not being sure what to do next, he was delighted when his father-in-law invited him to take on a tutorship at Oak Hill. In his diary Hickin records that he was to lecture on the Old Testament and church history, for which his brother-in-law, Grubb, would lend him his lecture notes.

This approach to teaching is borne out by the experience of Donald Lynch five years earlier when he was invited to teach Old Testament before having been interviewed or meeting the principal. When he said that this was the subject he felt least qualified to teach, the reply came, 'Oh, don't worry about that; you can "mug it up".' Fortunately for him and the students, Dr Stuart Barton Babbage, who later became principal of Ridley College, Melbourne, followed by a distinguished academic career in the USA, was appointed to the staff at the same time. He had been asked to teach liturgy, for which Lynch was better qualified, and so the two men agreed to swap subjects, and the principal gladly acquiesced.

In a report (presumably to the Kingham Hill trustees) of 14 October 1943 the principal described some of the challenges facing the college during the war:

> The times have enforced considerable changes here. The Conscription Acts limit us now to men over age or men unfit for some reason for any sort of National Service. We have at present at the two colleges together nine students. I am not yet sure how we can divide them. I intended to go by age – but one of the younger men who is dependent on grants has been told that the grant-makers wish him to count as London College of Divinity [as St John's Hall had now been renamed] and not Oak Hill as the principal of the latter hardly represents their views (no doubt this was not meant to come round to me). Of the nine men one is 38, one 32 and one 31 (and how the last got off service beats me), three are young men, one with an artificial hip, one with feet that can't march, and one with asthma. The remaining three are students who were here last year. One, and perhaps two, will leave at the end of this term. Two or three new students may come in January.[51]

Further references to dry rot and having to get a licence for the wood to repair it, and the difficulty of getting sufficient winter foodstuff for the cows, reflect the pressures of those times. In a postscript Hinde recorded that eight former students, now ordained, were serving in the forces as chaplains, while about ten who reckoned themselves still students were serving in the ranks of the services, and two of these had completed their courses and were ready for ordination.

The war continued for almost two more years until Japan finally surrendered in August 1945. The war had revealed to anyone who was willing to consider the evidence seriously the fallen nature of humanity, and it should not be surprising that people were now considerably more receptive to the Christian gospel. These years witnessed a very effective use of media to broadcast

---

[51] Handwritten report by Hinde dated 14 October 1943 in the college archives.

the Christian message. In 1941 C.S. Lewis gave twenty-five talks on BBC radio. His *Mere Christianity* was broadcast in early 1942 and Dorothy Sayers's *The Man Born to Be King*, which Hastings calls 'perhaps the most successful piece of religious work ever specifically written for radio',[52] was broadcast in 1941 and 1942. C.S. Lewis's best-selling *Screwtape Letters* was written in 1940 and by 1942 was in its sixth impression. In the words of Manwaring, 'suddenly in the space of a year or two, all the great truths of Christianity, including those of the actual devil and the personal return of our Lord, had become intellectually respectable'.[53] Charles Williams and T.S. Eliot also contributed to the Christian apologetic at that time.

Conservative Christian scholarship was also developing during the war years. In 1940 the IVF formed its Biblical Research Committee in order 'to remove the reproach of obscurantism and anti-intellectual prejudice from evangelical Christianity'.[54] It included in its membership Stibbs and Babbage. In 1942 the annual Tyndale Lectures were inaugurated and in 1945 Tyndale House in Cambridge was opened as a centre for biblical studies. Max Warren, secretary of the CMS, whom Bebbington classifies as part of the 'centrist school' of evangelicals, began the Evangelical Fellowship for Theological Literature in 1942 in order to encourage serious scholarship by younger evangelicals.[55]

The war ended with two more hopeful signs for a post-war revival of traditional Christianity in Britain. In 1944 Parliament enacted the Butler Education Act, which was designed to assure that the next generation were instructed in Britain's Christian

---

[52] Hastings, *History of English Christianity*, p. 388.

[53] Manwaring, *From Controversy to Co-existence*, p. 61.

[54] Bebbington, *Evangelicalism in Modern Britain*, p. 260.

[55] Bebbington identifies four 'schools of thought' among evangelicals at this time. 1) Liberal Evangelicals who identified with the AEGM (Anglican Evangelical Group Movement) 2) 'a centrist school tried to minimise the divide that had opened in the 1920s between liberals and conservatives' 3) moderate conservatives and 4) Fundamentalists. Ibid., pp. 251–2.

heritage. All schools were required to give religious instruction and begin the day with a non-denominational act of worship. In 1943 the Church Assembly set up a Commission on Evangelism under the chairmanship of the evangelical Bishop of Rochester, Christopher Chavasse. In 1945 a 172-page report entitled *Towards the Conversion of England* was published. The report stated that the aim of evangelism was 'so to present Christ Jesus in the power of the Holy Spirit, that men shall come to put their trust in God through Him, to accept him as their Saviour, and serve Him as their King in the fellowship of His Church'.[56] It argued that the psychological and spiritual needs of the age provided fertile ground for evangelization, and it reiterated traditional evangelical beliefs on basic doctrines. Manwaring comments: 'From an evangelical viewpoint, the report was a masterpiece of clear statement, not only on the needs and means of evangelism, but also on the essential doctrines of the faith.'[57] The report was extremely popular and was reprinted monthly for the next eight months.

In the meantime Oak Hill College was engaged in training the future ministers who could take advantage of the new opportunities. However, Hinde would not be leading the college into this new era, as he was now sixty-six years old. As the war drew to a close he began thinking carefully about the future. He had seen the need for more clergy to make up for the drop in ordinations during the war, and the likely increase in population. Recognizing that men who had spent up to six years in the forces following the age of eighteen would make his age limit of twenty-five years unrealistic, he had sought and gained permission to raise Oak Hill's age limit to thirty-five.

---

[56] Archbishops' Commission on Evangelism, *Towards the Conversion of England*, p. 1.

[57] Manwaring, *From Controversy to Co-existence*, p. 70. Hylson-Smith, *Evangelicals in the Church of England*, pp. 287–8 states: 'It reads like an Evangelical treatise and it helped to give prominence and official Church of England endorsement to the particular Evangelical emphasis which pervaded it.'

Meanwhile the council of the London College of Divinity (LCD) was occupied with considering their own future, which could not lie indefinitely at Oak Hill. As it was unlikely that they would be returning to Highbury, they needed to look for new premises, and in order to do this they needed to appoint a new principal. In the summer of 1943 they had approached the Revd Dr Donald Coggan, at that time Professor of Old Testament at Wycliffe College, Toronto, and he accepted their invitation, to take effect from 1 August 1944. The Oak Hill Newsletter of June 1944 welcomed him to the college, where St John's would remain for at least one further academic year. Living together on the same campus with two principals was not always easy but the arrangement seems to have worked well for both institutions.

In a statement to the trustees in January 1945 Hinde reported that there were in residence five Oak Hill students (of whom one was a pre-matric and another doing preliminary work before hoping to proceed to LCD), eleven LCD students, four recruits for the CMS under Coggan's direction, and two West Africans, living at the college as paying guests. He also stated, 'I am firmly persuaded my time here is about up, and that neither Mrs Hinde nor I can face up to it beyond this summer. We have no plans formed for the future, but we both feel very strongly we ought not, either in our own interests or in those of the college, to continue here.'[58] He subsequently accepted the living of Fairlight on the Sussex coast, where he continued to minister until retirement to Eastbourne three years later.

The same report outlined the problems a new principal would have to face, including need of a housekeeper (much of this work had been done by Mrs Hinde) and a handyman. During the war only immediate repairs had been permitted, so restoration was going to be expensive. With these considerations in mind Hinde suggested that the trustees seek a principal aged between thirty and forty-five, who should be an academic in contrast with his own pastoral gifts.

---

[58] Statement by Hinde in college archives dated 15 January 1945.

To the end Hinde maintained his watchfulness over the central affairs of the church in the Church Assembly. In February 1945 they debated the long-awaited report of the Archbishops' Commission on Training for the Ministry,[59] which led to the system of selection conferences. These began in the autumn of 1944 and were based on the War Office Selection Boards used to identify officer material. *The Record* reported Hinde as saying that the church was entitled to know something more about selection conferences. 'Who were serving as selectors?' he asked. 'This very important group of people were to determine now whether or not these candidates were to be accepted at the end of their training.' He was anxious that men who wanted to enter the ministry but had probably never taken matriculation and might be in their thirties, having first entered some business calling, should not be excluded from the schemes before them. These men might not be intellectually equal to those whose education had never been interrupted, but they could serve faithfully in the ministry and perhaps do more effective work because of their training in business beforehand. 'There is still a place in the church for an Amos as well as a shepherd lad like David,' he said. He also thought that the work of the detached theological colleges (those not based on a university campus) was insufficiently acknowledged in the report.[60] Such a speech reflects the experience he had gained from his work over the years with Oak Hill students.

In preparation for new leadership Hinde drew the attention of the trustees for the need of a governing council. He pointed out that the scheme drawn up by the founder provided for a council of twelve, of which the majority must be laymen, and over which the trustees should have an overruling power of veto. While he thought this suggested that trustees should not be included on the council, he recognized that it should include some trustees for convenience and smoother working. It would also have to be determined whether such a council would have any financial control. Correspondence in the archives shows that the final months of Hinde's principalship

---

[59] *The Record*, 16 February 1945.
[60] Ibid.

were taken up with the two matters of finding his successor and forming the governing council. The former task had been entrusted to a small committee (of which Hinde was not a member) who would report to the trustees (of which he was). He was apparently commissioned to approach potential candidates to enquire if they would be willing to let their names go forward for interview. At the same time he wrote among others to Max Warren (secretary of the CMS), Bishop Stephen Neill (at that time at Westcott House, Cambridge) and Julian Thornton-Duesbury (Master of St Peter's Hall, Oxford) to ask their advice as to suitable persons for the post.

The result of all this correspondence and the subsequent deliberations on the part of the trustees must form the substance of the next chapter. Meanwhile it is important to recognize the tremendous debt the college owes to its first principal. While he was very much a man of his time, he laid wise foundations for his successors. Recognizing his own limitations, he was an enabler of others, as was seen in his staff appointments, and he was a shrewd judge of men. Just as he was stubborn and outspoken in the defence of his principles, he was forthright in his assessment of students who he did not believe were qualified for the ministry. Writing to a bishop concerning one student he passed on his own private notes: 'X seems to have a poor opinion of what a parson should be or too high an opinion of what X is. He was in business where the sack was not likely because it was a family business; he seems to think consequently that we are indebted to him for contemplating Holy Orders. There seems however little evidence of vocation.'[61] This is typical of what he described as his plain, unvarnished opinion.

Hinde's name will always be associated with his stalwart opposition to the revised Prayer Book, and for that he was among those who were not considered for higher office in the church. Yet at Oak Hill he found the pinnacle of his life's work, and probably exercised a wider influence than he would have had on the bench of bishops. Maintaining his uncompromising stand for what he considered biblical truth, he did not flinch from involvement in

[61] Oak Hill archives, Hinde's letters.

the wider affairs of the church, and it is evident how ready he was to put forward an evangelical viewpoint on issues before the Convocation and the Church Assembly. He served by being an inspirer and encourager of others in days when the Protestant and Reformed cause in the Church of England was at a low ebb, and forces were at work which would delight to have squeezed it out completely.

On 8 May 1946 the trust minute book recorded a very understated tribute to the man whose insight, vision and leadership were responsible for the establishment of the college as well as its survival and growth during some of the most difficult years in recent British history:

> Prebendary Hinde after nursing and literally guarding the institution through those dangerous days of war has felt impelled to seek a more restful scene of work in a country parish, but he is happily still of our body of trustees and with us today. We are grateful for all he has done.[62]

---

[62] Minute book of the Kingham Hill Trust Corporation (8 May 1946), pp. 71–2.

4

Years of Expansion (1945–1960)

> Your Inspectors felt that Oak Hill was a thoroughly healthy Christian community – healthy in body, mind and spirit. Relations between staff and students and between each student and his fellows were obviously right. Courtesy towards the Inspectors was unfailing, and the more pleasing because it clearly reflected habitual consideration among staff and students for one another.[1]

This assessment of the Oak Hill community was written by the CACTM inspectors of October 1955. Their report was a testimony to the leadership of Leslie Wilkinson during his first ten years as principal. He had been appointed at a time when the college faced both challenges and opportunities. In reporting his appointment *The Record* commented on the challenge facing theological colleges to provide men who would be 'adequately equipped to fill the sorrowfully depleted ranks of the clergy'.[2] The war years had witnessed a dramatic drop in the number of men ordained. For example, the diocese of London, which averaged fifty ordinations a year before the war, had only two or three ordinations a year in the final years of the war.[3] The total number

---

[1] Church of England Record Centre AC/Coll/Oak/1, Report of Inspection of Oak Hill Theological College 19–22 October 1955.

[2] *The Record*, 10 August 1945.

[3] In 1947 Bishop Wand of London described the shortage of clergy in his diocese commenting: 'I am afraid that the facts are there, and there is little we can do at the moment to improve them. Two world wars

or ordinations fell from 562 in 1940 to 158 by the end of the war. As a result there was a significant drop in the number of curates and a tremendous need to increase rapidly the number or ordinands in theological colleges. The challenge of meeting that need would be aided by large numbers of men returning from wartime service, and in consequence the college expanded at a very rapid rate in the years following the war.

Hinde's hope that his successor should be more of an academic than himself was noted in the previous chapter, and correspondence in the archives shows that approaches were made to well-qualified academics on behalf of the trustees. However, they eventually decided to appoint another man in the pastoral mould, but who had also gained a reputation as an evangelist. Leslie Wilkinson had had good experience of pastoral ministry, first in inner-city Brixton during the years of the Depression, then in suburban Beckenham, and as an incumbent in Worthing during World War II. He had also served on the staff of the CPAS as their metropolitan secretary, and immediately prior to coming to Oak Hill had been their evangelistic secretary. This post was created with a view to mobilizing the church to take advantage of the opportunities that it was hoped would arise following the end of the war and the publication of *Towards the Conversion of England*. This involvement had given Wilkinson wide experience of the clergy and parishes of the Church of England, which he was to use for the advantage of his students when it came to placing them in suitable curacies and other appointments.

In introducing the new principal to the wider Christian public *The Record* described how his previous post had involved him in organizing and leading a series of student missions (in conjunction with IVF) in many of the large towns and cities of England.

---

[3] (*continued*) have reduced the number of the clergy, and it will be a considerable time before their ranks can be filled. We have been ordaining two or three men – not many more – at our ordination services in the last few years ... It will be a long time before we go back to the fifty or sixty at each ordination which used to be characteristic of this diocese.' Lloyd, *Church of England*, p. 515.

This had given him a great deal of experience in assisting students to become active in Christian work and to gain experience of evangelism in the parochial setting. On a visit to the college in the 1970s the then Bishop of Down and Dromore, George Quin, told how much he owed to his own participation as a student in one of Wilkinson's missions thirty years earlier. 'There was a man with the fire of the gospel in his belly,' he said.[4] It was not surprising then to find that during college vacations the new principal and fellow staff members took teams of students into parishes to conduct missions – a practice that has continued over the generations.

In the same interview in *The Record* Wilkinson expressed the dilemma that has dogged every college principal: the tension between giving students the necessary teaching to enable them to pass their examinations, and at the same time equipping them for the work of ministry. While recognizing that in an ideal world the latter would be done by a good incumbent during the first curacy, he spoke with feeling of those men who, having had no practical training while at college, went to serve with someone who never gave them any training, advice or help.

Since 1935 Rex Stredder, who had worked with Hinde in his Islington days, had been at the college acting as bursar/secretary, though the principal had carried much of the secretarial work on his own shoulders. Wilkinson brought with him from CPAS his secretary, Stephanie Sutcliffe, who proved an able assistant and helped to stimulate various developments that were to take place in the college during the next fifteen years. Among the first was the publication of *The Oak Leaf*, which made its appearance as a successor to the Oak Hill Newsletter at the end of the Christmas term 1946. This first issue contained a thoughtful response to the report on Training for the Ministry,[5] to which reference has been made earlier. This report had been somewhat dismissive

[4] Conversation remembered between Bishop George Quin and David Wheaton.

[5] 'The Final Report of the Archbishops' Commission on Training for the Ministry' published February 1944.

of the work of those colleges not situated in close proximity to a university campus. In response the new principal made a strong case for such colleges, arguing that the many attractions of university life could well encourage some students to treat their college as an hotel, and miss something in their training that could never be supplied elsewhere. While Oak Hill was near enough to London University to allow some students to attend special lectures there, he stated that he was glad that the college was self-contained. 'We certainly aim to keep the intellectual standard as high as possible, but would ever remember that it is but a means to an end,' he wrote. 'The end is that all the men who go from the college shall be "thoroughly furnished unto every good work". That meant the discovery of a way of Christian living and experience which needed a corporate life, and the opportunities of work, and worship and intercession together.'[6]

Wilkinson went on to challenge the idea that the undergraduate taking a degree course together with theological training should study for the two different components at different institutions. While recognizing that this might help some who could otherwise go stale with five years in one institution, he argued strongly for the kind of integrated course he had been developing at Oak Hill. In five years the ordinand could complete his degree studies together with the necessary papers of the General Ordination Examination (GOE) and also benefit from the practical side of training through lectures in pastoralia and homiletics, as well as the various evangelistic opportunities afforded by the college.

The same issue of *The Oak Leaf* gave details of a departure in the training that the college offered. From the outset it had been recognized that, while its constitution did not allow the college to accept graduates, a significant number of undergraduates had successfully completed the course leading to the Licentiate in Theology awarded by Durham University. Such men could then, if they wished, go to Durham for a further year in order to finish their studies for the BA degree. In March 1945 the Senate of Durham University had decided to terminate this agreement, and

[6] *The Oak Leaf*, Christmas term 1946, pp. 8–9.

for some time Oak Hill had been negotiating with London University to see whether they might be granted the status of an internal college of that university. The reply was that they were too small a unit to be granted that status. It was also probably felt that the staff was not sufficiently equipped academically for such recognition. However, as independent students and those at private institutions had for many years been allowed to submit themselves as candidates for the external degrees of that university, Oak Hill was able to offer a pathway through the London BA. This involved studying European History from AD 400–1914, Theology, English and Greek or Latin at intermediate level, and then taking final examinations in Ancient History, Ethics and Theology. This also met the requirement laid down by CACTM that all candidates under the age of thirty should obtain a university degree.

While Wilkinson was seen primarily as an evangelist and pastor, he was by no means inadequate academically, and responded to the criticisms of his predecessor made by the CACTM inspectors by taking no small part in the teaching programme. He lectured in both early and modern church history and worship, as well as pastoralia, and gave talks to first-year men on the minister's devotional life. The practice at the college was to begin and end each lecture with prayer, and students used to quip that if you did not know what the principal had been getting at in his lecture, you could always pick it up in his closing prayer!

Although there were ten students and two staff members in the college photo in 1944, by 1946 there were forty-six students in residence including the students from LCD. In the six years from 1940–45 the college enrolled a total of eleven new students. In 1946 there were twenty-three new students. Student numbers at both LCD and Oak Hill had expanded so rapidly that at the end of the summer term 1946 the two colleges (who had shared the Southgate campus during the war) were forced to separate because there was insufficient room for both. As LCD moved to temporary accommodation at Harrow, their principal, Donald Coggan, who later became Archbishop of Canterbury, expressed his appreciation for the welcome they had received at Oak Hill and commented on the fellowship that had been achieved. 'Together we prayed and played and worked, and together we learned something of the meaning of fellowship.'[7] Coggan and his staff were to face the task of rebuilding a college that had suffered enormous damage during the war.[8]

Although Oak Hill did not have the problem of repairing war damage, the challenge of providing adequate education for the rapidly expanding student body was formidable. The new principal recognized the college's dependence on God's provision when he wrote in the first edition of *The Oak Leaf*:

> It is becoming increasingly obvious that one of the greatest needs of the church at this time is man-power. Endeavours are being made, and funds raised, to assist those who have a call with their training. But even more vital than man-power, is the training which those who offer themselves for the ministry receive. Yet it is one thing to provide lectures and training, it is another thing that those who come to college not merely learn the details but enter into the spirit and experience of what is provided. We may sow, but it is God alone Who giveth the increase. We are dependent, therefore, on all our praying friends that by God's enabling we may accomplish the task He has given us to do for His Church.[9]

Wilkinson and his staff carried on this work in a nation plagued with shortages. Although loss of life was less than in World War I, civilian casualties were much higher and the cost of the war in the loss of economic assets was enormous.[10] The post-war years were years of austerity as scarce resources were devoted to rebuilding

---

[7] Ibid., p. 4.

[8] Davies, *Men for the Ministry*, p. 95.

[9] *The Oak Leaf*, Christmas term 1946, p. 2.

[10] 'External debts had increased by more that £3,350 million and Britain had sold £118 million of her overseas investments. Of the 18 million tons of shipping lost only two-thirds had been replaced.' David Thompson, *England in the Twentieth Century*, p. 202.

thousands of damaged or destroyed buildings and industry was converted from wartime to peacetime production. Bread and potatoes, which had not been rationed during the war, were briefly rationed and meat was rationed until the mid-fifties. However, despite the shortages, there was great hope for the future. An enormous building programme was begun, resulting in the construction of over one million new houses before 1951. People hoped that divisions in society, industrial unrest, poverty and insecurity would be things of the past. People talked about building 'a new Britain' and looked forward to the advent of 'a new world'.[11]

The post-war period was an era of considerable rebuilding for a church that had suffered massive physical damage during the war.[12] The new housing developments provided new challenges for ministering to a growing population. However, clerical resources were inadequate. Yet the general mood after the war was one of hopefulness for religious revival, and the initial reception of *Towards the Conversion of England* suggested there was real hope for the major campaign that the compilers of the report envisaged. Although the report became a best-seller,[13] received extensive publicity in the press, and was debated in the Church Assembly as well as being discussed in parishes and rural deaneries throughout the land, the Church Assembly refused to act on its recommendations. It even declined to set up the permanent Commission on Evangelism that the report proposed. Archbishop Fisher commented that 'everyone seemed to distrust schemes or organisations for the promotion of evangelism – and I share that distrust'.[14] Others were critical of the report's proposal

---

[11] Paul Welsby, *A History of the Church of England 1945–1980*, pp. 15–16.

[12] Bomb damage to churches in the major cities was immense. In the diocese of London only 70 of some 700 churches were undamaged and many had been completely destroyed. Welsby, *History of the Church of England*, p. 28.

[13] The first edition published in June 1945 sold out overnight and the report was reprinted eight times in the following year.

[14] Welsby, *History of the Church of England*, p. 46.

for a publicity campaign. Anglo-Catholics tended to view it as too evangelical while *The Record* attacked it for not being sufficiently evangelical.[15] The Revd A.W. Morton, a lecturer at Moore College, Sydney, who was visiting Oak Hill in 1946, gave his impression of the report in *The Oak Leaf* and offered his own solution to the challenge of evangelism:

> The report on evangelism, '*Towards the Conversion of England*', was a memorable document, but what has been done to implement it? Apparently little. There are conferences, discussion, retreats, house parties galore, but what contribution to the evangelism of the common man have they made? Here evangelical clergy and laymen have a special responsibility. Parochial missions with adequate preparation and adequate consolidation are the only answer.[16]

Although the report was largely ignored and quickly forgotten, a number of evangelistic campaigns did take place in the post-war period. Among the more successful was Bishop Wand's London diocesan mission in May 1949. However, it was a foreigner, using a method of evangelism that many considered alien to their culture, and teaching what they regarded as simplistic theology, who carried out by far the most successful campaign. Billy Graham came to Britain initially in 1946 and spoke at youth

---

[15] Selwyn Gummer, *The Chavasse Twins*, pp. 163–4. Welsby criticized the report for having 'little sense of the Church being prepared to "listen to the world" and to appreciate the world's own particular insights ... The report was full of confidence and displayed no doubts about the contents of the Gospel. It had great faith in the evangelistic power of education, believing that once the Gospel was taught and understood it had its own evangelistic momentum. It paid little attention to the social implications of the Gospel, preferring to place all its emphasis on personal commitment and displaying some reluctance to appreciate that Christian penetration into the structures of society could rightly be understood as evangelism.' Welsby, *History of the Church of England*, p. 46.

[16] *The Oak Leaf*, Christmas term 1947, p. 57.

meetings over a period of five months.[17] He returned in 1954 for a major crusade at Harringay Arena that lasted for 12 weeks and ended with a massive service at Wembley Stadium attended by 120,000. Even Archbishop Fisher, who initially had reservations about the crusade, attended the service and gave his blessing. It was a remarkable success. Hylson-Smith calls the results 'extraordinary', pointing out that 'it captured the popular imagination and throughout the crowds attending were enormous. More than 38,000 people went forward at the meetings in response to the appeals by the evangelist.'[18] Although the long-term results are more debatable, this clearly had a major impact on increasing the number of evangelical ordinands:

> Perhaps the most significant tangible impact of the Harringay crusade was its role in persuading an unusually large number of young men to enter the ministry, and to do so with explicitly evangelical beliefs and motives ... From that time until the present, according to knowledgeable Anglican churchmen, evangelical theological schools have consistently enrolled far more students than their liberal counterparts, and numerous key British church leaders, Anglicans and non-Anglicans alike, trace either their conversion or their decision to enter the ministry to the Harringay crusade.[19]

Oak Hill was particularly blessed. In the twelve years following Harringay, when students entering the college were asked how they had become Christians, the largest group cited the Harringay

---

[17] See William Martin, *The Billy Graham Story*, pp. 96–9.

[18] Hylson-Smith, *Churches in England*, p. 219.

[19] Martin, *The Billy Graham Story*, pp. 177–86. Martin presents a balanced assessment of the results of the crusade. Some of the evidence he cites is utilized by Iain Murray in his more critical assessment of the crusade. Murray believes the crusade played an important role in leading evangelicals to adopt new policies that were to prove divisive and destructive to the overall mission of British evangelicalism. Iain Murray, *Evangelicalism Divided: A Record of Crucial Change in the Years 1950–2000*, pp. 56ff.

crusade.[20] This must have been an immense encouragement to those who had organized and supported the crusade, including the vicar of St Mary's, Islington, the Revd Maurice Wood. After he became principal of Oak Hill, the 1965 edition of *The Oak Leaf* included an article in which seven students testified to the impact of Harringay on their faith. Although most of the seven had had some contact with church before they heard Billy Graham, it was his preaching that changed the direction of their lives. Five of the seven are still in the ministry almost half a century later, so the crusade clearly had a lasting effect in their lives. Wilkinson recognized the significance of the crusade before the college experienced its fruits. In the 1954 *Oak Leaf* he called the Harringay crusade 'the most significant happening of the year for this neighbourhood, as indeed, I believe, for the whole country ... As a result we have found it easier to talk about the gospel and opportunities for presenting the personal challenge of the Christian Faith seem to be increasing.'[21]

As can be imagined, the students were not slow to follow their principal's enthusiasm for evangelism. While there were regular opportunities for ministry, such as taking ward services in local hospitals and prayers in the local remand home, the college opened itself up for evangelism. Some of the students who had forged links with the colleges of London University realized the potential for evangelism among the hundreds of overseas students who came over to study in the capital. The hayloft in the old barn on the farm was made safe, and through the winter months a regular series of 'barn squashes' was held, to which local church youth groups brought their friends and the college staff and student body provided evangelistic speakers. From time to time there were also student initiatives to take the gospel to the local residents in Southgate by running open-air meetings near the tube station on a Saturday afternoon. A further opportunity for outreach was afforded by the Wesley Club, a group of students who

---

[20] Ian Randall, *Educating Evangelicalism: The Origins, Development and Impact of London Bible College*, p. 95.

[21] *The Oak Leaf*, 1954, p. 3.

enjoyed singing together. They especially enjoyed the hymns of the Wesleys with their robust doctrinal themes, and would visit churches in the London area to present a programme of such hymns with appropriate evangelistic comment, testimony and preaching.

It was not only the Harringay crusade that encouraged evangelism. The Lambeth Conference that met in the summer of 1948, the first for eighteen years, issued a clear call for an increase in evangelistic efforts. The opening encyclical letter, to be read aloud in every church, included the following plea for mass evangelism:

> The supreme task of the Church today is to win the nations of Christendom back to the knowledge of God ... and to take the good news to those who have not yet heard it. We call upon our people to engage in this campaign and to put themselves into training for it. God, in His mercy, has given to us in our Conference a clearer vision of His will and purpose for His Church and of its mission to the world. To these we bid you dedicate yourselves.[22]

In addition the media showed commitment to Christian values. In 1948 the director-general of the BBC declared that 'The BBC ... bases is policy upon a positive attitude towards Christian values ... The whole preponderant weight of its programmes is directed to this end.' The BBC was committed to making 'Britain a more Christian country' and to 'avoiding anything which might appear to undermine Christian morality and by fostering the understanding of the Christian religion'.[23] The Butler Education Act of 1944 had also been intended to restore Christianity 'to its true and traditional place in English education'.[24]

However, other developments threatened to undermine traditional Christianity. In 1947 Bishop Barnes of Birmingham

---

[22] Lambeth Conference 1948, p. 17, from Lloyd, *Church of England*, p. 492.

[23] Welsby, *History of the Church of England*, p. 50.

[24] Edward R. Norman, *Church and Society in England 1770–1970: A Historical Study*, p. 402.

published a book rejecting most traditional teaching as well as the authority of the New Testament, presenting Jesus as primarily a good man and a moral teacher.[25] By 1947 'responsible attacks' on the Christian faith were permitted by the BBC. Yet at the same time there was an increasing acceptance of traditional Christianity among intellectuals, and writers such as C.S. Lewis were extremely popular. Hastings comments: 'The odd thing about the 1950s is the cohabiting of these two intellectual in-worlds, the religious and the agnostic, each self-assured, each apparently thriving, each rather sneeringly dismissive of the other.'[26]

In spite of such threats to conservative Christian beliefs and values, conservative evangelicalism thrived during the 1950s. In 1958 Stephen Neill wrote:

> The conservative evangelicals have also greatly improved their position. Extremely well organised in the university and the public schools, disciplined, precise in their beliefs and impetuous in their propaganda, they have made a deep impression on a younger generation which seems to demand a definite answer to its questions and to its doubts. This group has begun to take much more seriously than it did intellectual questions and the problems of scholarship. All the theological colleges maintained by this wing are full. Some of the authorities of the Church seem to feel anxiety over the possible

---

[25] W.R. Matthews, an admirer of Barnes, maintained that 'He had no doctrine of the Incarnation or of the Atonement.' He further stated that Barnes's teaching on the divinity of Christ could be summed up as follows: 'Men saw that Jesus Christ was a very good man, so they called him son of God.' Welsby, *History of the Church of England*, p. 53. Archbishop Fisher stated that the book 'so diminishes ... the content of the Christian faith as to make the residue which is left inconsistent with the scriptural doctrine and beliefs of the Church in which he holds office ... If his views were mine, I would not feel that I could still hold episcopal office in the Church.' Hylson-Smith, *Churches in England*, p. 229.

[26] Hastings, *History of English Christianity*, p. 496.

> effects on the life of the Church of this phalanx of 'fundamentalist' believers.[27]

Neill's contemporary analysis is supported by modern historians who attribute the revival of conservative evangelicalism to the impact of the Harringay crusade, the growing strength of evangelicalism in the universities, the development of conservative evangelical scholarship, the significant role of John Stott, and the increase in the number of evangelical ordinands.[28] However, not all was plain sailing. An invitation by the Christian Union at Cambridge to Billy Graham to lead a mission there had led to a correspondence in the pages of *The Times* as to whether 'fundamentalism' had any place in the universities. The debate led to publications on both sides of the argument, and John Stott offered a scholarly response to efforts to attach the fundamentalist label to conservative evangelicalism.[29]

In the wider circles of evangelicalism there was a desire for the setting up of a Bible college, to be based in London, which could offer training aiming at the highest levels of scholarship. It is significant that both Wilkinson and Stibbs were involved in the early stages of planning for what later became London Bible College (LBC).[30]

Oak Hill staff members also made significant contributions to the revival of conservative scholarship. The Christian unions at Oxford and Cambridge had a custom of inviting a leading evangelist to give a 'freshers' sermon' at the beginning of each

[27] Stephen Neill, *Anglicanism*, p. 401.

[28] Barclay, *Evangelicalism in Britain*, pp. 60ff.; Bebbington, *Evangelicalism in Modern Britain*, pp. 249ff.; Hastings, *History of English Christianity*, pp. 453ff.; Hylson-Smith, *Evangelicals in the Church of England*, pp. 287ff.; Manwaring, *From Controversy to Co-existence*, pp. 96ff.

[29] See A.G. Hebert, *Fundamentalism and the Church of God*; J.I. Packer, *Fundamentalism and the Word of God: Some Evangelical Principles*; J.R.W. Stott, *Fundamentalism and Evangelism.*

[30] For further details see Randall, *Educating Evangelicalism.*

academic year, and for a number of years this distinction was shared between Wilkinson, John Stott and Maurice Wood. Meanwhile the forties and fifties saw Stibbs's pen most active. Following the publication of *Search the Scriptures*[31] and the *New Bible Commentary*,[32] in which he had played a major part, he had produced a trilogy published by IVP entitled *Understanding God's Word*, *Obeying God's Word* and *Expounding God's Word*.[33] The Church Book Room Press had also published his *The Church: Universal and Local*,[34] and all were selling well on the Christian Union bookstalls. In consequence both principal and vice-principal (Stibbs used to delight in quoting that he was the man who made a virtue out of being a vice!) were in frequent demand for Bible teaching or evangelistic activities in the universities, and their ministry attracted many graduates.

A significant factor in the advance of conservative evangelical influence in the Church of England was the growing number of evangelical ordinands. At the 1957 Islington Clerical Conference its president, Maurice Wood, pointed out:

> We are now producing more candidates for ordination than any other group, and the future is ours ... We must tell this to ordination candidates who are being dissuaded from offering for ordination for fear of conscientious difficulties ... The future belongs to us, for in parish after parish the gospel is being proclaimed by clergy and laity working in a new harmony, men and women are coming to a saving knowledge of the Lord Jesus Christ through regular, homespun, parish evangelism, ordination candidates are coming forward in growing numbers and our eight evangelical theological colleges are fuller than ever before.[35]

---

[31] A.M. Stibbs (ed.), *Search the Scriptures*.
[32] F. Davidson, E. Kevan, A.Stibbs and D. Guthrie (eds), (London: IVF, 1953).
[33] London: IVF, 1950, 1955 and 1960 respectively.
[34] London: 1950.
[35] *Church of England Newspaper*, 11 January 1957.

Wood's optimism about the future was reflected in the experience of Oak Hill. In the early 1950s the college had been granted permission to accept graduates, and that decade in particular saw the student body developing with a healthy mix of graduates, undergraduates and non-graduates. In July 1952 the principal reported to the Kingham Hill Trust that the fifty-four students then in residence were equally divided between graduates and non-graduates. Stibbs encouraged individual students, especially theological graduates, whose previous studies would exempt them from some of the papers of the GOE, to undertake research projects of their own choosing. Some of these were reproduced in *The Oak Leaf* and reflect the breadth of the students' theological concerns. There are articles on Sunday observance, reunion schemes, the church and the working classes, holiness, theology and practice of infant baptism, disestablishment, child evangelism and the problem of suffering, to name but a few.

To teach such a challenging cross-section of ability Wilkinson showed great initiative. The departure of Coggan and the members of the LCD in 1946 had left a big gap in the academic staff, and Wilkinson's first appointment – that of the Revd J. Stafford Wright (who later left to become principal of the Bible Churchmen's College, subsequently renamed Tyndale Hall, in Bristol) to teach Old Testament – was a highly successful one. Wilkinson was keen to encourage younger men with a possible future in theological teaching, and so in 1946 he appointed two lay junior staff, Alan Cole and Richard Allen, who were later to be ordained. Cole later had a distinguished career in theological teaching in south-east Asia and Australia, while Allen contributed to the college with his keen social conscience and deep interest in the political scene. He was so involved in the political scheme that he stood for Parliament in the early 1950s as a Liberal candidate. Generations of Oak Hill students remembered him for his comments on current affairs, delivered in the dining hall during Thursday lunchtime, and it was no surprise that, after leaving in 1953 to train for ordination at Wycliffe Hall, he should have become warden of St George's Crypt in Leeds. His early death in an accident on the M1 was a great loss to the world of evangelical social action.

While at the college Cole gained his London BD and MTh degrees as well as completing the work for his PhD at Trinity College, Dublin. When he left in 1950 the principal looked out for other students who were doing postgraduate work, and so in ensuing years Jim Packer (Stafford Wright's successor at Tyndale Hall, and later first principal of Trinity College Bristol)[36] and Andrew Walls, who later became Professor of Religious Studies at Aberdeen University, took up the role of tutor minimus at the college. When Stafford Wright moved to Bristol in 1951 he left a serious gap among the ranks of the senior staff. However, once again the principal's flair in making excellent appointments came to the fore, when he appointed the Revd F. Derek Kidner, who was at that time vicar of Felsted in Essex. Kidner had been a professional musician before ordination, had gained firsts in economics and theology at Cambridge, and was to make his mark as an Old Testament scholar, contributing several volumes to the IVP series of commentaries. He also chaired the panel that produced the hymnbook *Christian Praise* in 1957, and was on the committee behind publication of the *Anglican Hymn Book* in 1965. He was a great wordsmith, and his lectures and sermons were well remembered for their apt words and pithy phrases.

Two years later Wilkinson made the first appointment of a student to the staff when Ronald Herniman took over the mantle of Allen. The brief given him was teaching in the realm of philosophy and the philosophical aspects of Christian doctrine, as he had been studying the subject at Birkbeck College under professor C.E.M. Joad, gaining first-class honours in the London BA. Significantly the principal's words to him on appointment were 'I want you to teach the men to think'. David Field, who later returned to the Oak Hill staff, recalls the first meeting of a fellowship group when Herniman, their tutor, asked why the new members had chosen to come to Oak Hill. To David's answer,

---

[36] For a description of this year, see chapter 3 of Alister McGrath, *To Know and Serve God: A Biography of James I. Packer*.

'To win souls for Jesus,' the response came, 'What is a soul?' When in the following year David Wheaton, who graduated in classics at Oxford and was currently studying for the BD at LBC, was appointed on a part-time basis to teach classical and New Testament Greek (becoming full-time the following year), the team was completed. It remained unchanged until the principal's death in 1960.

Hinde had expressed concern that his successor should have sufficient support from ancillary staff, but this was not easy in the immediate post-war years, particularly in the kitchens, where Mrs Wilkinson and Miss Sutcliffe frequently found themselves responsible for catering and cooking for the expanding numbers. A solution was found in 1950 when Dr and Mrs Bume joined the staff and were to carry these responsibilities for the next eleven years. They were Jewish refugees from Austria. She had been a singer with the Vienna State Opera, while he had been a university teacher with a DSc degree. Jokingly, students would on occasion refer to the academic standing of their staff with the throw-away comment 'Even the chef has a doctorate and speaks six languages!' Their experiences during the war had led the Bumes to value the peace and quiet of the Oak Hill surroundings, where they were provided with a flat in the basement, and joined in the social life of the college. When a new chapel was dedicated in 1957 Kidner especially composed an anthem to be introduced by a flute obligato played by Dr Bume.

Hinde had flagged up the need of a houseman to carry out the practical tasks in the college, and Wilkinson appointed Arthur Taylor to this post. He was to become something of a legend during his twenty years of service to the college. Generations of students saw him as a suitable target on whom to practise their evangelistic skills, but he steadfastly resisted them all. It was Wilkinson's death, and the way his family reacted to it, that brought him to faith in Christ, and he thus became the first of several of the ancillary staff who became Christians through their involvement in the life of the college.

The principal's wife supported the work of the college. Fortunately, she was in a position to help, as most of the time the Wilkinsons' children, Michael and Elizabeth, were away at boarding school. Michael went on to university and then cemented the links between the founder's two establishments by marrying Caroline Cooper, the daughter of the warden of Kingham Hill, while Elizabeth married a former curate of Cockfosters, Jeremy Pierssené. Wilkinson had also brought his widowed mother with him to Oak Hill, and she took on the role of housekeeper. Students of those days remember the care she took of their bed linen and towels, and it was not until she was well into her eighties in 1957 that Winifred Cohen, a widow, with her daughter, Jane, was appointed to relieve her of these duties.

The principal's duties were not confined solely to the needs of the college: there was also the farm to be considered. While the day-to-day running of the farm and gardens was supervized by staff in that department, the principal was regarded as being in charge, and every report he submitted to the management committee had details of produce supplied to the college or sold to local outlets. There was even an analysis of egg production by the hens, and staff members had part of their salaries made up in kind with the supply of milk and vegetables. It became a standing joke among them as to how healthy they should be in the early spring when for weeks the gardens seemed to produce a diet of spinach and rhubarb only. Originally, the overseers of this department were two staff who had begun their service at Oak Hill in the days of the Baring Youngs. Fred Boland had joined the farm staff in 1888, and in 1943, when he retired, he was presented by King George VI with a bronze medal and certificate from the Royal Agricultural Society in recognition of his fifty-five years' service on the one estate. He died in 1952, but his sister, who had been in domestic service to the Baring Young family, lived on in the Lodge until she moved to a local Church Army nursing home in 1972.

During the forties and early fifties the gardens and farm were in the charge first of Harry Taylor, and then of David Morgan, both of whom left in order to widen their experience elsewhere. In 1958 Roy Brown was appointed, and he stayed until the farm finally closed in 1982. Roy was a farmer by background, and was a committed Christian. He and his family made a valuable contribution to the life of the college during their twenty-four years' service. Under him the herd of cattle flourished, and for several years won the shield for the champion herd of Middlesex, while he also built up the chicken stocks to the degree that they were supplying eggs to many local residents as well as to the college kitchens. The Browns were also generous in their hospitality, and many students remember with gratitude the evenings spent in Farm Lane sharing fellowship with Roy and his first wife, Evelyn, and, after her death, his second wife, Ann.

A number of workers also came to assist. Sid Carrington and his wife lived in the Garden Cottage (as it was called) for over twenty years. Joyce Brown shared with him in the work of the dairy until it closed. She then transferred to the domestic staff, and spent her remaining years of service in the kitchen. Alfie Taylor, who will be remembered by generations of students and staff, cared for the ornamental gardens in the immediate vicinity of the college. This he did in the afternoons, after working by night at the Wood Green London Transport bus garage maintaining tyres. An exploding tyre had rendered him partially deaf: a disability he could at times use to advantage! His pride and joy was the display of geraniums in the conservatory, which he brought to perfection for the golden jubilee celebrations in 1982.

This expansion of staff led to the first major building project of the Wilkinson era. Over the years the trustees had bought two houses in the neighbouring De Bohun Avenue to house the bursar and the houseman. The Hernimans had lived in the old Garden Cottage (demolished during Maurice Wood's principalship), but needed a larger property to accommodate their growing family, and so the trustees obtained planning permission to build on the estate. In 1954 Acorns was built opposite Garden Cottage, and when subsequently both Morgan and Wheaton expressed their intentions of getting married it was decided to sell the properties off campus and, with the proceeds, to build two pairs of semi-detached houses further down Farm Lane.

All these developments were facilitated by the creation of a separate management committee for the college. After the several unsuccessful attempts by Hinde to set up a college council, the minutes of the Kingham Hill Trust record on 14 November 1945 that the management committee should be reconstituted with Lord Roche in the chair and with the Revd (later Canon) Talbot Mohan and Messrs Kinahan and Keith as members.[37] The principal and bursar were to be in attendance and should prepare suggestions for the agenda. This committee should meet regularly – not less than once a term. Records available suggest that this scheme worked well for the next twenty-five years, until the setting up of the college council. Problems could arise when those who controlled the work of the trust did not go regularly to the college to see for themselves the work that was going on there, but the college was very fortunate that successive chairmen made it their business to make regular visits to the college. The practice of inviting the principal, together with the warden of the Kingham Hill school, to attend the trustees' annual meeting at Kingham Hill and report on their establishments enabled them to draw the attention of the trustees to any particular needs or situations. The college was also fortunate in having a succession of chairmen of the management committee, and subsequently the college council, who gave generously of their time to the affairs of Oak Hill, and were eloquent in pleading its cause at meetings of the trust. One such was Canon Mohan, secretary of CPAS, who was chairman from 1949 until 1968.

The college has benefited over the years from the expertise brought on to its governing bodies by the dedicated laymen who served in various capacities. Prebendary Dick Lucas was a great help through his work among businessmen in the City of London at St Helen's, Bishopsgate: from among his congregation came several who rendered invaluable service to the college as members of the management committee, the subsequent college council and the Kingham Hill Trust. These included G.F. (Geoff) Rocke, MC, director of a City firm; Douglas Scott, a gentleman farmer; Peter Dale, a City banker; and David Monro, a partner in a firm of

---

[37] It is difficult to say in what way this committee was reconstituted, as there are no records available to give evidence of its previous existence.

solicitors. Successive chairmen of the trustees continued the high standards of interest in and involvement with the work of the foundations set by Lord Roche and his son, the Hon. T.G. Roche, QC.

While Wilkinson had extended the scope of the college to include graduates and was keen to raise the academic standard of those being trained, he was no less aware of the needs of the less academic – the sort of men the founder had in mind in his benefaction. In 1952 he produced a memorandum for CACTM, recognizing that there were two types of non-graduates in the college: those who could derive benefit from the standard course leading to the GOE; and others for whom such formal academic training was unsuitable. 'At present', he wrote, 'the clergy are trained by middle class people for middle class parishes ... The only men who can really understand the working classes and fully sympathise with them is a working man – not an ex-working man.'[38] He proposed to train men, preferably of working-class origin, for a lifetime of evangelistic and pastoral ministry in industrial parishes. He used an interesting military metaphor in arguing that they should be seen as highly trained specialists, not to be wasted in spheres of ministry for which they had not been trained, yet not for that reason to be thought in any way inferior: 'No general willingly uses his sappers as infantry except in grave emergency, and this does not imply that sappers are inferior to infantry. On the contrary, they are experts.' He therefore proposed a scheme for part-time training where the candidates would remain in secular employment, with a training centre located in an industrial area or possibly on a new housing estate. Prime attention should be given to character training, while intellectually candidates should be given a good grasp of biblical teaching, apologetics, and the ability to deal with the difficulties faced by many ordinary people. In this visionary plan Wilkinson showed more affinity with the Bethnal Green scheme implemented by Ted Roberts in the 1970s than with the

---

[38] Paper on *Non-Graduate Training* by L.F.E. Wilkinson, dated 1952, in the college archives.

ministerial training courses (MTCs) that have developed since the late 1950s. It is interesting that the first Kingham Hill Fellow, Ian Bunting, was to propose a similar plan in 1987.[39]

The only concession made to those who might find the GOE tough was the scheme allowing men over thirty to submit essays rather than having to sit for examinations. Interestingly there was one occasion in the mid-fifties when Archbishop Fisher sponsored an Oak Hill candidate with a covering letter saying 'I do not wish you to examine this man, but set him on a guided course of reading. He would never pass a written examination, but I am convinced that he is of the stuff of which good pastors are made, and I intend to ordain him!'[40]

The number of married students increased during the Wilkinson era. Up until now, little concession was made to them, as the pattern of college life was still basically that of a monastic institution. It began with chapel at 7.20 a.m. (7.05 a.m. for Holy Communion on saints' days) and ended at 9.00 p.m. from Monday to Friday. Students were also expected to be in college from 8.30 a.m. until after 1.00 p.m. on Saturdays, and at communion at 7.45 a.m. followed by breakfast on Sundays. Wives and fiancées might live in the neighbourhood, but were not permitted to be in college during the working week in case they distracted the men! First-year students had to live in as bachelors even if they had only recently been married. Annette Silvester (whose husband later returned to join the staff) recalled an occasion when she was so desperate to see her husband, who had had to leave her to reside in college after only a year of married life, that she crept down the drive for a clandestine visit during forbidden hours. To her horror she saw the figure of the principal approaching her up the drive, and was so terrified of the consequences if she was discovered that she dived painfully into a holly bush until he had passed. This situation was eased only when Derek Wooldridge challenged the system: he had been married just before entering training, and flatly refused to leave his wife in this way. To the

[39] See chapter 7, p. 229.
[40] Letter in former students' files in the college archives.

staff's surprise their principal allowed him to live with his wife in their flat off campus. It is difficult to see why these rules were made, except that the college was anxious to show that as an evangelical institution it could be no less disciplined in the area of ministerial formation than the more celibate colleges of the Anglo-Catholic tradition. Married men whose wives had had to remain at home, often in the further parts of the country, were, in addition to the half-term break from Friday lunchtime to Monday morning, allowed one 'married men's' weekend away from college each side of half-term.

An editorial in *The Oak Leaf* as late as 1955 highlights the concern felt among students. Commenting on the impression gained that those in 'higher circles' wished clerical celibacy to be regarded as intrinsically good and therefore an idea to be sold to candidates for ordination, the article continued:

> It seems not unreasonable to suggest that the feeling thus, rightly or wrongly, gained, reinforcing the desire of a young man in love to be married as soon as possible, is at least a contributory factor to the 'brisk activity' to which we have referred (congratulations had been offered to no less than eight members of the college who had recently become engaged), but quite obviously the decision to marry during training is not carelessly taken. It involves, for the majority, the problem of finding satisfactory accommodation for the remaining pre-ordination period, or the alternative one of living apart for most of the first months, or years, of married life. It involves, too, financial problems additional to those of the ordinary student. In theory, at least, it might also be supposed to affect the quality of work achieved, but whether this is so in practice is questionable. Indeed, the problems of marriage while still at college may well be fewer and less serious than those of a reluctantly prolonged courtship.[41]

The anonymous author concluded by tempering his plea for an official policy statement from the House of Bishops with expressing the fear that the apparent trend in current 'official'

[41] *The Oak Leaf*, 1955, p. 4.

opinion might not produce the answer for which he was looking. Oak Hill students were well aware that bishops felt that the first year of ministry, which began with ordination to the diaconate and culminated with 'priesting', was so important that candidates were told that they must get married not less than three months before their being made deacon and not less than three months after 'priesting'.

To cater for the growing number of wives and fiancées the Wilkinsons organized an annual weekend after the end of the Lent term when wives or fiancées were invited to the college. With their partners they could see the lifestyle that lay before them under the guidance of an experienced clergy couple, along with input from the staff. In 1947 three wives had spent the closing days of the term with the rest of the college. They were subject to the normal college routine, including the rising bell at 6.15 a.m. Three years later the first of the annual weekends was held solely for students and their wives or fiancées, to which many look back with gratitude for the help and advice given.

From this developed the Bible study group for wives and fiancées living in the neighbourhood, which Joy Wheaton started in the late fifties. It was held in her home, Acorns, which was thought to be sufficiently far away from the college for the men not to be distracted! In due course Margaret Wood took over this group in the Woods' flat in the college.

As well as lectures in the morning, and sometimes early evening, students were expected to attend chapel twice a day from Monday to Friday for morning and evening prayer, with Holy Communion on saints' days. On one evening each week there would be a visiting preacher drawn from various traditions of the church, and prior to lunch there was a further twenty-minute devotional slot either in chapel or in various rooms when prayer groups supporting different missionary or other interests would meet. On those occasions the staff would also meet for informal prayer for the needs of the college and student body.

Saturday morning began with an hour's prayer meeting after breakfast for the whole college when a variety of issues could be addressed. Those present for the 1955 CACTM inspection well recall how the inspectors, on hearing that there was going to be a prayer meeting (which they thought very un-Anglican), decided they had better stay to see what happened. As soon as the meeting was open for extempore prayer an earnest student began praying for the inspectors who (as he thought) had just left. He was not sure of their spiritual position, and prayed urgently for their conversion. The prayer was suddenly drowned by a member of staff who, aware of the presence of the inspectors, developed a coughing fit.

The inspection of 1948 had drawn attention to the urgent need of a larger chapel. The inspectors had commented that the room then in use was 'neither suitable in appointment nor adequate in size'. They were concerned that the present overcrowded conditions did not encourage all students to kneel during the prayers.[42] The situation was partially alleviated when the room was extended by the removal of the wall dividing it from the next room. The next inspectors commented:

> The chapel is a light and well-ventilated warm room. Its appearance is not distinctively Anglican. The Holy Table has no ornaments or covering but two service books lie flat on it, one at each end. A picture of the Last Supper is mounted on the oak panelling behind it. A large and finely printed Bible on the lectern is open towards the congregation, except for the actual reading of the lessons when it is turned towards the reader.[43]

This last piece of symbolism had become a tradition of the college, to make the point that the minister's task is to open the Scriptures to his people.

The 1955 inspectors stated that they had been told by the principal that the building of a new chapel would begin in the near future, and this happened in 1956–7, when the trustees generously agreed to make this the focal point of the college's silver jubilee celebrations. The new building was dedicated by

[42] Report of 1948 CACTM inspection in the college archives.
[43] Report of 1955 CACTM inspection in the college archives.

the Archbishop of Canterbury in the afternoon of 11 July 1957. In the morning there had been a thanksgiving service in Cockfosters Church (even the new chapel would not have been adequate to seat the large numbers of former students and supporters as well as the present college body). The preacher was the Bishop of Liverpool, the college's episcopal visitor, and the Bishop of St Albans was present to pronounce the blessing. This was followed by a lunch in the church hall, attended by 220 people, including the bishops of London, Liverpool and Barking.

The new chapel had the same simple dignity as the old one but was considerably better proportioned. The east end had a slightly curved apse covered for the most part by a large blue and gold hanging, in fact the remnant of material that had been specially woven for the coronation of Queen Elizabeth II. The architect, K.C. White, felt its symbolism (oak leaves surrounding a crown) was highly appropriate for the chapel. There was amusement over the fact that the new building was thought to straddle the diocesan boundaries of London and St Albans, thereby permitting the principal to do what one bishop might not like in the other bishop's half of the chapel. It had originally been thought that the furniture from the former chapel could be transferred to the new one, but when this was done it was seen to be out of proportion. Consequently, a new holy table, lectern and minister's pews were constructed in a pattern of light and dark oak. These were matched by a pulpit, a gift from former students.

The archbishop duly arrived for the afternoon's dedication service, which was conducted with due ceremony. In his address he picked up the fact that the college's foundation stemmed from the Prayer Book controversy of 1928, and he chose to stress from his text (Acts 2:42–7) that the Church of England was by its nature evangelical, fundamentalist, modernist, pentecostal, catholic and eschatological. Laying stress on the fact that the college should be looking to the future and not to the past he claimed that all Anglicans should be Protestants against error, and reformers, yet in order to be reforming the church must also be catholic. This, he stated, should be the attitude to adopt in the revision of canon law, one of the major features of his time at

Canterbury and an area in which he had already crossed swords with the principal.

Following the Reformation the classic dress of the clergy of the Church of England had been the cassock and surplice, with scarf and hood of their degree, and until the early years of the twentieth century most bishops had required their ordinands to robe in this way for the ordination service. However, in the late 1940s certain bishops of more advanced Anglo-Catholic views, notably Wand of London and Kirk of Oxford, had insisted that their ordinands wear stoles, a custom introduced by those wishing to show the church's affinity with Rome on this occasion. Several men had felt uneasy about this – they would never otherwise use the stole, and wearing different vesture for different services would be a denial of the unity of the ministry of Word and sacrament to which they were being ordained. In addition the use of the stole had been deemed illegal in a judgement given by the Judicial Committee of the Privy Council in 1871 (the so-called 'Purchas Judgement'), and in spite of its subsequent widespread use there was still a degree of doubt as to its legality. This was one of the issues Fisher hoped to resolve by revising the canons to legalize all forms of vesture. Lambeth Palace library has considerable correspondence on the subject, not least from Wilkinson, in its archives. The result was a joint approach from the principals of the evangelical colleges. In response the archbishop wrote to all diocesan bishops and college principals to the effect that in future no candidate should be refused ordination solely on the grounds of being unwilling to wear the stole.[44]

In challenging such practices that were becoming increasingly widespread in the church Wilkinson maintained his position firmly but charitably. He wrote:

> We shall continue to say we are in no sense a Party College. We love the Prayer Book and the Articles. The only thing we do not do is be swayed by the current opinions and vagaries about them which may

---

[44] Lambeth Palace library records, see Fisher 109 and 210.

> exist in the Church of the day. We believe that the ordinary Englishman enjoys and responds to the simple Prayer Book services when they are explained to him and when they are reverently and worshipfully rendered in the Parish Churches of our land.[45]

However, even in Wilkinson's day there were those who would like to have seen the college closed. After attending a CACTM meeting Wilkinson told his staff how he had sat beside an archdeacon who did not know who he was, but, on hearing mention of the name of Oak Hill, had burst out: 'Oak Hill – the place ought to be wound-up!'

'My dear sir', replied Wilkinson, 'you know what happens when you wind up a clock. It goes all the better!'

In many cases bishops or their directors of ordinands did their best to dissuade candidates from coming to Oak Hill because it was too 'definite', and the ordinands' belief in the infallibility and supremacy of Scripture was often challenged. When the inspectors visited the college in 1955 they avoided controversial subjects with the staff, but spent an afternoon grilling the senior and vice-senior students as to why they had come to the college. It appeared that the inspectors' picture was that the college was a kind of evangelical sausage machine to which students came to have their doctrinal views shaped, whereas in fact they were choosing to come because they already held those views. In view of such commitment it is not surprising that during Wilkinson's principalship the number of men who dropped out during training was remarkably low. There were still a small number of pre-matrics each year, and occasionally they would not be recommended by a selection conference, but an encouraging number went on to complete the GOE and in some cases to obtain a degree.

Even so, the college was far from being a monolithic institution. *The Oak Leaf* records meetings of the Unicorn Society, a debating society covering a wide range of subjects, while there

---

[45] *The Oak Leaf*, 1951–2, p. 4.

were branches of the more liberal SCM as well as the conservative IVF in the college. Many students of this era will recall with affection the various 'coffee schools' that met after lunch to hammer out doctrinal and ecclesiastical affairs.

Although the principal referred to the inauguration of a student committee in 1947,[46] this had already for several years been well served by a succession of senior students. To modern ears it will appear strange that these were appointed by the principal after consultation with the staff and without any democratic input. But the system worked well, and all of those so appointed, several of whom were to achieve high office in the church later on, worked loyally to act as a bridge between the academic staff and the student body. It reflects the stature of those joining the college after wartime service that one of the early senior students, S. John Hill, had already been awarded an MBE!

Nor was life at Oak Hill always serious. There was a Pooh Club, which enjoyed reading the works of A.A. Milne. The annual garden party, when the whole college spent the morning tidying up and getting ready for the influx of visitors, was preceded by an informal parade of a light-hearted nature. The principal's birthday was usually an opportunity to present him with something appropriate, such as a Doctor of Divinity's hood made of extremely gaudy crêpe paper.

Sport was also a regular feature of the college life. The fifties were the heyday of activity among the London colleges. The London Theological Colleges Athletic Union included King's (Anglican), Richmond (Methodist), New (Congregationalist), Spurgeon's (Baptist), LCD (Anglican) and the interdenominational LBC. This organization arranged friendly and league games in soccer, rugby and cricket, and in the summer term all the colleges travelled to the King's ground at Mitcham for an intercollegiate athletics meeting. Many students and their partners will also remember with gratitude the trustees' provision in 1947 of three hard tennis courts,[47] which became the scene of

[46] *The Oak Leaf*, summer term 1947, p. 34.
[47] *The Oak Leaf*, Christmas term 1947, p. 50.

many a fierce battle for the singles' and doubles' cups, presented at the end of each summer term. Gardening teams also levelled an area by the old wing for a deck tennis court, and throughout the year the facilities for table tennis were in frequent use.

Rivalry on the sports ground led also to various pranks between the colleges. On one occasion students arrived for breakfast to find that all the knives and forks from the dining hall had been spirited away overnight by a raiding party from LCD, who by then were in their new premises at Northwood. Those were the days of cooked breakfasts, and the attempt to consume fried bacon without the necessary cutlery caused much merriment. A subsequent raiding party was not so successful. They came over by night to Southgate and laid their plans in the shadow of a wartime pillbox, which still stood in the corner of the football field. Unknown to the plotters this was occupied by an elderly tramp who heard all their plans, and, once they had set off to carry out their schemes, telephoned the police, who arrived on the spot to greet the would-be intruders, who were sent back home after due cautioning!

Nor were such activities solely intercollegiate. One newly engaged student made it known to his contemporaries that he was looking forward to his fiancée's first visit to the college one Saturday afternoon. While he went down to meet her at Southgate station, his study was emptied of all its furniture, and one of the two horses the principal's wife kept in the front field was carefully led in. When the student proudly threw open the door and stepped back for his fiancée to enter, she was greeted by the horse's hindquarters!

An activity that evoked mixed reactions was gardening. Every student was expected to spend one afternoon each week working in the gardens: this could include tending the actual gardens or working on the farm. One visitor to Southgate enquiring in a shop for the college was told that they knew of no theological college locally, but they knew there was an agricultural one because they had seen the students working in the grounds! While the college benefited from the farm produce, such supplies could occasionally be excessive. One autumn in the eighties saw a particularly bumper crop of apples. The cook was congratulated for her recipe for apple surprise – one that did not use apples!

PERSONALITY PROFILE

Denis Shepheard (1928–92) was born in a Wood Green council house, the sixth of nine children. He joined the Royal Navy at sixteen, and had served ten years when he fell from a rooftop, causing an injury to his ankle that ended his naval career. During eighteen months of treatment he sought a purpose in life and believed the answer lay in becoming a vicar. His search took him eventually to St Cuthbert's Church in Wood Green, where Old Oak Douglas Clark was the incumbent. He was introduced to the gospel, and at a showing of the Billy Graham film *Souls in Conflict* he suddenly saw the truth about Jesus and the cross.

As he had been called to ordination before his conversion, he gained the four O levels required for entry to Oak Hill, and joined the college in 1956. He did not find study easy, but his motivation was so strong that he succeeded in passing the GOE, and he became a popular member of the community.

Upon ordination Denis served two curacies in Kent – four and a half years with Douglas Clark in Folkestone, and two years in Southborough. He then moved to All Souls, Langham Place, first as chaplain to the Oxford Street stores, and then as warden to the clubhouse.[48] His health suffered at this time, and a year passed before he become vicar of Loudwater, High Wycombe, in 1972.

In 1981 he accepted an invitation from CPAS to join their staff as an evangelist. Most of his missions were to single churches or parishes. He seldom took a team with him, because his vision was to stir up evangelism within

---

48 A centre run for young people on premises belonging to All Souls at the back of New Oxford Street. Traditionally one of the curates was put in charge of this outreach.

the churches rather than bringing in a group of visitors to do this for them. He continued in this work until his sudden and early death in 1992.

Wilkinson was concerned that his students should have a good all-round training. In those days, when most assessment was by examination, the college conducted written examinations in all subjects in the penultimate week of each term. This allowed the tutors to mark in the final week, during which a variety of speakers would be invited to come and address the student body on different subjects. These could range from the church overseas to children's and youth work, industrial relations or moral welfare matters. Final-year students were encouraged to sit the GOE in March, and then the summer term was entirely devoted to practical pastoral training. This would include a week's course in teaching principles and techniques, given by trained teachers from the National Society (this was offered to all the Anglican theological colleges) and backed by hands-on experience in local primary and secondary schools. Students also spent a week with local probation officers attending the courts and learning something of the type of problems they may have to handle. Many leavers found this one of the most valuable parts of their final term.

Cultural matters were not overlooked, and one of the first visitors Wilkinson invited to the college was the well-known portrait painter Frank Salisbury, who gave an illustrated lecture on the portraits he had painted. Staff of the Royal School of Church Music paid regular visits to the college, and Oak Hill was often represented at the courses they ran for ordinands. The 1955 CACTM inspectors concluded their report by commenting that:

> It seemed symbolic of the college that, on the last evening, your Inspectors should have been entertained in a tutor's flat where the cook, Madame Bume, sang a Mahler song-cycle to Mr. Kidner's expert accompaniment. Only sickness prevented Mr. Bume (PhD) from adding his flute obligato. Could anything be more civilised! The men of the college were good to look at, easy in manners, good to talk with; and your inspectors all agreed that, if they were looking for

> curates, they would have no difficulty in finding in this college men who would be fully acceptable in respect of personality and spirit quite as much as in respect of their academic training.[49]

The same inspectors commented that the students had no difficulty in passing the GOE, and that the prospect of the examination did not appear to loom too large. They were impressed with the general atmosphere that prevailed in the lecture room. The lecturers were competent and informed, questions being invited, and great pains were taken to make the teaching informed and relevant. They praised the new emphasis being given to philosophy by Herniman, whom they noted to be a 'lecturer of first-class promise'. It was a loss to the church that he did not remain in theological teaching, concluding his ministry as Archdeacon of Barnstaple. Examination results show that in most years there were very few who had to resit papers in the GOE, and seldom any failures in the various examinations of London University. In *The Oak Leaf* of summer term 1949 the principal was pleased to report that all six entrants for the London BA finals were successful, two (R. Halse and A.J. Liddon) gaining first-class honours.[50]

Wilkinson, as well as Hinde and those principals who have followed them, was concerned to produce godly pastors and teachers to preach the gospel and build up the body of Christ in the parishes of this country and further afield. There are consequently many Old Oaks who over the past seventy years have exercised a faithful ministry in lonely and difficult places: the fruit of their labours is known to God alone. It is therefore somewhat invidious to single out individuals for mention, but in the interests of this record attention needs to be drawn to those trained in Wilkinson's day who went on to serve the church at home and overseas in significant ways. They include bishops Dick Lyth (Kigezi), John Carter (Suffragan Bishop of Johannesburg), Michael Baughen (Chester), Gavin Reid (Maidstone) and Geoffrey Turner (Stockport), and archdeacons Don Whitbread

[49] 1955 CACTM inspection report.
[50] *The Oak Leaf*, summer term 1949, p. 34.

(the Arctic), John Delight (Stoke), Ron Herniman (Barnstaple), Jim Slater (Winnipeg), William Filby (Horsham), Gerald Kaye (Patricia) and Tom Walker (Nottingham). Tony Capon and Richard Gill became principals of the Montreal Diocesan Theological College and Bishop Gwynne College in the Sudan respectively, while Anthony Thiselton was successively Principal of St John's College, Nottingham, St John's College with Cranmer Hall, Durham, Professor of Christian Theology at Nottingham University and Canon Theologian of Leicester Cathedral. Fred Crook was appointed general secretary of the Commonwealth and Continental Church Society and David Bubbers to a similar role with the CPAS. In addition Peter Street, Philip Gascoigne and Denis Shepheard served on the staff of CPAS as staff evangelists.

Wilkinson's interest in the wider Anglican Communion had also been fostered by a visit to Australia in 1952, when he had undertaken a wide-ranging ministry in the diocese of Sydney and visited Moore College to see something of the work going on there. Following that visit, Archbishop H.W.K. Mowll appointed him as his commissary and it was rumoured that when he retired Wilkinson was being considered as his successor. However, when asked from time to time by his colleagues whether he would like to be elevated to the bench of bishops his reply was always 'I'd rather be training than ordaining men!' The college's links with Australia were fostered by a number of Australians who came over to Oak Hill for training, including Max Bonner, David Smith and David White (son of the 'Jungle Doctor' of Mvumi).[51] Former students from this period who emigrated to take up ministry in Australia included Philip Blake, Clive Brown, Bernard Gook and George Robinson.

In the Lent term of 1955 the trustees gave the principal leave of absence to visit Rwanda. For some time he had been suffering from heart problems, and it was hoped the warmer climate would

---

[51] Paul White had been a missionary doctor at Mvumi Hospital in Tanzania. Based on this experience he wrote a series of *Jungle Doctor* books, which had been published by Scripture Union and made into filmstrips, and were very popular in the 1950s.

be of benefit. He had for years been a keen supporter of the Rwanda Mission (CMS),[52] and for some time was chairman of its council. He had followed with interest the progress of the so-called East African Revival,[53] and some of their emphases were to be found in his addresses at the Keswick Convention, where he was a regular speaker from 1949–59.

In the wake of World War II the college had made its own contribution to reconciliation by sending regular food parcels to the Evangelical Academy at Brunswick. In 1949 the *Landsbischof* in whose diocese it was situated addressed the college over lunch about the situation in Germany then and the work of his diocese. As a result two of their students came over and spent part of the summer term at Oak Hill and wrote an article describing the work of their institution. They concluded, 'It is a grand feeling for us being in this country to get an impression that we are all one in Him, our Lord and Saviour Jesus Christ: one large unity between nations, races and denominations through Him Who said, "Whenever two or three are gathered together in My Name, I shall be with them." '[54]

History was made when the first ordination service was held in the college chapel on St John the Baptist's day in 1948. This was an evocative moment for Alan Stibbs. As commissary to the bishop of East Szechwan (the diocese in which he had served as a missionary) he presented a student, William Picton, to be ordained by the bishop of that diocese, to whom the bishop of St

---

[52] Today known as Mid-Africa Ministries.

[53] A holiness movement of the forties and fifties, emphasizing the need for repentance before the cross and mutual confession of sin. Brokenness was one of its key words, emphasizing 'Not I, but Christ', with the human figure bent in the shape of the 'c' of Christ rather than upright. It started among the missionaries in East Africa, and was sometimes called the 'Ruanda Message' (sic – at that time Ruanda was spelt with a 'u' instead of the current 'w'). This movement is documented in H.H.Osborn, *Fire in the Hill* (Crowborough, East Sussex: Highland, 1991).

[54] *The Oak Leaf*, summer term 1949, pp. 40–1.

Albans had graciously given permission for the service to be held in his diocese. Picton was one of a number who during the Wilkinson years responded to the call to serve overseas, in what was in those days regarded as the mission field, but today would be described as overseas provinces of the Anglican Communion.

In 1952 Wilkinson asked whether the terms of the trust deed would permit him to admit clergymen from overseas provinces of the Communion who could benefit from a year's training in the United Kingdom in order to hone their skills for positions of leadership back in their own dioceses. This was readily granted, and it soon became evident that these men contributed as much to the life of the college as they gained from it. The first person to benefit from the bursary was the Revd Elia Khoury, who came from the Anglican Church in Jordan for the 1952–3 academic year.

Subsequent years have found one or more students from overseas studying at the college, and they have been remembered with affection by their peers. One such student was Silvanus Wani, who later became Bishop of Madi and West Nile. After Idi Amin had arranged the assassination of Janani Luwum, Wani was elected by his colleagues to succeed him as Archbishop of Uganda. In an article published in the 1956 *Oak Leaf* Wani describes the reservations he had over having to cope with the English language and British customs and cold weather. He found the reserve preventing people from talking to one another on a bus or train quite strange, though he found people very helpful when it came to asking for help or directions. During the winter months he found he had to keep moving round in order to keep warm, and at night he was still cold, even though he was supplied with six blankets. He summarized: 'My stay at Oak Hill has been a very happy one as a whole, because the friendship and spirit has been very warm, the study of the Bible very profitable, and the whole atmosphere very blessed.'[55] Don Whitbread, who started his studies at Oak Hill and then transferred to Emmanuel College,

[55] *The Oak Leaf*, 1956, p. 18.

Saskatoon, and later became Archdeacon of the Arctic, wrote from Emmanuel that he missed the recognized time for quiet he had enjoyed at Oak Hill, along with all the great spiritual emphasis on Bible analysis, prayer meetings, student fellowship and prayer partnership.[56]

Prayer partnerships were introduced by Wilkinson to encourage the student body to get to know each other, and to avoid cliques or men associating solely with those of like mind. Every student was paired each week in term time with one other member of the college, and they were expected to meet together at least once during the week to exchange news of each other's situation with a view to supporting one another in prayer. Some men found it so helpful that they would make it a practice to find a time for such prayer daily. The practice was valued so much that when ACCM (the Advisory Council for the Church's Ministry, the successor of CACTM)[57] organized a day's workshop on Spirituality in Ordination Training in 1980 David Wheaton was invited to contribute a paper on the subject.[58]

An indication of the wide range of backgrounds brought together at the college, which made this scheme so invaluable, came out in a survey conducted by one of the students, subsequently written up in *The Oak Leaf*. Conducted in the spring term of 1953 it revealed that of the fifty-two responding to the mock census, forty-four had been in the forces and thirty-nine had held down a secular position prior to coming to college. Only sixteen were products of the public school system, and only nine came from north of Derby. Ten students were married, twenty-two used the *Book of Common Prayer* in their devotions and a similar number possessed Calvin's *Institutes*. Most went to the cinema, but of the fifteen who never went all were among the thirty teetotallers in the college. Other facts discovered were that twenty-four

---

[56] *The Oak Leaf*, Christmas term 1948, p. 101.

[57] The body that supervized theological education underwent one of its several name changes in 1966: CACTM became ACCM.

[58] Published under this title as *ACCM Occasional Paper no. 9* in January 1981.

were blood donors and fourteen birdwatchers, while only four wanted the Church of England disestablished and only six wished to see the abolition of infant baptism.[59]

Wilkinson introduced another valued and regular part of chapel worship by encouraging regular prayer for former students. Four Old Oaks were remembered in turn at every service held in the college chapel. He also opened the Sunday services of Holy Communion to the growing college community of wives and fiancées, as well as ancillary staff, by holding one or two services each term in mid-morning.

Perhaps the best remembered of Wilkinson's innovations in the chapel will be his inauguration of the Commissioning Service, held for all students leaving the college for ordination. For those who found their cathedral ordination perhaps a little formal and daunting, this ceremony, held in the intimacy of the college chapel among those with whom they had lived and worked, was much appreciated. In it those who had been awarded permission to wear the college hood would make their first appearance wearing it, and their names and curacy appointments would be read out. Opportunity was provided to pray, and then, as their bishops would be giving them a New Testament on being made deacon and a Bible at their priesting, the principal gave each leaver a copy of the Prayer Book (candidates from other provinces, e.g. the Church of Ireland, would be given whatever was appropriate for them). The flyleaf bore the inscription:

> *[Name] on Ordination as Deacon and in remembrance of the fellowship in which you have lived at Oak Hill; as a pledge of our prayers and as a reminder that the life of worship is the first essential of fruitful service.*

For most these closing words summed up what they had seen in the life of their principal.

Over the years a steady number of Irish ordinands chose to come to Oak Hill. Such candidates were normally expected to train at

[59] *The Oak Leaf*, 1953, p. 10.

the Divinity Hostel in Dublin, but those of stronger evangelical convictions held out to go to Oak Hill because they valued its stronger emphasis on biblical teaching. Some of their bishops also felt that allowing some of their ordinands to train in England made their dioceses less insular and brought some fresh thinking into their clergy. The Irish contingent were remembered with great affection by their contemporaries, and they even persuaded some of their peers to cross the Irish Sea to take up ministries.

An interesting example of the influence the college has had on other provinces can be seen in those Canadians who trained at Oak Hill. The Revd Gerry Gregson went over to Canada just after World War II to pioneer Scripture Union's work there. He met Harry Robinson, whom he encouraged to come to Oak Hill and read for the London Diploma in Theology. On return to Canada, Robinson was influential in the call to ordination of Jim Slater (later Archdeacon of Winnipeg), and steered him to Oak Hill for his training. As rector of St Margaret's, Winnipeg, Slater guided Alistair Petrie to come to Oak Hill. Petrie later became rector of Brentwood Bay on Vancouver Island, and there a member of his congregation, David Butterworth, heard the call to ordination and came to Oak Hill.

Experience of ministering in different parts of the country had taught Wilkinson the importance of clear diction. He reported in the first edition of *The Oak Leaf*:

> The voice plays such an important part in the work of the ministry, that the management committee felt that elocution training should take a prominent place in a man's course. Mr. Ripper, L.R.A.M., M.R.S.T., L.C.S.T., who has had many years of experience in voice training and speech therapy is coming to the college for two hours a week so that all men will have at least one or two years' regular training ... This elocution work is part of the normal curriculum of the college, so that no extra fees are charged for it.[60]

[60] *The Oak Leaf*, Christmas term 1946, p. 15.

Further encouragement for students to work at reading aloud was given in the form of a competition held annually, later to be endowed in memory of Phyllis Johnston, the wife of Peter Johnston, the first person from Oak Hill to be ordained. Other prizes were given for an essay set each year on a given topic and awarded in memory of the founder. Prizes were also given annually for those who distinguished themselves in their results in the GOE.

Wilkinson's enthusiasm for the Keswick Convention led to his opening the college grounds for a week each June for a North London Keswick Convention. A large marquee, seating a thousand, was erected, and each evening speakers from the Keswick platform were invited to address a congregation drawn from parishes and free churches in the neighbourhood, and even farther afield. The meeting was held in Oak Hill grounds usually during the last week of the summer term so that students who might not be able to afford the time or the expense of going up to the Lake District for a week could have the benefit of its teaching. This continued from 1953–81, when it was transferred to Cockfosters Church, and was particularly valued by people converted during the Harringay and Earls Court (the 1966 Billy Graham crusade) Crusades and who had found little Bible teaching in their own churches.

A further innovation designed to cement the relationship between the two branches of Baring Young's foundation was a regular visit to Kingham Hill School. This began in 1952, and would take place in the summer term, when there would be an opportunity to play cricket either against the school or one of the theological colleges from Bristol.

Wilkinson also served the wider Church of England by chairing the Church Society Trust, which he saw as an opportunity to place some of his former students in parishes that were seeking an evangelical ministry. Other interests included the chairmanship of the governing body of two women's training colleges, St Michael's House at Oxford and Ridgelands Missionary College, as well as the Church Society Council. He was also a vice-president of IVF, the Crusaders' Union and CPAS. While he had never written a book, his addresses at the Keswick Convention were regularly published in *The Life of Faith* and *The Keswick Week*. Keen to exploit the developing technology of his day, one of his great hobbies was producing and showing colour transparencies, particularly of his visit to Rwanda. The Church Society published two filmstrips devised by Wilkinson to give clear Anglican teaching on infant baptism and Holy Communion. He also used sets of slides and a filmstrip to illustrate the work of the college.

With the student body having grown to a regular number of sixty-plus there was scope for a further appointment to the academic staff. The principal was given permission by the trustees to look for someone ideally to teach in the field of church history and thus relieve him of some of his heavy workload. On Tuesday 13 December 1960, after a period of indifferent health, Wilkinson seemed to be on the mend, and was full of enthusiasm as he appeared at last to have found the right person to join the staff. Later that day he walked across the road to post the day's letters. Shortly afterwards his body was found by the pillar box, where he had suffered a fatal heart attack. The college had suffered an enormous loss, and the staff and students felt it deeply. One of his colleagues wrote this fitting tribute:

> No principal could have been more loved by his students, who showed their affection most openly by making him the focus of their corporate wit. At college concerts he continued to be guyed unmercifully. And he never ceased to enjoy it, even when subjected to outrageous ragging. He was big enough to play and be made the fool without the slightest loss of dignity. At one moment he would convulse an audience as the village idiot and, at the next, move the congregation with a preaching of the Cross. He was always the principal. Not because he stood upon a position, but because he claimed wholehearted respect. To be in his company was to be at ease; but no-one thought to take the tiniest liberty. There could be no clearer proof of respect for his judgement than that given by the numbers who came back to discuss a second curacy and even a second living.[61]

---

[61] *The Oak Leaf*, 1961, pp. 7–8.

5

New Programmes and New Buildings (1961–1971)

> It was a great pleasure to welcome the new principal to the reunion lunch. After the meal, he spoke concerning future plans for the college. We are sure that under his leadership we shall see many of the plans and schemes begun by Prebendary Hinde and Mr Wilkinson growing even more, as well as new ideas coming in.[1]

In June 1961 Maurice Wood, the new principal, spoke to the annual reunion of the Oak Hill Association. The reporter who wrote the above account of that speech would not be disappointed: Wood both continued the 'plans and schemes' begun by his predecessors and introduced new programmes. The search for a new principal had begun less than a month after the sudden death of Wilkinson, and the appointment of Wood was announced in February 1961. However, he was not able to take up his duties until the end of the summer term. Stibbs served ably as acting principal during the interim. Although the appointment was made quickly, those concerned had considered a number of names before they unanimously agreed to recommend Wood to the trustees.[2] It was an excellent choice. The college was entering an age that was to prove

---

[1] *The Oak Leaf*, 1961, p. 36.

[2] On 12 January 1961 Canon Mohan, the Chairman of the Management Committee, presented a list of names suggested by various people. 'After detailed discussion of each, two short lists each of three names was approved.' The chairman was authorized to contact candidates on

vastly different from the placid and largely traditional era that preceded it. Wood proved to be the ideal leader to meet the challenges of the sixties.

One of his great strengths was his vision for evangelism, having already established a reputation as a committed evangelist. He was ordained in 1940 and after serving a curacy at St Paul's, Portman Square, had spent two years as a naval chaplain and in the course of service with the Royal Marine Commandos had been awarded the Distinguished Service Cross. When the war ended, he was appointed to St Ebbe's in Oxford, where undergraduates flocked to his church. In 1952 he was offered the position of vicar and rural dean of Islington, accepting the position because of the potential he saw for evangelism. He set up lay leadership training courses to help promote evangelism. His lectures at those courses were published in 1955 in a book entitled *Like a Mighty Army*,[3] and he also produced a series of *Islington Booklets* designed for evangelistic purposes. The first of them, entitled *How Can I Find God?*, was a reprint of a sermon that he had preached at St Mary's, Islington on 15 August 1954, which had been broadcast. It presented the Christian gospel in simple terms using very effective illustrations from real life and included a prayer of commitment. Other booklets followed dealing with questions such as the guidance of God, assurance, methods of Bible study and comfort in sorrow.[4]

Wood was well known for his readiness to take every opportunity to pass on these booklets and he continued to do this after he became principal. One staff member recalls being on a train with his face hidden behind his newspaper when the door of the compartment opened. He heard a very familiar voice

---

[2] (*continued*) the first list to see if they were willing to be considered, to interview each of them and to inform the council 'who would submit their choice for appointment to the trustees for their approval.' Minutes of the Oak Hill Management Committee, 12 January 1961.

[3] London: Marshall, Morgan and Scott, 1957.

[4] While he was vicar of Islington he also wrote a very useful book, *Your Suffering*, after being bereaved of his first wife.

offering him a booklet. It seems that Wood often used train journeys as an opportunity for evangelism, walking the length of the train and politely offering a booklet to people in each compartment. He even handed out booklets to new members of the Oak Hill staff. Margie Lane, who joined the staff in 1968 to work in the kitchen, recalls that 'When I first went to work at Oak Hill, the principal gave me this little pink booklet on how to become a Christian.'[5] It is not surprising that Wood was one of the leading supporters of the Harringay crusade and according to his own testimony he only missed one night: 'We finished parish duties, we got into my little car with any of our young people who were counsellors and free to come and we drove up the hill just to get to the end as they finished preaching, so we counselled straightaway. Those were great days!'[6]

Wood also brought the college into greater involvement in the wider Church of England. He was active in the Church Assembly, served as proctor in Convocation, was a member of the Archbishops' Commission on Evangelism, and served the posts of secretary and later vice-chairman and chairman of the Theological Colleges' Principals' Conference. He had good relations with people from other traditions, including those with whom he had major theological differences, and invited visitors to Oak Hill who were not necessarily sympathetic to the conservative evangelical position. For example, in March 1963 the new Archbishop of Canterbury, Michael Ramsey, an Anglo-Catholic who had been extremely critical of Billy Graham, visited Oak Hill. He took tea with the staff and their wives in the principal's flat, unveiled a portrait of the Queen and preached at evening prayer in the chapel. Afterwards

---

[5] Margie, who was to remain on the staff for over thirty years, saw Maurice Wood again at Gordon Bridger's going away party in 1996. When she said to him 'Do you remember Maurice, you gave me a little booklet on how to become a Christian?' He said 'Do you mean this one?' and handed her the same booklet. Interview with the Lanes, 31 May 1999.

[6] Interview with Wood, 4 May 1999.

he answered questions in the common room and invited the entire college to Lambeth Palace for afternoon tea. On 14 May that year according to *The Oak Leaf* 'the whole college, plus wives who were able to come' went to Lambeth Palace where they had tea, a tour of the palace and evening prayer in the palace chapel at which the archbishop preached.[7] Wood also invited the Roman Catholic Prior of Cockfosters to dine at the college. According to Wood's account:

> I led Dom Edmund Jones in. It was all very formal in those days, you all wore gowns for meals in the evening, and all the students were standing there when we came in to the top table. So I said we are very privileged to have our next door neighbour across the road at *Vita et Pax* calling on us and we welcome him to dinner. This caused an enormous turmoil in the college.[8]

By inviting a Roman Catholic priest to dinner the principal was very much in accord with the new relationship between Protestants and Catholics resulting from the Second Vatican Council, and the link with the priory at Cockfosters continued until the community moved to Turvey Abbey, Bedfordshire, in the early eighties.

Wood also supported the proposed Anglican–Methodist re-union scheme that many other evangelicals viewed with suspicion, maintaining 'we have got to live with the ecumenical movement'.[9] However, this did not mean an uncritical acceptance. Rather he insisted that evangelicals needed 'to preserve biblical truth within this and any further reunion schemes'. He commented: 'we must pin-point our disagreement with such views on priesthood, episcopacy and sacraments as seem to go beyond or fall short of biblical truth, anglican formularies or the forty-four sermons

---

[7] *The Oak Leaf*, 1963, p. 17.

[8] Interview with Woods: Vita et Pax was the local Roman Catholic priory.

[9] Maurice Wood et al, 'Some Considerations for Evangelicals' in Peter Morgan (ed.), *The Anglican–Methodist Conversations: An Evangelical Approach*, p. 9.

of John Wesley'.[10] In the end the proposals were defeated in July 1969 – the Church Assembly was unable to achieve the requisite seventy-five per cent majority.

Wood was called to lead the college when the future seemed bright for theological education. During the fifties the number of ordinations rose steadily, and this trend continued in the early sixties.[11] In 1960 there were more ordinands than there were places in the existing theological colleges and the Church Assembly discussed the possibility 'that a new and larger theological college might soon be needed'.[12] In 1960 the Southwark Ordination Course began as a non-residential course to train men for the ordained ministry while they continued in their secular employment. In the same year the Church Assembly commissioned a well-known sociologist, Leslie Paul, to conduct a study of the existing system of clergy payment and deployment, published early in 1964 under the title *The Deployment and Payment of the Clergy*.[13] Although the report was highly critical of the present system and recommended some radical changes[14] it was optimistic in its expectations about the number of likely ordinations in the coming decade. Basing his projection on the positive statistics of the late 1950s Paul assumed that by the beginning of the next

---

[10] Ibid, pp. 10–11. In March 1963 Wood also expressed his support for the union in the Church Times: 'If different views can be held both in tension and in love within the Church of England,' he wrote, 'the tradition of both clerical and lay evangelism, which is the historic heart of Methodism, is as much at home in the Church of England as Anglican Evangelicalism.' *Church Times*, 1 March 1963.

[11] The annual number of ordinations increased from 441 in 1954 to 632 in 1962. Leslie Paul, *The Deployment and Payment of the Clergy*, p. 290.

[12] Bullock, *History of Training*, p. 125. In the discussion it was pointed out by the Bishop of Lincoln that twenty-nine men could not find places and seventy-nine were training in colleges outside England.

[13] London: Church Information Office, 1964.

[14] The report contained sixty-two recommendations; among them were the abolition of the 'Parsons Freehold' and the patronage system.

decade there would be a thirty per cent increase in the number of ordinations. He expected that the number of ordinations would gradually increase every year and that in 1971 there would be 831 ordinations.[15] Seldom has a projection been so inaccurate. In 1971 there were 393 ordinations. Ten years after the Church Assembly had discussed the need for a new theological college the same body was faced with the need to close a number of colleges.[16] Paul's report completely misjudged what would happen in the sixties because it was based on projecting the positive statistics of the past decade into a new decade characterized by a radically different ethos.

The sixties were an era of prosperity and permissiveness and the moral restraints of the past were gradually eroded. Abortion became legal by the end of the decade and divorce facilitated. Advertising, films, and television became more sexually explicit, while the introduction of the contraceptive pill in January 1961 helped to encourage sexual promiscuity. In this new world the old institutions seemed terribly out of date. Many rebelled against the restrictions of the past. Clements notes that 'it was a tenet of the early 1960s that the most suspect things were those which were apparently beyond question'.[17] All this affected the church in a dramatic way. It was not ready for the new challenges.

In one sense the church contributed to its own decline by its reaction. Rather than proclaiming an unchanging Word of God, many (including office-holders who received a great deal of publicity) lost confidence in that message. Consequently they adjusted and revised it to fit what the many in society already believed. In the effort to make theology relevant to modern man they abandoned much of traditional Anglicanism. In 1961 Don Cupitt was shaping the radical theology that would give him so much media attention in future years. In 1961 he published a short article in *Theology* entitled 'Four arguments against the

---

[15] Paul, *Deployment and Payment*, p. 298.

[16] Bullock, *History of Training*, p. 131.

[17] Keith W. Clements, *Lovers of Discord: Twentieth-Century Theological Controversies in England*, p. 175.

devil'. He argued that belief in the devil was a holdover from a superstitious age, but in the present age 'the time has come to banish superstitious fears for ever'. By doing so 'Christian theology could now finally win the age-long battle of monotheism against the enslavement of man by superstitious fear.'[18] Five years later Cupitt, now Dean of Emmanuel College, Cambridge, led a retreat attended by representatives from each of the twenty-five Anglican theological colleges. He again suggested that belief in a devil was a relic from a past age and should be discarded. However, he did not seem to convince the audience. According to Hugh Dibbens, the Oak Hill student who attended, 'Don Cupitt's suggestion that it was outmoded to believe in a personal devil provoked a general protest, and the devil was quickly reinstated.'[19]

In March 1963 the publication of John Robinson's *Honest to God*[20] had a massive impact. It sold nearly a million copies in the next three years, went through three impressions in the month of March alone and was translated into numerous languages. Robinson, then Bishop of Woolwich, wanted to find a way to preach the Gospel to modern man and to reach those for whom the historic Christian faith and the language in which it was presented had no meaning. Unfortunately, the impression the book left in the minds of many was that the bishop had himself abandoned the Gospel. He had put himself in the place of the modern agnostic and asked all the hard questions an agnostic might ask about the Christian faith. The answers Robinson then gave were neither clear nor were they in accord with what a bishop who had made a commitment to the Scriptures and to the Anglican formularies should believe. Lloyd states: 'all this meant not only a repudiation of many sacrosanct words and phrases of traditional theology, but also,

---

[18] Don Cupitt, 'Four Arguments against the Devil', *Theology* vol. 64 (October 1961), p. 415.

[19] *The Oak Leaf*, 1966, p. 22.

[20] London: SCM.

and more, a repudiation of much of the whole traditionalist way of looking at God and his world'.[21]

Although the *Honest to God* debate generated a great deal of public attention it does not seem to have affected those whom Robinson was trying to reach. Clements points out 'that there was interest in the public at large was clear enough. But the representatives of "non-religious man" did not seem to be particularly impressed.'[22] Wood, who knew Robinson well, recalls meeting with him after the publication of *Honest to God*, giving him a copy of an *Islington Booklet* and saying:

> I've read your book. Do you not think that from your perspective, you could take a booklet of the size of *How Can I Find God*, and write a simple booklet that sets out the steps to faith and explains how a seeker can come to faith from your point of view. It could be something that you could give to people as I give my booklet to people who are seeking Christ?[23]

In response Robinson 'just chuckled', but if he hoped to achieve his objective of communicating the faith to modern man he would have been wise to have followed Wood's advice, because *Honest to God* seems to have had the opposite effect. Gilbert believes that rather than helping to reach those who were outside the faith, '*Honest to God* was a vital event in the making of post-Christian Britain.' He stated that 'it is impossible, a decade-and-a-half later, not to conclude that the publication hastened the decline of British Christianity and actually increased the estrangement from the secular culture of that waning religious tradition which the bishop sought to make more preachable'.[24] Whether or not this

---

[21] Lloyd, *Church of England*, p. 605. One of the most useful and fair discussions of the contents of Honest to God is found in Clements, *Lovers of Discord*, pp. 178ff.

[22] Clements, *Lovers of Discord*, pp. 196–7.

[23] Interview with Wood.

[24] Alan Gilbert, *The Making of Post-Christian Britain: A History of the Secularization of Modern Society*, pp. 121–2.

is correct, it is clear that the decline in most church statistics continued and even accelerated after 1963. Six years after the publication of *Honest to God* Anglican confirmations had fallen by 32.2 per cent, ordinations dropped by 24.8 per cent in five years and baptisms fell from 55.4 per cent of live births in 1963 to 46.6 per cent in 1970. For the first time marriages solemnized in the Church of England fell below 40 per cent.

The most effective response to Robinson from an evangelical viewpoint was Jim Packer's *Keep Yourselves from Idols*,[25] but the debate received a very fair assessment in *The Oak Leaf* where Alan Holloway (a lecturer in doctrine and philosophy) reviewed *Honest to God* making the point that noone should dare to discuss or pronounce on it without having read it carefully and sympathetically.[26] Philip Crowe (a lecturer in the gospels and Greek) also concluded a letter to the *Church of England Newspaper* by saying 'by all means let us criticise the answer if, and only if, we are prepared to face up to and grapple with the question'.[27]

This situation meant theological colleges, including Oak Hill, would be competing for a declining number of ordinands. However, evangelicals seem to have been least affected by what Hastings calls 'Robinsonianism', maintaining that 'as a group they came through the sixties in far the best shape'.[28] While others were losing confidence in the traditional Christian message, evangelicals remained firm in their faith in the gospel and their commitment to tell others the good news. In his penultimate presidential address at the Islington Clerical Conference at the beginning of the decade, Wood exhibited the type of enthusiasm, innovative spirit and confidence that helps to explain the continuing strength of evangelicalism. He challenged evangelicals to 'stand for public morality', to 'be concerned with social problems' and 'to seize every new opportunity for evangelistic activity'. He encouraged them to reach out to 'the millions who are outside

---

[25] J.I. Packer, *Keep Yourselves from Idols.*

[26] *The Oak Leaf*, 1964, p. 32.

[27] *Church of England Newspaper*, 26 April 1963.

[28] Hastings, *History of English Christianity*, p. 552.

any place of worship on Sunday' through innovative methods of evangelism including the use of television and large open-air services at seaside resorts. He also urged them to become more involved in the Church of England, stating 'there is a fresh realisation of the need of spiritual revival not merely in our own evangelical fellowship, but throughout the Church of England'.[29]

Although Wood was very optimistic about the future, in the same speech he commented on the divisions developing among evangelicals that could hamper the cause of evangelism, mentioning specifically the growing strength of those whom he accused of as having 'ultra-Calvinist' views and who questioned the need for evangelism. In addition the second Billy Graham crusade in 1966 was marred by divisions between those who, like Wood, were enthusiastic supporters and those who questioned the usefulness of this type of evangelism.[30]

Another source of division came from an unexpected quarter. In 1961 the *Church of England Newspaper* carried a number of articles and devoted several editorials to strange phenomena being experienced in the American Episcopal Church that came to be called the charismatic movement or neo-pentecostalism. By 1963 this experience had reached these shores and evangelicals were being confronted with a new movement which, while having much in common with classic evangelicalism, also had major differences.

The charismatic movement differed radically from what Hastings calls 'typical 1960s religion', which was 'antisupernaturalist' and 'found little or no relevance in miracles, angels, heaven and hell' or 'petitionary prayer'. The charismatic movement in contrast 'was intensely supernaturalist ... pretty fundamentalist in regard to the Bible and ... preoccupied with intercessory prayer'.[31] Despite its positive aspects, as the movement grew in strength it led to divisions among evangelicals and

---

[29] *Church of England Newspaper*, 15 January 1960.

[30] See the report *On the Other Side*, published by the Evangelical Alliance, 1968.

[31] Hastings, *History of English Christianity*, p. 557.

conservative evangelicals became very suspicious of it. They feared that it relied on experience rather than scriptural teaching and were concerned that the so-called 'gift of tongues' often seemed to be the result of very contrived methods. They were also concerned that doctrinal differences with others who had experienced charismatic renewal, such as Roman Catholics, were often ignored in the 'euphoria of shared experience'.[32]

Although evangelicals were experiencing internal divisions in these years, in April 1967 the first National Evangelical Anglican Congress, which met at Keele University, displayed remarkable solidarity. Over a thousand people attended and conservative evangelicals made a commitment not only to remain within the Church of England, but also to take a more active role in it at every level. In addition the Keele statement stressed support for participation in the ecumenical movement, the need for social responsibility and a commitment to 'work towards the practice of a weekly celebration of the Sacrament as the central corporate service of the Church'.[33] It affirmed many of the policies and beliefs that Wood had pursued during his first six years as principal. During this time Wood appointed an outstanding teaching staff, introduced a number of innovative programmes, and continued to stress involvement in evangelism. The members of the college community were also very much aware of the controversies that plagued the church. Staff members and students commented on the questions being debated and contributed their own point of view in articles in both *The Oak Leaf* and *Churchman*. The openness of the debate that went on within the college and the diversity of opinion contrasted with the popular and largely uninformed image of the college. Those who had only a superficial acquaintance with the college were sometimes more influenced by the caricature of conservative evangelicals than the evidence.

Paul Ferris included a description of life at Oak Hill in his book about the Church of England.[34] He presented a picture of a

---

[32] Hylson-Smith, *Evangelicals in the Church of England*, p. 334.

[33] Hastings, *History of English Christianity*, p. 554.

[34] Paul Ferris, *The Church of England.*

singled-minded community unwilling to ask the hard questions. Commenting on the student body, he suggested that 'most of the 60 or 70 insiders in residence at Oak Hill will mellow after a few years in parishes; but, having come because this offered them the type of Christianity they wanted, they will continue to bear the stamp of the college.' Ferris reported that 'Oak Hill doesn't go in for the intellectual gymnastics at times verging on agnosticism found at other colleges. Nor is there much doubt, as there is in widening theological circles, that the Bible is reporting historical fact.' The principal was described as 'one of the strong men in the conservative evangelical wing', and one of Wood's lectures is quoted in which he supposedly stated that 'we're marked men on the devil's list'. Ferris commented: 'the devil is not a convenient bit of mythology in his life'.[35] Although his account was probably accurate in what he reported, the tone of his remarks gave an image of the college that was to a great extent inaccurate.

Another book to comment on Oak Hill in the sixties was written by two sociologists, Robert Towler and Tony Coxton. Using the methods of sociological analysis they compared student attitudes and beliefs at five theological colleges representing various traditions – Oak Hill, Queen's, Birmingham, Mirfield, Westcott House and St Chad's, Durham. Their careful study presented a more accurate picture of the college, even though they were not in agreement with what the college taught. They maintained that there were two types of clergy: those they labelled 'puritan' were pious, enthusiastic and conservative, in contrast with the 'antipuritan' or the 'irreligious type', who were opposed to much of what the puritans found important. The obsession of the puritans with piety, worship and church activities was to the two authors distasteful, since the antipuritans had a much greater involvement in the secular world.[36] Oak Hill differed from all the other institutions in that it had a large percentage of puritans (nineteen out of

---

[35] Ibid., pp. 34–9.

[36] Robert Towler and A.P.M. Coxton, *The Fate of the Anglican Clergy: A Sociological Study*, pp. 100–101.

twenty-two fell into that category) and only one antipuritan. They also found Oak Hill unique in that its students were willing to criticize each other's as well as the staff's conduct and religious behaviour. The writers also viewed the college as committed largely to 'practical training' in comparison with the other colleges and gave Oak Hill high marks for the way in which it trained professional ministers. They pointed out that 'in many ways Oak Hill provided the practical training required by a religious professional', but they also maintained that 'all the emphasis was on preparation for the life of a full-time church worker, with little notice being taken of the specifically clerical character of their ministry'. They maintained that Oak Hill students were being trained for particular tasks – namely, to reach the unconverted and to build up the life of a local church community – and the college aimed to equip its students to undertake these tasks with maximum efficiency.[37] They concluded that 'Oak Hill was best suited to preparing men to serve churches under new conditions in which the emphasis might be firmly on the congregation, but it was narrowly evangelical.'[38] However, although they assumed that the conservative suburban churches might flourish in the short run, they were convinced that in the long run they believed 'the future will be with the radicals'.[39]

Although a good deal of what Towler and Coxton wrote about the college was true they also failed to see the full picture. The image of the college that emerges is that of an institution populated by serious, single-minded puritan types who were hardly prepared to confront the real challenges of the modern world. They used the methods of modern sociological research to confirm the popular image of the college, but the image presented was far from accurate. Those who came to know the college better had a very different image. For example, the CACTM inspection team of 1962 noted in its report that 'we

---

[37] Ibid., p. 169.
[38] Ibid., p. 203.
[39] Ibid., p. 205.

found greater variety of opinion on religious topics than might have been anticipated in a college of such definite tradition'.[40] Furthermore, as is pointed out below, the college community was well aware of what was happening in the wider world and addressed the contemporary problems of both church and society.

It should not be surprising that the Oak Hill community did not conform to the popular image when one considers the quality of the staff and the students they taught. Wood inherited a staff that included two outstanding biblical scholars in Kidner and Stibbs. The death of Wilkinson necessitated the use of a number of visiting lecturers including John Stibbs, Alan Stibbs's son, who lectured in modern church history. Hugh Silvester, a final-year student who had achieved impressive examination results, lectured in Christian doctrine in place of Herniman, who had been ill and unable to teach.

Wood already had in mind a possible replacement for Herniman. On 9 March 1961 he wrote to John Taylor, then an incumbent in the Chelmsford diocese, exploring the possibility of his joining the staff. In a follow-up letter Wood described the type of staff he was seeking to build at Oak Hill:

> I need not only someone who will give the men plenty of good, solid, academic food, as I know you would, but I also need the quality of home life that you and Linda can provide, so that these young men, many of them just married or getting married, can by the grace of God learn from our homes a little bit about Christian married life. In the same way, I want to build a staff who will each take real trouble over a proportion of the men committed to their charge from a pastoral point of view.[41]

[40] Central Advisory Council for the Ministry Inspections Committee, *Report of the Inspection of Oak Hill College*, 14–17 November 1962, p. 4.

[41] Letter from Wood to John Taylor, 16 May 1961, in college archives.

Wood was not able to convince him to join the staff until 1964, but he clearly had the right man in mind: John Taylor would bring to the staff both significant academic gifts and a truly pastoral heart.

Herniman moved to parish work in June 1961. At the same time Dr and Mrs Bume, who had served the college as cooks for eleven years, retired. Stephanie Sutcliffe also left after sixteen years of devoted service to the college when the new principal brought in his own secretary, Anne Burton, from Islington. Miss Sutcliffe's leaving was very distressing to many, and Stibbs had written to Wood:

> Apparently on Sunday morning the men, who as volunteers help Miss S. prepare the Sunday lunch, found out she had been given notice to quit. She, apparently in conversation with them about the future, was emotionally overcome at times – something quite unlike her. The news has stirred a wave of feeling that her departure is unthinkable and would only do un-Christian damage to her and cause grievous loss to the college.[42]

This sensitive letter did not lead to reinstatement, and after serving the college so well for so long she left.[43] Unfortunately, this would not be the last time a long-term employee left in unhappy circumstances, and the college has not always shown wisdom or understanding in these matters. After Miss Sutcliffe's long service as college secretary, during the next decade four different persons held the position.[44]

---

[42] Letter from Stibbs to Wood, 7 May 1961, in college archives.

[43] A tribute to Miss Sutcliffe in *The Oak Leaf* gave the details of her valuable service in many areas, commenting, 'Miss Sutcliffe gave a new dimension to the word [Secretary]. Few realise just how hard working she has been, and how wide-ranging have been her activities. She never sought the front rank, but was ever a tower of strength behind the scenes.' *The Oak Leaf*, 1961, p. 12.

[44] In addition to Anne Burton they were: Stella Cranmer (January–August 1965); Jane Bundey (September 1965–July 1967); Miriam Cragg (August 1967 –June 1972).

The college found it difficult to find a new cook. After attempting to resolve the problem with the use of a catering firm, Maureen Finding was employed as senior cook and Jeanette Roberts as second cook.[45] Herniman was eventually replaced by Alan Holloway, an Old Oak who came from parochial ministry at Chalk in Kent to lecture in doctrine and philosophy. Wood also received permission to appoint an unmarried tutor. However, in the 1961–2 academic year he had to manage with a somewhat depleted staff with only Stibbs, Kidner and Wheaton as full-time tutors. Fortunately, the college was blessed with some gifted part-time lecturers. Holloway, who was unable to join the staff for a year due to family commitments, served as a part-time lecturer, as did John Stibbs, who would continue his valuable service to the college for much of the Wood decade. He came to lecture in church history on Saturday mornings and also instructed all first year non-graduates in study methods and English. The Revd Douglas Paterson taught worship, the Revd Arthur Poulton, rector of East Barnet, taught New Testament Greek and John's Gospel, while Miss H. Brettell taught voice and speech to students in their final two years. In addition Dr Leon Morris, warden of Tyndale House, previously vice-principal of Ridley College, Melbourne, gave a series of lectures on the atonement.

In the following year Wood began the building of his new staff. Holloway joined the full-time staff and John Simpson, curate of Christ Church, Orpington, was appointed as a single man to lecture in church history and worship. In addition, Philip Crowe, a Cambridge graduate who was also to serve as curate of Christ Church, Cockfosters, joined the staff to lecture in the Gospels and Greek as Wheaton took up the living of Ludgershall in Buckinghamshire. This process eventually resulted in nine staff appointments in a decade. Wood clearly had a gift for selecting talented young men who were later to rise to high positions in the church. Two became bishops, one of

---

[45] Principal's report, 2 February 1962.

whom became Archbishop of Canterbury, four became heads of theological colleges or courses, one a cathedral dean and another became a director of education.[46]

Wood's appointments were made largely at his own discretion. When asked how he found so many quality people and whether he advertised or interviewed a number of potential candidates, he responded 'I had a very wide knowledge of the evangelical world, so I knew the sort of quality people I could pick from.'[47] He also listened to the advice of his senior colleagues. David Field was one of those quality people selected in this fashion. According to Wood, 'at Stibbs's suggestion, I dug out this rather shy young man and appointed David, who was an enormous success at the college'.[48] On joining the staff Field reports that he 'felt quite overawed by my colleagues'.

Although appointments were made in a very informal manner the college was run very formally. According to Field:

> There was a pecking order. Maurice ran the college under fairly tight control; he had been in the armed forces and he was very definitely the commander in chief. At staff meetings, we used to sit in the staff room around the table in order, and the junior member of staff would sit on Maurice's right to take the notes and as you got a little more senior you moved around the table, so the vice-principal sat on his left. Of

[46] George Carey, Bishop of Bath and Wells 1987–91, Archbishop of Canterbury from 1991; John Taylor, Bishop of St Albans 1980–95; Philip Crowe, Principal, Salisbury and Wells 1988–95; David Field, Dean of Oak Hill Ministerial Training Course 1988–95; John Goldingay, Principal, St Johns College, Nottingham 1990–97, Professor of Old Testament, Fuller Theological Seminary, Pasadena, California from 1997; Chris Byworth, Warden, Cranmer Hall, Durham 1979–83; John Simpson, Dean of Canterbury 1986–2000; Alan Holloway, Director of Education, Gloucester Diocese 1988–92. The ninth appointee was Hugh Silvester who was equally talented, but who died young in 1980 while serving as vicar of Holy Trinity, Platt.

[47] Interview with Woods.

[48] Ibid.

> course, we always used to walk into lunch in order, so I was last. There was a fight at the back because George Carey was fairly junior, not as junior as me, and he wanted to be last, and between us, I'm afraid, we were a little rebellious and used to shuffle our places and destroy the neat order.[49]

Oak Hill was blessed with an equally talented and diverse group of students. Among those who studied between 1960–70 seven later became bishops, three college lecturers or university professors, one a cathedral dean and another an archdeacon. Other students were to serve in the leadership of the church's official bodies and missionary and parachurch organizations. Many who were committed parish ministers served as rural deans and some were honoured by being appointed honorary canons.[50]

---

[49] Interview with David Field, 15 May 1999. Maurice Wood also had a very informal side to him that was noted and especially appreciated by the non-academic staff. Margie Lane called him 'a fun character'. She recalled that he would join the non-academic staff for coffee because he said they had better biscuits that the students. She added that 'he always used to make himself at home with us in the coffee room ... whether he was the same with students and academics as he was with us I don't know ... But he certainly was good fun.' He also did not consider it below his dignity to help in the domestic work. When the houseman was off work for a period of time and the ladies were unwilling to clean the men's toilets, the principal got a bucket and mop and cleaned the toilets himself. 'He said, "Well, I worked on a ship, if I can work on ship I can work here, same thing." ' Interview with the Lanes, 31 May 1999.

[50] This is based on sampling over 400 names so it is possible that a number who achieved high position have been overlooked. The names of those referred to above with their dates at Oak Hill are – bishops: Geoffrey Turner, 1960–63; Roy Williamson, 1961–3; Cyril Ashton, 1964–7; Terence Kelshaw, 1965–7; David Gillett, 1966–8; John Went, 1967–9; George Cassidy, 1970–72. Archdeacon: Gordon Kuhrt, 1965–7. College lecturers: Edmund Gibbs, 1958–63; Gary Gibson, 1962–4. Cathedral dean: Michael Bunker, 1959–63. Directors of CMJ: Anthony Higton, who also founded 'Action for

Exterior of the new academic centre – 2000.
(Richard Hanson)

Oak Hill college front entrance in winter prior to building of the chapel in 1957.
(source unknown)

C.E. Baring Young, the founder.
(Salmon & Son, 169 Hampstead Road, London)

A.W. Habershon, principal of Oak Hill College (Bohun Lodge), 1928–32.
(Habershon family)

H.W. Hinde, first principal of Oak Hill Theological College, 1932–45.
(David Grubb)

L.F.E. Wilkinson (left), principal 1945–60, and A.M. Stibbs (right), staff member 1937–71 and vice-principal 1938–65.
(source unknown)

Archbishop George Carey (centre) with past and present principals (left to right) G.F. Bridger, D.H. Wheaton, M.A.P. Wood and D. Peterson.
(David Rogers)

Archbishop Carey dedicating the academic centre in the new lecture theatre.
(David Rogers)

Students working on the farm in the 1950s.
(source unknown)

'Farmer Brown' watches the Queen Mother planting a tree to commemorate the opening of the first married quarters for students.
(Charles Adams of Southgate)

Wartime scene: staff and students with tin hats and stirrup pump.
(supplied for the college archives by the late Prebendary Donald Lynch)

Maurice Wood and students lead an open-air rally in Trafalgar Square in March 1967. Those taking part (left to right) are David Gillett, Jim Chelton and Maurice Wood.
(David Gillett)

Study facilities at Bohun Lodge 1928.
(1928 Bohun Lodge prospectus)

'Wilkie' teaching in the 1950s.
(Cameracraft of Palmers Green)

A student seminar in 2000.
(Richard Hanson)

Inside the modern library.
(Serota Photography 2001)

The chapel prior to 1949.
(source unknown)

The chapel today.
(Richard Hanson)

The students came from a wide range of educational and social backgrounds, and African students added to this diversity. Their richness of spiritual life, profound faith and trust in their Lord in the midst of hardships was an inspiration. In 1965 the Evangelical Fellowship of the Anglican Communion initiated a bursary scheme that helped to finance African students for the next quarter of a century.[51]

Students regularly wrote articles and reviewed books for *The Oak Leaf*, revealing an independence of thought and willingness to ask the hard questions that would hardly fit the stereotypical image of the Oak Hill student. For example, in 1961 Martin Stevens, a second year student, wrote an article on Calvin's doctrine of the atonement, which he pointed out 'has become a controversial issue in the present day'. After accurately summarizing the views of those, including the Puritan writer, John Owen, who maintained that Calvin believed in the doctrine of limited atonement, he argued in opposition to many Calvin scholars of his day, including James Packer, that Calvin taught a doctrine of universal atonement.[52] In the same issue Hugh Silvester wrote an article entitled 'What is Truth?' calling into question the use of the term 'infallible' and arguing

---

[50] (*continued*) Biblical Witness to our Nation', 1965–7; Jos Drummund, 1968–70. Originator of 'Walk of 1000 Men' Daniel Cozens, 1968–71. Director of Church Society: David Streater, 1966–8. General Secretary of London City Mission: James McAllen 1964–6. Director of Archbishops' Council's Ministry Division: Gordon Kuhrt, 1965–7.

[51] The scheme began when Amos Betungura, a student at LCD, suggested to two lecturers that evangelical parishes could form a link with someone selected by a bishop in a growing church of the Anglican Communion. They would bring this person to a theological college in England to gain a further qualification and be equipped to train others. The parishes would provide the finance, together with hospitality during the vacations. John Stott then made this part of the work of the Evangelical Fellowship in the Anglican Communion.

[52] Martin Stevens, 'Limited Atonement: A Note on the Theology of John Calvin', *The Oak Leaf*, 1961, pp. 21ff.

that it would be in accord with what the Bible actually taught to use the term 'wholly reliable'.[53]

PERSONALITY PROFILE

John Went read classics and theology at Cambridge. In 1967 he attended a meeting addressed by Wood: he found him an inspirational leader and decided to apply to train at Oak Hill. As his previous studies exempted him from much of GOE he decided his time could be well spent learning Hebrew with John Taylor, whose Bible expositions, together with those by Alan Stibbs, he remembers with great affection and gratitude.

He married Rosemary in 1968, but in those days Oak Hill was not suited to married students. Apart from their Monday evening fellowship, wives were allowed in college only once a month. John used to go home to breakfast with his new wife after chapel, for which he was rebuked, but somehow continued the practice!

His five-and-a-half-year curacy at Emmanuel, Northwood, was served under David Bubbers and Richard Bewes and proved an enriching experience. There followed an incumbency at Holy Trinity, Margate, where he and Rosemary saw much spiritual and numerical growth. An invitation in 1983 to become vice-principal of Wycliffe Hall came as a surprise, but led to six stimulating years training men and women for the ministry. How theological colleges had changed since the 1960s!

After a further seven years as Archdeacon of Surrey he was consecrated Bishop of Tewkesbury in 1996. John Taylor was the preacher and Maurice Wood joined in the laying on of hands.

John thanks God for the excellent foundations for Christian discipleship, ministry and mission laid at Oak Hill.

[53] Hugh Silvester, 'What is Truth?', *The Oak Leaf*, 1961, pp. 26ff.

Wood began his term of office with a record number of students. During the 1960–61 academic year there were sixty-nine students in residence. Although twenty-eight left in June, thirty-one new students entered the college in September 1961. The seventy-two students then in residence were the highest number in the history of the college and by April all the places for the following year had already been filled. In his principal's report to the management committee Wood optimistically suggested that it was 'fairly probable' that in October 1962 they would have 96 students and there was an 'outside possibility' of 107 students. He concluded that:

> Our past planning on the basis of a student body of 65–69 is now unrealistic: and an increase of BD men means a 4 or 5 year course, and so even more pressure on space. 90–100 would seem a realistic figure for 1964 with a possible 85–90 as a balanced estimate for 1963.[54]

The large increase in enrolment for BD candidates was projected partially on the basis of the initial success of one of Wood's 'new visions', the so-called Cambridge scheme for BD candidates. This scheme gave students reading for the BD the opportunity to spend a year in residence initially at Tyndale House and subsequently at Selwyn College while attending lectures given by the Cambridge University faculty. They returned once a fortnight to Oak Hill for detailed supervision with one of the lecturers and, as the college had a ten-week term to Cambridge's eight, they spent the first and last weeks of each term in residence at Oak Hill. In the initial year three students participated. In his report to CACTM Wood stated that the programme was greeted with 'very positive feedback from the students'. Among others he thanked 'the Rev Gordon Bridger, who has acted as chaplain to the group'.[55] Wood also reported to the management committee after the completion of the first year that 'the men were gaining a very good name for Oak

---

[54] Principal's report, Michaelmas 1961. Typically Wood was a bit overly optimist. The actually number of students in October 1962 was 78.

[55] ACCM/COLL/OAK/1 report to CACTM by the principal on the One Year Cambridge Scheme.

Hill in Cambridge'. Tyndale House authorities were also pleased. The students, they said, had made 'such a difference to Tyndale House', adding 'we hope you will maintain this scheme and give us more men next year'.[56]

In order to meet the expected increase in enrolment and the growing need for places for ordinands, Wood proposed to the management committee that they set up a working party to study the possibility of a northern daughter house,[57] and/or expansion at Oak Hill. At its next meeting that body stated that 'it was quite impossible for the trust and the management committee to take any part in the scheme for a northern college' and therefore they appointed a subcommittee, which included Wood, 'to explore the possibility of providing extra accommodation'.[58] The committee report revealed that there was great need for expansion. In addition to inadequate living accommodation for students 'the library is housed in two small rooms which have also to serve for lectures ... the dining hall is much too small and when wives are invited to meals the difficulties are increased'. This latter comment illustrates that wives were now playing a fuller part in college life.

After consultation with Mr White, the architect, a scheme was proposed that would provide for ninety men at a cost of £107,000. However, the trust limited spending to £75,000. The architect was asked to work within the new limits and he drew up plans which included a new dining hall, a new block for students, additional lecture rooms, a library and improved studies for tutorial staff. The plans were approved by the management committee and the trustees as well as CACTM by October 1962. In the ensuing months a number of problems arose. First, the

---

[56] Principal's report, Michaelmas 1961.

[57] Founding another evangelical college in the north had been under consideration for some time. Wilkinson made some attempts to get one started. At the time the Management Committee was asked to consider this, Alderman Garnett of Lancaster had offered his family home as a site for a college.

[58] Management Committee minutes, 17 February 1961.

college faced the problem of raising the funds. The trustees promised £20,000 and CACTM agreed to contribute £30,000, with the stipulation that the college must agree in writing not to exceed seventy-two students in the future. They also recommended that the additional £25,000 be borrowed and the loan paid back by adding a sum to the student fees.

The suggested limitation on numbers led to protests both from Oak Hill and the principals' conference that met in January 1963. They supported Oak Hill, believing the principle of autonomy was at stake. The trustees also refused CACTM's suggestion of raising the additional money by borrowing; consequently, the architect was asked to revise the plans to conform to the new cash limits. New plans were then submitted retaining the dining hall and residential block, but with fewer bed studies and no new lecture hall or modernization of the existing facilities originally planned. However, negotiations with CACTM resulted in some softening of their position. In May 1963 the principal reported to the management committee that it was agreed 'that the maximum number of students is to be 75 (including the Cambridge scheme) plus or minus 3'.[59] In the 1963 *Oak Leaf* the principal was able to report triumphantly:

> Following a year's negotiations we can now report that the rehabilitation scheme is approved and agreed. The Kingham Hill trust are generously providing £20,000, and the Church Assembly through CACTM £30,000, for a new dining and assembly hall, (an octagonal building at the left hand edge of the terrace, with glorious views across the valley) and a new block of twenty-five large study-bedrooms and a study in the wing, or a new room, so that we are not trying to increase our total numbers beyond about seventy-five, but to provide good accommodation for efficient work in surroundings which are modestly comfortable. We shall then have a fine new library in the present dining hall. The building will take a year.[60]

[59] Ibid., 10 May 1963.
[60] *The Oak Leaf*, 1963, pp. 30–31.

While the building project was in the process of negotiation the college underwent a CACTM inspection. Responses to the preliminary questionnaire revealed that in 1962 fifteen per cent of the students were graduates and twelve per cent were undergraduates studying either for a BA or BD at London University. The college was teaching six separate courses. These included: a three-year GOE course; a two-year older man's GOE course; a two-year postgraduate GOE course; a London BA course that normally took five years; a London BD course that normally took four years and could include the Cambridge scheme; and a one-year older man's course for men over forty. It was reported, however, that the London BA was to be dropped because 'it throws too great a burden on the teaching facilities, and takes men out of college life'. In addition the principal taught homiletics and pastoralia and lecturers met with their students for tutorials. It is not surprising that with this heavy teaching load the inspectors were somewhat critical of teaching methods, noting that in some cases 'notes were dictated' and 'in other cases the lectures comprised largely bare facts that students ought to obtain for themselves out of text books'. The vice-principal received high praise for 'lively' teaching of Greek and the principal was commended for homiletics lectures that revealed he 'was not at all afraid of ideas that might seem different from too narrow an interpretation of evangelicalism'.[61]

While the inspectors were impressed with the Oak Hill students and with the college overall, commenting 'we found a healthy Christian community',[62] they were particularly critical of three things. First, and not surprisingly, they felt the library resources were inadequate:

> The library building is much too small, so that the books themselves have to be stored in three different rooms. This makes a

[61] ACCM/C/Oak/1 Report on inspection of Oak Hill College, 14–17 November 1962.

[62] Ibid. They were also 'impressed by the smartness of appearance of the students', commenting 'in what other College is it the accepted tradition for all to wear lounge suits at dinner once a week?'.

> difficulty in finding particular books. The whole library system badly needs overhauling, and we were glad to learn that one of the new tutors has this in hand. There is an annual grant of £180 – none too much in view of the present price of books and of the 'leeway' that has to be made up. Naturally most of the books reflect the particular emphasis of the College, but many of these are sadly out of date. The books need severe pruning; many of them are housed just under the lofty ceiling and many could well be withdrawn to make room for more modern works.[63]

They were also critical that the 'provision for keeping the students informed of the world around them' was inadequate. The newspapers available in the common room (*The Times*, *Guardian*, *Daily Telegraph* and *Daily Mail*) were called a 'safe selection' that would not prepare students to minister in a society where 'such papers have a minority circulation'. In addition there was no college television and although it was acknowledged that the principal made an effort 'to acquaint the men with the religious opportunities of TV' the inspectors 'did not find any emphasis was put on understanding this medium in its wider impact on modern society'.[64]

The inspectors were also somewhat critical of college worship, although clearly the college could hardly be said to have neglected this. Morning prayer was said or sung at 7.20 a.m. on Monday, Wednesday and Thursday. On Tuesday and Friday the day began with a Scripture exposition preceded by the collect of the day and the second and third collects of morning prayer. On Saturday morning students were able to sleep in a bit, because a college prayer meeting was held at 9.15 a.m. Morning prayer was followed by a half-hour of quiet time before breakfast. Evening prayer was at 5.40 p.m. every day except Wednesday, when there was a full service at 7.10 p.m. with a visiting preacher. On Monday evening there was an abbreviated service followed by

---

[63] Ibid.

[64] Ibid.

singing practice led by Kidner. Students led morning and evening prayer services. In addition, students held prayer meetings at various times during the week. Holy Communion was celebrated on Sundays and saints' days and once a month there was a communion service to which wives were invited. Although Wood stated in the questionnaire that the word 'compulsory' was not used in connection with worship, it was 'understood that all men would come to all services'. He added, 'this works extraordinarily well, because the men do enjoy their worship'.[65] Surprisingly, the inspectors did not feel this pattern of worship quite met the standards they expected of ordinands because morning prayer was not said on Tuesdays, Fridays and Saturdays. They also suggested that Bible exposition should follow the office.[66]

The inspection also revealed what today would be considered a draconian policy with regard to married men. According to the report by 1962 over half of the students were married, yet the same regulations persisted as during the Wilkinson era. They were required to live in college for the first year, but with the principal's permission could live out in their second and third year as long as the residence was not more than three miles or fifteen minutes' journey away. They were still expected to be at college from 7.20 a.m. to 9.15 p.m.

Margaret Wood held a wives' 'training evening' every Monday. There were three main aims in mind: 'Firstly to help them become part of a warm and strong college fellowship; secondly to help herself and them to grow together as Christians with special emphasis on Bible studies; thirdly to help them gain confidence for their future as a clergy wife.' She worked out a two-year

---

[65] Questionnaire for 1962 inspection visit.

[66] The inspectors also questioned the fact that the college used its own specially designed lectionary to fit the three terms of the college year. Although they understood the motive behind the lectionary they cautioned that 'the implication is that the recital of Morning and Evening Prayer is something for term time only, which will not be a help to men in fulfilling their obligation regarding daily Morning and Evening Prayer after ordination.' Ibid.

course, and credits Joy Wheaton with giving her a valuable piece of advice: 'Help them to be familiar with and know their Bibles. It will always stand them in good stead whatever the future holds for them.'[67] Stibbs was particularly helpful in preparing materials and together she and, in due course, Eileen Carey prepared the questions for the sessions. Each year *The Oak Leaf* included a report on the rich and varied activities of this group.

Fortunately, the principal and members of the trust and the management committee were far-sighted enough to realize the arrangement for married students was not satisfactory, and the next major building project was to be housing of married students. In May 1965 T.G. Roche, the trust chairman, presented the management committee with a scheme to build houses for four married students. The committee agreed that 'if the money could be found, it was an excellent idea'.[68] The proposal took some time to materialize but in July 1968 the trustees agreed to provide up to £30,000 for the building of six married quarters. The work on the new houses began in February 1969 and on 14 May 1970 the Queen Mother officially opened the six new houses in what was then named Mohan Close. At the opening, which received wide press coverage, Wood did not miss the opportunity to point out the need for evangelism. He spoke of 'the need for more men for the ordained ministry at a time when the nation desperately needs the gospel of Christ'. He also stated that 'the church needs evangelists and pastors to win, teach and equip the people of God to be witnesses and workers for Christ in His world'. The Queen Mother replied that 'never in the history of our beloved country has the challenge offered to the Anglican Church been greater, or the need for more recruits to the ministry more pressing'.[69]

In the same edition of *The Oak Leaf* that described the Queen Mother's visit the principal announced that the trustees were planning to provide additional married student housing by 'turning

[67] Interview with Woods.
[68] Management Committee minutes, 14 May 1965.
[69] *The Oak Leaf*, 1970, p. 19.

some rooms in the old wing (freed by married men sleeping out) into flats for couples without children'. He added that 'we are resolutely tackling the real opportunities of training family men full-time on site, and bringing wives and fiancées more and more into the life of the college community. Nothing succeeds like success and applications from married men increase all the time.'[70] The college, in fact, was too successful in attracting married students. Within a decade it would acquire a reputation as a 'married students' college' and have problems attracting single men.

During the eight years between the first inspection and the completion of Mohan Close the college confronted the movements within church and society discussed earlier. Although the inspectors criticized the college for not keeping the students 'informed of the world around them', the articles in *The Oak Leaf* between 1963 and 1970 suggest that they were well aware of what was happening outside the college. Various issues of *The Oak Leaf* included articles by staff and students on race relations, the technological revolution, ministry in the new towns' ecumenical relations and current theological trends exemplified by the *Honest to God* debate and Paul report. These writings display both a breadth of understanding and a desire to appreciate the standpoint of those whose views they criticized.[71]

Oak Hill experienced a number of major staff changes between 1962–70. In 1964 Kidner resigned to become warden of Tyndale House, leaving only Stibbs from the staff that Wood had inherited. Stibbs also announced that he intended to resign at the end of that summer term. Although Wood was able to persuade him to stay another year, he was already preparing for his successor as vice-principal. In April 1964 he announced that he was in touch with John Taylor to serve as Kidner's replacement in Old Testament and he recommended that he be appointed as lecturer and vice-principal designate.[72] In September 1963 Holloway suggested to

---

[70] Ibid., p. 5.

[71] *The Oak Leaf*, 1963, pp. 5, 12, 33; 1964, pp. 32, 35; 1966, p. 6; 1967, p. 6; 1969, pp. 8–12; and 1970, pp. 29–31.

[72] Principal's report, 22 April 1964.

the principal that he appoint another promising young man as a part-time lecturer. Holloway wrote:

> I should think George is our man for the BD and DipTh, and the answer to our long-standing prayers on the subject. I had a long session with him this afternoon, and he confirmed that he has done quite a lot of reading on the incarnation and trinity and is very keen on the subject. He is really eager to have a go, it seems. I left it that the next step would be taken by you, as you will know the best move to take.[73]

The principal agreed with Holloway's suggestion and the twenty-six-year-old George Carey, who was serving as curate at St Mary's, Islington, joined the staff as a part-time lecturer in the 1963–4 academic year. He continued as a part-time lecturer for two more years. The college was clearly pleased with his contributions and in June 1965 Wood wrote offering him 'a place on our permanent, residential staff from lst September 1966'.[74]

In his first year as a full-time staff member, Carey contributed an article to *The Oak Leaf* that revealed a very balanced attitude towards the growing charismatic movement. Entitled 'A Lesson from the Past' it applied the lessons of history to the twentieth century in assessing the movement. While maintaining that 'only a foolish person would deny that God has brought the pentecostal movement to birth in the twentieth century', he warned against the abuses of ecstatic gifts which in the second century had resulted in their disappearing from the regular life of the church. He concluded:

> The lesson from the past is twofold. On the one hand those who claim the baptism of the Holy Spirit may find their experience withdrawn if it divides the body of Christ ... On the other hand those who lightly discount the claims of others may find themselves in the same

[73] Note from Holloway to Wood, 17 September 1963.
[74] Letter from Wood to George Carey, 9 June 1965.

> situation as Von Harnack. He knew a great deal about the doctrine of the Holy Spirit, but how little in terms of actual experience![75]

Stibbs also wrote about the charismatic movement in the same year. In the winter 1966 edition of *Churchman* he published an article entitled 'Putting the Gift of Tongues in Place'. In typical fashion he examined carefully all the relevant texts, concluding that although the Bible tells us 'not to forbid speaking in tongues', we are also told to 'earnestly desire the higher gifts', the greatest of which is love. 'Such apostolic injunctions', he asserted, 'will keep speaking in tongues in place.'[76] Although Stibbs in no way indicated that he rejected the charismatic movement as an act of God, he was clearly concerned about the overemphasis on some spiritual gifts.

By this time Stibbs had retired as vice-principal and become a part-time tutor. Although he would continue to serve the college until shortly before his death, his semi-retirement was an event of enormous significance in the history of the college. He had served on the staff for twenty-eight years and as vice-principal for twenty-seven years. His outstanding gifts as a lecturer and a biblical expositor, his deep humility and profound faith made him a legend in his own time, and he was appreciated not only in evangelical circles but throughout the church. He was an outstanding example of what Charles Baring Young meant when he spoke of being a witness to the Word. His name has been and will continue to be associated with what the college can be when it is true to its founder's ideal. The grateful trustees offered to build a house for him on the estate, but he and his wife preferred to remain in the Farm House. It was agreed that they should continue there rent free, and, in the event of his death, Mrs Stibbs could stay as long as she wished.[77] Wood wrote this tribute to Stibbs in the 1965 *Oak Leaf*:

---

[75] *The Oak Leaf*, 1967, p. 20.

[76] Alan Stibbs, 'Putting the Gift of Tongues in Place', *Churchman*, vol. 80, no. 4 (1966), p. 303.

[77] They also gave them a gift of money and a West Country painting.

> Staff and students, past and present, remember him with great thankfulness, deep affection and personal gratitude. First, as befits a scholar and a Cambridge first, he has meticulously quarried and clearly presented the great nuggets of Biblical truth which came alive to us in his lectures, sermons, and Bible Analyses. Secondly, he has lived out in practical holiness and transparent humility, the lessons first taught him by the revelation of the Holy Spirit, and then shared with us. Thirdly, he has demonstrated in every word and gesture and attitude, his unshakeable conviction in the Divine authority and inspiration of Holy Scripture.[78]

Stibbs also had a sense of humour. When invited to assume the title of senior tutor in biblical studies upon his retirement he responded 'May we add the word Basic – Senior Tutor in Basic Biblical Studies – STIBBS?'[79]

A number of other staff changes took place in the last half of the decade. Crowe left in 1967, and an article in *The Oak Leaf* entitled 'As the Crowe Flies' expressed the appreciation of the college for his services both as a lecturer and promoter of missions. He was also lauded for his skills on the football field.[80] Wood already had another gifted young man in mind to take his place. In November 1967 he wrote to the Bishop of London asking his permission to use the curate at Christ Church, North Finchley,[81] a young man named John Goldingay who had gained a first in theology at Oxford, to teach Greek two mornings a week. Wood displayed almost prophetic insight when he suggested to the bishop that 'John

---

[78] *The Oak Leaf*, 1965, p. 2.

[79] Mohan, *History of Oak Hill College*, p. 103.

[80] George Carey's contributions on the football field were also recognized in *The Oak Leaf* in his final year. The article stated: 'Colours were also given to that veteran (that means old) of Oak Hill football, George Carey,' who was 'made an honorary member of the Junior Common Room'. The writer gave 'thanks to George for his years of service to Oak Hill football'. *The Oak Leaf*, 1970, p. 39.

[81] The Revd Harold J. Parks, who had declined an invitation to join the staff in 1961, was the vicar.

Goldingay is clearly a man whose eventual work may well involve theological college teaching'.[82] The bishop reluctantly agreed and Goldingay joined the staff part-time in 1967. He later came to live at the college while completing his MTh, teaching and helping with tutorial care.

The college had greeted two new bursars at the end of the decade. Stredder resigned because of his wife's health and was replaced by J. Desmond Dugan who had been lay co-ordinator at All Souls, Langham Place. He left in 1970 and was succeeded by R.J.G. (Dick) Hobson. In the previous year Holloway left the staff after seven years of service to take up the position of chaplain and senior divinity lecturer at St Paul's College of Education, Cheltenham. The principal appointed Christopher Byworth, who was on the staff at Holy Trinity Platt in Manchester, to join the staff in the 1970–71 academic year. In the same principal's letter welcoming Byworth to the staff, Wood expressed the college's gratitude to two of his other appointees leaving to take up new positions. George Carey and John Goldingay left to join the staff of LCD, which had recently relocated to Nottingham.

In 1969 Stibbs's 'shy young man' also joined the staff. Not expecting to stay very long, David Field asked his wife, Margaret, 'not take the pins out of the curtains because I'd be done in less than a year'. He added 'I didn't think I could teach.'[83] It is fortunate that his judgements in other areas were better. He was to remain on the staff for a quarter of a century and brought many of the same gifts as the man who had recommended him. He was not only an outstanding teacher, adding Christian ethics to the teaching of Greek, but he also contributed to the wider church through his writings, which dealt with contemporary issues in an honest, clear and uncompromising fashion. Like Stibbs he was a self-effacing, humble man who preferred to let others take the leadership positions. However, God called him to serve both as

---

[82] Oak Hill archive letter from Wood to the Bishop of London, 30 November 1967.

[83] Interview with Field, 15 May 1999.

vice-principal and acting principal as well as dean of the non-residential course. He also helped to achieve validation from the Council for National Academic Awards and, before he left the staff, he would play a vital role in saving the college from closure during the Bridger decade.

Anyone joining the Oak Hill staff quickly found out that in addition to being teachers they were expected to contribute to the college's outreach programme. It is not surprising that throughout Wood's term of office evangelism was a central concern of the college. In the 1967 principal's letter Wood expressed his firm conviction that the gospel was relevant to the changing and complex world of the 1960s. He stated that the aim of the college was to equip students to go out into the world 'with sensitivity to the perplexities and complexities in the church in the world, but with quiet assurance that "the faith once delivered to the saints" is relevant and powerful to transform men today'.[84] Students regularly went on missions to parishes, participated in the 1966 Billy Graham crusade and engaged in street evangelism. In the summer term the principal took leavers to Speakers' Corner in Hyde Park to teach them open-air evangelism.[85] Students also met with Christian students at Southgate Technical College and used films to evangelize non-Christians. David Gillett reported on a major evangelistic effort in Trafalgar Square in March 1967:

> The day was a howling gale as we put the banners up, but in the afternoon not a sign of rain. Counsellors arrived from 2 pm and went out armed with hand bills, and at 2:45 the amplified organ loaned for the occasion filled the square with well-known tunes. 'The Followers', the first of three groups, got the afternoon off to a swinging start and the crowd numbered over 2,000. During the next two hours in spite of cold weather many stayed and others came and hundreds of non-Christians heard the gospel. We came away thrilled, having made

---

[84] *The Oak Leaf*, 1967, p. 3.
[85] Letter from Wood, 25 April 2001.

> mistakes no doubt, but very conscious that on that day at Trafalgar Square God had been at work.[86]

In the 1964–5 academic year the college produced an attractive prospectus that set out in very clear terms its purpose. It is interesting to note that in stating its purpose the trust deed was interpreted as teaching 'in harmony with orthodox protestant and evangelical Anglicanism, as found in the official formularies and biblical doctrines of the Church of England'. In addition to the academic course, the practical nature of the training was emphasized:

> Although the college sets, and seeks to maintain, the highest academic standards, it also aims to prepare men to be effective ministers of the Word and Sacraments, and to be equipped at every point to meet the challenge of presenting Christ to men in the present day complexities of life.[87]

The prospectus also stressed the provision for married students, although it was produced before married student housing was available, and mentioned the advantages of a campus located in a country environment. The prospectus also stated that 'each student is expected to spend two hours each week working in the gardens, woodlands or farm, so as to take an active part in the upkeep and improvement of the estate'.[88] Some of this work was carried out under the direction of Roy Brown, under whose able management the farm continued to provide milk and eggs, total egg production in 1961 reaching 159,000. Even after the farm had closed Oak Hill was better known to some local people for

---

[86] *The Oak Leaf*, 1967, p. 4.
[87] Oak Hill College prospectus, p. 11.
[88] Ibid., p. 16. The prospectus also listed fees as £340 per year. Fees had risen from £250 in 1959 to £282 in 1962. In 1963 the increased rates caused by new building and the added cost of lighting and heating made it necessary to increase fees to £340. In 1967 they were raised to £450 and in 1970 to £475.

the farm than for the college.[89] Farmer Brown, as he was called, did not always appreciate the student help because some were neither enthusiastic about the work nor able to distinguish vegetables from weeds. On the other hand, there were those who valued the opportunity to discuss spiritual issues with him, which they did not feel able to take to their tutors, and many a time of prayer was spent with him.

In 1966, when church leaders began to express concern about the falling number of candidates coming forward for ministry, Wood introduced another new vision. At the trust's January meeting the Bishop of Tonbridge reported on the 'disquiet felt by CATCM' about this problem and warned that it might mean the closure of some theological colleges.[90] Although the most serious drop in numbers was still to come,[91] a plan was put forward by Wood to confront the problem, to be put into place after the Billy Graham crusade. The programme, entitled 'Opportunity Knocks', was announced at the CPAS annual meeting in April 1966. It was to be organized by CPAS and had the approval of the other theological college principals. The programme was based on the assumed success of the coming Billy Graham crusade through which it was hoped 'not only individuals but whole parishes will be quickened by the Holy Spirit, and a whole new potential for the ordained ministry may well be discovered.'[92] The plan was to send staff members from the theological colleges with two students of differing backgrounds for parish weekends. They would arrive in the parish on a Saturday evening equipped with literature, filmstrips and tape recordings. The staff member

[89] Student Daniel Cozens was asked to paint two signs to be placed outside the farm to advertise the sale of milk and eggs. They are now in the college archives.

[90] Minutes of meeting of the Kingham Hill Trust, 3 January 1966, p. 2.

[91] The figures for ordinations give some idea of the drop in the number of candidates. In 1963 there were 636 ordinations. By 1972 there were only 362 ordinations. During that time seven theological colleges were closed.

[92] *The Oak Leaf*, 1966, p. 7.

would preach and students would speak of their experience in the Sunday morning service, repeating the procedure in another parish in an afternoon or evening service. Vocational weekends to present the challenge of ministry to university Christian unions were also planned in an all-out effort to stir people throughout the nation to respond to the call to ministry.

As would be expected, Oak Hill was fully involved in the Opportunity Knocks campaign.[93] An Oak Hill filmstrip was produced including shots of corporate worship, prayer meetings and sports activities as well as 'the highly photogenic principal, staff, present students and cows'. In addition there were shots of Stibbs's Bible analysis to 'underline the emphasis placed on the exposition of scripture'.[94] In December 1967 the principal reported that 'the academic staff and myself have made 29 visits to parishes during the year'. He commended the staff, who 'in addition to all their work in the week ... have taken teams of students to various parts of the country with marked success'.[95] At the end of 1967 there were many positive signs. Parishes had been welcoming, many people had heard the appeal, and many questions were answered. The weekends were to continue throughout the decade, being renamed Christian Service in 1969, but the overall results are difficult to estimate.

In the same year work at Bohun Lodge was re-launched under the title of the 'Cadet Scheme', providing an opportunity for younger single men who sensed a calling to ordination to acquire any qualifications they would need at Oak Hill. In 1969 it was reported that Bill Seaman, an Old Oak, was raising funds to support students who did not qualify for grants.

In February 1968 the college experienced another inspection. The report submitted by the college to the inspectors gives the impression that the staff were terribly overworked. Six full-time members and three regular visiting lecturers were responsible for

---

[93] The Management Committee agreed to pay the expenses of students travelling to these events.

[94] *The Oak Leaf*, 1966, p. 6.

[95] Principal's report, 1 December 1969, p. 1.

seventy academically diverse students.[96] The great variety of course options included: a three-year GOE course; a three-year GOE incorporating the London University Diploma in Theology in the second year; a two-year essay scheme for GOE candidates over thirty; and a five-year course combining the London University BD with the GOE. Graduates in theology did a two-year GOE course including a specialist study under supervision, or they could do work for an advanced degree. Non-theology graduates could combine the GOE with a diploma or degree in theology. Candidates over the age of forty could by arrangement with their bishop take a one-year course of reading, lectures and essays. Cadet students needing to pass GCE subjects at O or A level with a view to ordination training did most of their studies at Southgate College, but participated in Oak Hill's life and worship and could receive special tuition from the staff for the GCE in Religious Knowledge. In addition all ordinands were expected to include pastoralia, homiletics, mission and unity, social and ethical studies, pastoral psychology, and youth and children's work in their studies. Some of these courses were taught by visiting lecturers. Nevertheless, the pressure on staff members must have been immense. For example, during Lent term 1968 George Carey offered lectures in five areas: analysis of the four gospels for first year men; content and criticism of the Pauline corpus for BD and diploma candidates; the Greek text of John's Gospel for BD and diploma candidates; Christology and Trinity in the New Testament for diploma candidates; and the doctrine of

---

[96] Of the sixty-three ordinands eleven were graduates (five in theology) and eight were undergraduates reading for degrees. There were also seven non-graduates with professional qualifications and thirty-eight other non-graduates. Of the seven non-ordinands four were ordained men (three from Africa), and three were cadet students working for their qualifications to enable them to train at Oak Hill. They were also diverse in age: eighteen were under 25, twenty-one were between 25–29, eleven were between 30–39, ten between 40–49 and three were over 50. Thirty-three students were married, seven were engaged and one was a widower.

the Incarnation and the Trinity for BD candidates. He was also responsible for the library, and took part in college missions and Opportunity Knocks. Fortunately, most were young, or they would never have survived!

The inspectors recognized that 'each member of staff has a heavy load of teaching' but were still critical of teaching methods and suggested a number of 'essential' changes. These included avoiding dictation of notes, giving students handouts of texts, which they could discuss, and drawing on the 'rich variety of experience' of the older men with a 'more inductive approach, particularly in the sphere of ethics'. The inspectors' first recommendation therefore was that a 'review of teaching methods' take place. While noting that 'there had been useful reconstruction of the library' since the last inspection they still felt more needed to be done, also recommending that the annual library grant be increased from £240 to £400. In addition, they repeated the last report's criticism of worship. Although there were now only two days of the week when the daily office was not said in the morning (Bible analysis was now held only on Thursdays) they still felt it should be included six days of the week. In addition they suggested that chapel attendance was not as good as it might be and that 'regular use of the Anglican Cycle of Prayer might enrich the men's prayerful concern'. The other three recommendations included making the junior common room more effective in college life, providing married quarters and 'an increased measure of consultation over pastoralia'.[97]

At the time of the inspection a major report entitled *Theological Colleges for Tomorrow* was published. The college principals had requested an independent investigation of the crisis facing them as the number of candidates continued to fall. The study was undertaken by a small group chaired by Sir Bernard de Bunsen. It recommended fewer and larger theological colleges with 120 students as an optimum and it proposed the amalgamation of some colleges and the closure of others. It also suggested that

---

[97] Report of inspection of Oak Hill College, 14–17 February 1968.

most of the colleges should be situated near universities where they could draw on the resources of departments of theology, and at least one integrated ecumenical college should be established without delay. It was suggested that the number at Oak Hill be increased to ninety, with no suggestion that it be amalgamated with any other college.

This should have delighted the trustees and the principal, but it did not. At their meeting on 13 July the trustees were given a summary of the contents of the report and how it would affect Oak Hill. The major concern of the trustees was the cost of expanding to ninety students, as this would involve building work and a larger teaching staff. Since the present seventy-two places were not filled they questioned whether the larger number was feasible. The principal thought that if ACCM (the successor of CACTM) closed the pre-theological colleges and Oak Hill took more cadets, it would be possible to fill the places. However, in the 1968 *Oak Leaf* he was quite critical of the report. He pointed out that even though Oak Hill was treated very favourably, 'we find no complacency in this, for other fine colleges have come under the axe, or are ripe for such demolition'. He added wryly that a report proposing the reduction of colleges from twenty-seven to twelve or fourteen would immediately be called 'the Bunsen Burner'. In typical Wood fashion he chided the compilers of the report for not having enough faith in the potential of evangelism. They were, he argued, basing their estimates on how things are today rather than considering the potential ordinands who might come forward from 'the thousands of people converted through the Graham Crusades of 1966 and 1967 who are already maturing into local leaders and potential ordinands today'.[98] To his great credit he expressed outrage at the way in which the public report was affecting the colleges listed for closure or amalgamation:

> Recruitment by the 'axed colleges' has almost stopped overnight; student morale has been severely affected; no contingency planning

[98] *The Oak Leaf,* 1968, p. 13.

> for academic staff has been suggested; and headlines in many local papers have disrupted domestic and other staff ... Although these possible weaknesses happen not to affect our Oak Hill situation very much, the immense contribution of many colleges to the total life of the church demands sympathy from the more fortunate to those under this 'cloud of unknowing.'[99]

A quarter of a century later Oak Hill would be named as an 'axed college' in another report and the sympathy expressed by others then was greatly appreciated.

In the two years following the report's publication the church debated how to respond. In February 1970 the Church Assembly agreed to set up a committee to prepare a scheme for reorganization of the theological colleges. In October 1970 a committee chaired by Bishop Runcie of St Albans gave its report. The so-called Runcie report recommended the closure of some colleges, the amalgamation of others and leaving the remainder as they were. The principal was able to state that the reference to Oak Hill in the report was 'delightfully terse', since the college received only two lines in a sixteen-page document. The report recommended that the number of places at Oak Hill remain at seventy-two. The council[100] expressed its gratitude to the Lord that the college had survived the two years of uncertainty so well with the recommended numbers undiminished, and 'that our position remains strong and undisturbed'.[101]

---

[99] Ibid., p. 14.

[100] The Management Committee changed its name to College Council in 1969. When completing a questionnaire from ACCM, it was noted that 'This questionnaire gave rise to the use of the name "Management Committee" for what was in effect a council, and it was decided that in future what had been the "Management Committee" should be called the "College Council".' Management Committee minutes, 7 March 1969.

[101] Oak Hill Council minutes, 23 October 1970. For a considerably more detailed account of those two years of uncertainty see Mohan, *History of Oak Hill College*, pp. 116ff. Bullock, *History of Training*, pp. 138ff. provides a brief account of what happened to each of the theological colleges in the years following the Runcie report.

Although the Runcie report recommended that Oak Hill continue having seventy-two places, the college was having difficulty in filling them. In 1968 there were still thirty-one new students, but in 1969 numbers dropped to twenty-one, and in 1970 there were only eighteen. In 1971 there were fifteen new full-time students and two students joined the newly established Auxiliary Pastoral Ministry (APM) course, another one of Wood's new visions. He explained how he came up with the idea as follows:

> When we were doing our Opportunity Knocks weekends, it became obvious we were dealing with men who loved the Lord, who had the sense of call, but who might either on the one hand not be academically able for a rigorous academic course of the quality that ACCM was demanding, or secondly, could not have got away from home and their work ... so I began to feel that we really must provide something for them. We had to argue our case with the ACCM Council. They were always suspicious of what Oak Hill was trying to do next; they knew we were full of ideas and full of initiatives and we did have quite a time with ACCM.[102]

Wood's idea was not new. As mentioned earlier the Southwark Ordination Course, designed to allow employed men to train over a three-year period by attending evening and weekend lectures, was established in 1960. When the church authorities began to consider expanding this type of training, Wood recognized that Oak Hill might be an ideal location. In November 1969 he reported that the bishops were considering a report from ACCM 'on the selection and training for the auxiliary pastoral ministry'. This was a plan for 'self-supporting priests' and the possibility of training for a 'retirement ministry' for men over fifty-eight. He suggested that a working party be set up to consider the implications for Oak Hill of what he called 'a radical change in future patterns of ministry'. He reminded the council that a north-west

[102] Interview with Wood.

training scheme was being set up 'with this in mind' and along 'Southwark lines' and suggested that Oak Hill with its 'experience on a very large scale of training married men' might have something to contribute in this area.[103] A working party chaired by Timothy Dudley-Smith and including the principal, vice-principal and Sir Timothy Hoare was set up. A plan for training was drawn up, and the working party recommended that it be approved to begin in 1971 with no more than six men. On 21 January 1971 the trustees resolved 'in principle that the scheme should be tried out for three years to see if it works'.[104] In May 1971 Wood reported that ACCM had granted 'provisional approval'.[105]

Not everybody was fully supportive of the APM scheme. Some members of the college council expressed 'a certain disquiet ... with regard to some of the theological implications of the proposals'. A concern that the APM ministry 'would harden the division between clergy and laity, and at the same time produce anomalies in the relation between lay readers and APM trained men' was also expressed.[106] In addition it was not very popular with the staff. Field reports that 'Maurice was very much in favour of it but I don't think anyone else in the staff room was. It was an extra add-on to our work and we didn't need any extras. The Oak Hill staff were not terribly keen to be involved; we thought we had enough to do, and I was one of those.'[107] Since the staff could not take on additional work Hugh Silvester, who had served as a part-time lecturer in place of Herniman, was brought in to supervize the new programme. In February 1971 the council was informed that Silvester had accepted the position. It was to be Wood's last appointment.

---

[103] College Council minutes, 28 November 1969.
[104] Minutes of the Kingham Hill Trust, 21 January 1971. The proposal was published in full in the 1971 edition of *The Oak Leaf*, pp. 7–8.
[105] College Council minutes, 20 May 1971.
[106] Ibid., 19 February 1971.
[107] Interview with Field.

As Silvester returned from east Africa, where he was chaplain at King's College, Budo, Wood received another appointment.

Wood's service to the wider church had been recognized in 1969 when Bishop Stopford of London had collated him to be a Prebendary of St Paul's Cathedral, as Hinde had been before him. In June 1971 he received from Downing Street the invitation to become Bishop of Norwich, an appointment not without controversy. Owen Chadwick points out that in 1970 the Archbishop of Canterbury, Michael Ramsey, was under pressure to appoint a conservative evangelical bishop because they were now 'so strong in the church ... that it was wrong if they were unrepresented on the bench of bishops'. Ramsey asked the Archbishop of York, Donald Coggan, to suggest three or four conservative evangelicals 'who would be capable of the office of diocesan bishop'. Wood's name was among those recommended and, of course, Ramsey knew him personally from their earlier visits and the Church Assembly. Chadwick writes:

> The question was difficult; for a conservative evangelical was in the nature of the case an uncompromising person, and dioceses preferred ecumenical minds which were not too uncompromising. However, Ramsey was sure that the claim was right, and in this way Maurice Wood became the Bishop of Norwich in 1971.[108]

Two of the canons of the cathedral protested against the appointment. Even though they recognized 'a need to strengthen the conservative evangelical voice on the bench of bishops ... They thought that in the long run such an appointment would increase parties and division in the church.' Ramsey defended Wood's appointment by pointing out that it 'would be bad for the church if all the bishops were central churchmen' and stressing that the important question in an appointment is whether the person selected is 'capable of uniting and leading the particular diocese'.

---

[108] Owen Chadwick, *Michael Ramsey: A Life*, p. 134.

He added 'I believe that in the present case that condition is present.'[109]

The appointment was announced at the end of summer term 1971. It is fitting that one of Wood's last activities as principal was to write to Stibbs on 27 May 1971 asking him again to take Bible analysis, to teach homiletics in the first term and to help with the APM group. A note in the 1971 *Oak Leaf* announcing that Stibbs would no longer be lecturing in GOE subjects after Hugh Silvester arrived expressed the gratitude of 'generations of students and staff, who continue to say "thank you" from the depths of their hearts'. It was also noted that '[Stibbs] has just completed 100 academic terms, and has never missed a lecture through illness!'[110] However in May 1971 Stibbs fell ill and the principal expressed his regret that 'you are a bit under the weather'. He also told him that 'your future and Mrs Stibbs's future in the Farm House is assured, as you know, regardless of how much or how little you are able still to do in the way of lecturing'.[111] By the time Stibbs learned of Wood's appointment he was very ill, but continued to pray for others and display his wry sense of humour. When a student came to him very excited about the news that the principal was to be made a bishop he found Stibbs with a class picture praying for each student individually. When the student asked 'Have you heard, Mr Stibbs, that the principal is going to be the new Bishop of Norwich? Don't you think that's wonderful?' Stibbs's reply was 'We shall see!'[112]

The Wood decade had come to an end. He had not only maintained the traditions of the college through difficult times but had introduced new programmes and presided over major building works that radically changed the physical face of the college. Throughout his term of office he was optimistic about evangelical theological education. In 1969, when ACCM and the Church

---

[109] Ibid.

[110] *The Oak Leaf*, 1971, p. 5.

[111] Oak Hill archive letter from Wood to Stibbs, 27 May 1971.

[112] Interview with Wood.

Assembly were anticipating and discussing college closures, Wood wrote in *The Oak Leaf* 'I am ... an optimist about theological colleges, and I believe the church needs to be equally optimistic about them, for a long time to come.' However, in the same article he pointed out that changes were necessary to meet the challenge of changing times. He suggested that in the future there would need to be 'new ways of selecting candidates ... new dimensions of training ... new patterns of assessment ... [and] new forms of ministry'. In order to continue being an effective witness to the Word in the next century Wood recognized that the college would have to train men who were prepared to face new conditions and continue to proclaim an unchanging gospel. 'As in the First, so in the Twenty-first Century', he wrote, 'presbyters must be rock-men, and our training, with its necessary academic withdrawal, must be increasingly subjected to harsh realities.'[113]

At the end of his term of office the college also adopted a new motto. Wood felt that 'Be right and persist' should be supplemented with a biblical motto. After consultation with the staff he suggested to the council in November 1970 that 2 Corinthians 4:5 be adopted as the aim and purpose of the college: 'For we do not preach ourselves, but Jesus Christ as Lord, and ourselves as your servants for Jesus' sake.' The council approved and this motto was duly adopted.[114]

Although Wood had a vision for the future and endless energy to pursue his goals he could not have accomplished his objectives without the support of the gifted and dedicated men who served on the management committee and the Kingham Hill Trust. Those who served unselfishly devoted large amounts of their time to the work of the college. This was especially demanding during the Wood years because of the building projects and the new programmes. Wood was also supported by an able academic

---

[113] *The Oak Leaf*, 1969, p. 27–8.

[114] For some years the founder's crest including the family motto continued to appear on the college notepaper, but the biblical text was used to express the college's aim and appeared in prospectuses and later on the stationery.

staff and a committed non-academic staff. Secretaries, cooks, housekeepers, groundsmen and maintenance staff were vital for the running of the college, and, although they seldom received recognition, the college was blessed with very able and dedicated people. Among the many who helped to keep the college functioning was Sid Coleman. Sid's 'versatility and competence'[115] in his first year of service was praised and the college was to be well served by his many skills during the years to come.

In their meeting on 3 July 1971 the Kingham Hill trustees were informed that Wood had been appointed Bishop of Norwich. The chairman proposed that a sub-committee be set up to prepare a shortlist of possible new principals for submission to the council, which would interview them on 27 July. At the Annual General Meeting of the Kingham Hill Trust Corporation four days later the chairman paid tribute to the outgoing principal stating that 'his departure will be a serious blow to the college he has served so well'. He concluded 'we must pray that a worthy successor may be found'.[116]

---

[115] College Council meeting, 20 May 1971.

[116] Minutes of the annual meeting of the Kingham Hill Trust Corporation, 31 July 1971.

6

Growth and Diversification (1971–1986)

'Hold fast to Christ, David! Hold fast to Christ! He is the only Foundation!' The scene was a ward at Highlands Hospital, now demolished, and the speaker was Alan Stibbs. David Wheaton had been to visit him, bringing news of various former students he had recently met at an Old Oaks' reunion in the north of England. Stibbs had lost the power of speech after a stroke, but after his visitor had read the Scriptures and prayed with him, Stibbs regained speech sufficiently to utter these few words – as far as his widow knew, those were his final words. Later Wheaton was to learn from Wood that when he had asked whom Stibbs would like to see succeeding him the reply was that it would be very 'pleasing' (a favourite word of his) if Wheaton were appointed. Whether Stibbs had this in mind when speaking the above words cannot be known, but the experience confirmed the new principal's sense of divine calling in taking up his new work.

During the nine years he had been away from the college Wheaton had had a variety of responsibilities that led him to feel that he had a contribution to make in the field of theological teaching. His first living on leaving Oak Hill in 1962 had been a small country parish where he had learned important lessons about pastoral care. He served also as assistant chaplain to a maximum security prison in the neighbouring parish, and ran the youth work for a number of villages as deanery youth chaplain. Four years later he had quite unexpectedly been invited to follow another Old Oak, Kenneth Prior, as vicar of St Paul's, Onslow Square, in central London. As well as the well-to-do residents, this part of South Kensington was home to numbers of students and young people beginning their professional careers, living in shared flats and single bedsits, and the church had some two hundred of these young people on the membership list of their young people's group. While leading this work Wheaton had also been appointed chaplain to Brompton Hospital, and had seen that ministry develop with people finding faith in Christ and communicants increasing. A newly introduced Christian radio programme was relayed over the hospital's system. This variety of pastoral experience was something he felt that he could share with the students, and he had also built up a knowledge of clergy and parishes he could use in advising on possible curacies

Wheaton had concerns over the way men were being trained for ministry. Preparation for becoming the omnicompetent one-man band still seemed to be the norm. He had seen the way in which bishops were beginning to develop ideas of team ministries, but felt there was a fallacy in what they were doing when the concept of the team was limited to that of ordained ministers working in neighbouring parishes. Experience with his previous congregation had taught him that the ideal ministry team was grown from one congregation where clergy and laity could work together in a fruitful partnership, encouraging and developing one another's gifts from a common understanding of the Gospel. A new and much more exciting role was to be found this way – that of being a resource; helping Christian men and women to grow to maturity in knowing and exercising their faith. He valued the insight of the Bishop of St Edmundsbury and Ipswich, who had said:

> The job of the ordained servants of the church is to equip themselves in every way possible to equip the lay people to fulfil directly their call. This is the primary task of the ordained ministry. They therefore give themselves to the pastoral care and counselling of the laity and they build them up in faith through Word and sacrament. This is how I see it. The laity are not there to back up the clergy; the clergy are there to back up the laity.[1]

---

[1] Bishop Leslie Brown, chairman of ACCM, interviewed by that body prior to the 1968 Lambeth Conference.

Such sentiments may seem commonplace today, but when they were first voiced they were regarded as almost revolutionary. Wood had expressed them in his vision for mobilizing the laity of Islington deanery, and it was Wheaton's concern to see the coming generations of ordinands receiving adequate training to become effective team leaders and members.

The situation facing the new principal in the college, the wider church and society at large was far different from that which Wood had faced. The fifties had been a time of euphoria: the country was recovering from its wartime privations and entered into the 'never had it so good' boom. For the college, as we have seen, these were years of growth and expansion, with the numbers of ordinands climbing back towards their pre-war levels. However, the sixties saw the numbers of students in the theological colleges, including the evangelical ones, fall dramatically, and the reappraisal following the de Bunsen report had led to the closure of several colleges, among them St Aidan's, Birkenhead, and Tyndale Hall, Bristol. However, the latter was saved by going into merger with Clifton and Dalton House (a training college for women's ministry) to form Trinity College.[2]

Archbishop Coggan had drawn attention to this decline, and attempted to explain a possible reason in the following terms:

> We have presented a God too small for this space age, a God Who would seem to be a sort of over-sized ecclesiastic, interested in little else than ecclesiastical matters. We have all too often failed to present a Christ magnificent in the greatness of His love and power, vast in the scope of His redemption. No wonder there is uncertainty of belief, a failure to commit oneself for life.[3]

Certainly the Church of England's agenda at the time justifies his comment. Church Assembly sessions had been taken up with completing the work of canon law revision started during Fisher's

---

[2] For details of these closures see Bullock, *History of Training*, pp. 138–43 and McGrath, *To Know and Serve God*, chapter 8.

[3] York diocesan leaflet, September 1966.

archiepiscopate and endless debates over liturgical revision and the synodical government to be introduced in the autumn of 1970. Meanwhile the nation was facing the run-down of its heavy industries (ship-building, coal, steel and the production of cars, lorries and buses), which had been at the heart of its economic resurgence after the war.

Once again unemployment figures rose, additional tensions leading to the race riots of the early eighties. With governments of either hue appearing unable to tackle such problems it fell to the church to set up an Archbishops' Commission on Urban Priority Areas, which in due course produced the report *Faith in the City*.[4] This drew attention to the sense of deprivation experienced by so many, but received no thanks from those who regarded it as interference by the church in the state's domain. However, it did have an effect on Oak Hill in the appointment of the first Kingham Hill Fellow, as will be seen later.[5]

These factors, together with the changing moral climate of the sixties, the dramatic rise in the rate of inflation in the early seventies, the ever-present threat of a nuclear holocaust and the introduction of the credit card led many in all sections of society to adopt the prevailing philosophy of 'live now, pay later'. Such a society was intolerant of the traditional Christian values of self-control, chastity and faithfulness within marriage. A generation had grown up largely out of touch with the Christian faith, and the increasingly popular television sitcoms portrayed the clergy either as pleasant but ineffectual, or characters whose morals belied their profession. Citing the loss of one million members from the church's electoral rolls between 1930–68 Hylson-Smith comments:

> There was less regard for distinctively Christian beliefs and values. Churches were treated with increasing disregard as institutions with clearly perceived functions and roles. Church leaders were held in

---

[4] *Faith in the City: The Report of the Archbishop of Canterbury's Commission on Urban Priority Areas* (London: Church House, 1985).

[5] See page 229.

> less honour, given less respect and accorded less authority as representing the churches and the Christian faith. There was a widespread ignorance of the basic facts concerning the person of Christ, the Bible and what it contained and taught, Christian doctrines, and Christian practices, and such knowledge was in any case quite frequently considered unnecessary; and there was a pervasive indifference to all matters of the doctrine, and even of the morality, proclaimed by the churches.[6]

Many evangelicals hoped that the appointment in 1973 of two of their number (Donald Coggan and Stuart Blanch) as archbishops would help to combat these trends. Much of Ramsey's energies during the latter part of his archiepiscopate had been taken up with abortive negotiations for reunion with the Methodists, and now it was hoped that the new leadership would focus more on the need for evangelism. They launched a 'Call to the Nation' as an attempt to bring the Christian church and its message back into the mainstream of national life, but unfortunately it appeared to bear little fruit beyond reassuring church members that there were some leaders who still had confidence in the gospel.

Challenges to orthodox belief came from the writings of Don Cupitt as well as John Robinson's *The Human Face of God*,[7] Maurice Wiles' *The Remaking of Christian Doctrine*[8] and *The Myth of God Incarnate*, edited by John Hick.[9] The Doctrine Commission's publication of *Christian Believing*[10] drew attention to the increasing divide between those who saw the Christian faith and life as a 'voyage of discovery' and those who saw it as a response to the objective revelation of God though his Word written in the Scriptures and revealed in

---

[6] Hylson-Smith, *Churches in England*, p. 211. The whole chapter (7) gives an informative picture.
[7] London: SCM, 1973.
[8] London: SCM, 1974.
[9] London: SCM, 1977.
[10] London: SPCK, 1976.

Christ. James Barr in his *Fundamentalism*[11] launched a direct attack on the conservative evangelical position maintained by Oak Hill and its sister institutions.

Perhaps the greatest furore over the inroads of liberalism came with the nomination in 1984 of David Jenkins to the see of Durham. Jenkins had been Professor of Theology at Leeds University, but now made no secret of the fact that he no longer believed in either the virgin birth or the empty tomb, leading many within the church to protest against his nomination. In particular the orthodox clergy in his diocese were dismayed at the prospect of having a bishop who no longer professed the faith they were committed to proclaim. Evangelicals in the north-east expressed their distress that a person with such heterodox views should be considered as a candidate for the episcopate, where part of his task should be to 'uphold the truth of the Gospel against error'.[12] Their call for support from other evangelicals was discussed at a conference of the staffs of the evangelical Anglican colleges in September 1984 without any action being taken: subsequently the Oak Hill staff passed a resolution in their support, which was communicated to them.

Disillusionment with a hierarchy who appeared no longer to believe in the church's historic formularies, and suspicion of an establishment who no longer seemed able to get to grips with the many problems confronting society, may have been among the many factors that led to the dwindling numbers offering for ordination, particularly in the Church of England. Some who might otherwise have offered for ministry became Free Church ministers or sought to exercise leadership in the burgeoning house and community churches.

As a counterbalance to these developments the Billy Graham Evangelistic Association convened a Congress on World Evangelization at Lausanne in Switzerland in 1974. Wheaton attended and became one of the thousands who signed the Lausanne Covenant whereby those participating committed

---

[11] London: SCM, 1977.

[12] ASB service for the ordination of a bishop.

themselves not only to furthering the work of evangelization throughout the world, but also recognizing the social implications of the Gospel. Many evangelicals had repudiated the spread of the so-called 'social gospel' by liberal theologians in the earlier part of the century, but the experience particularly of the Latin American and other third-world theologians present called for a re-think of the whole issue. The impact of such thinking on the Oak Hill community is reflected in *The Oak Leaf*, whose 1972 issue focuses on 'green' issues and the implications of the population explosion. The following year's publication gives a plug for the Evangelical Urban Training Project in Everton, Liverpool, which was being developed by Old Oak Neville Black and which anticipated the response to *Faith in the City*.

Another noteworthy happening during this period was the convening of a further National Evangelical Anglican Congress at Nottingham in 1977, ten years after the significant event at Keele. Once again the college played a notable part: staff members, especially Ian Cundy, were involved in writing and editing the preparatory study material,[13] and it was former student Anthony Thiselton[14] who brought a new word into the vocabulary of many evangelicals – hermeneutics. He expanded on the subject in his book *The Two Horizons*.[15] Although twice as many were present the impact was not generally reckoned to be as great as that of Keele, with the subsequent statement reflecting the fact that many of the subjects discussed showed divided opinions even among those who took Scripture as their guide. Perhaps the clearest reminder came from John Stott in his affirmation that the designation 'evangelical' should be retained

---

[13] See J. Stott, I. Cundy and B. Kaye (eds), *Obeying Christ in a Changing World*.

[14] Thiselton had been on the staff of Tyndale Hall and was at that stage lecturing in biblical studies at Sheffield University. He later became successively principal of St John's College, Nottingham, St John's College, Durham, and Professor of Christian Theology at Nottingham University.

[15] Exeter: Paternoster, 1980.

because 'we evangelicals are Bible people ... and we are Gospel people'.[16]

The sixties had seen the expansion of higher education in the UK on a scale never known before. New universities and polytechnics sprang up overnight as governments recognized that, with the fading-out of industry, the future of the economy lay in educating the coming generation to take advantage of the developing world of scientific discovery and technological advances.

Apart from these external factors, the new principal was faced immediately with other problems. Having just received a new curate, for the first term of the new academic year he continued to minister in his parish and hospital, coming out to Oak Hill one day a week to teach, interview students and chair the staff meeting. Taylor, as vice-principal, ran the college in a most competent fashion. But although it could run for six months without a principal, it could not function effectively for twenty-four hours without a cook! Fortunately Wood performed one of his last services to the college in that connection: in a telephone call to an incumbent concerning a proposed curacy he is reputed to have said, 'You need a curate and I need a cook!' Sue Morley, who was then studying in Leeds to become a cook/caterer, joined the domestic staff.

Following the review of the colleges at the end of the sixties ACCM had said that any college that had more that ten per cent of its ordinand places empty should be considered as a candidate for closure. When Wheaton took up his post there were forty-seven students in residence. The college's ceiling of ordinand places had been set at seventy-two, so it was in fact less than two-thirds full. There were several reasons for the decline in numbers entering the college (admissions had fallen from twenty-eight in 1968 and twenty-one in 1969 to thirteen in 1970 and 1971).[17] The main reason was the move of LCD from Northwood

---

[16] For a fuller appraisal of NEAC 1977 see Bebbington, *Evangelicalism in Modern Britain*, pp. 249–51; and Hylson-Smith, *Evangelicals in the Church of England*, pp. 290–93.

[17] Vice-principal's report, 26 November 1971.

to Nottingham, becoming St John's College, under the dynamic leadership of its new principal, Michael Green, who had recruited George Carey and John Goldingay to his staff. Married men had in particular not wanted to face two moves during their period of training, and so numbers at Oak Hill may have been artificially inflated during the years 1968 and 1969, with an increased enrolment for St John's starting in 1970.

The practicalities of the APM scheme mentioned in the last chapter still had to be worked out by the college. For the first year there were only two students on this course, which was helpful, as Silvester was then able to take on more teaching in the college while working out the details of the APM syllabus and arranging with his colleagues to share in its teaching. He took over the teaching of the doctrine syllabus previously covered by Stibbs, and became responsible for the running of the parochial training scheme both for full- and part-time students.

While recognizing that there was a place for such a course, and that it was right that the facilities of the college should be made available for it, Silvester was never convinced that it was the best form of training for the ministry. More than once he asked friends, 'Would you be prepared to put your life in the hands of a surgeon who had studied only at night school for three years with a few weekends thrown in?' When it looked as if, for reasons noted elsewhere, the church was likely to steer more of its ordinands in the direction of training on courses rather than at colleges, he gave an address to the Islington Conference on the importance and value of residential theological training.[18] The college also watched with interest the development in Bethnal Green of a scheme launched by another former student, Ted Roberts. He had noticed how residential training could take a man from an inner-city area and put him in a middle-class environment with the result that he would feel ill at ease to go back to his roots to minister. As vicar of St James-the-Less he had, with the support of his bishop, Trevor Huddleston, identified

---

[18] Subsequently published by CPAS as Fellowship Paper 284: *Theological Colleges – The Future?*.

seven men in his congregation whom he felt to have the gifts and character for ministry, but whom he proposed to train at grass-roots level in the parish. Six of them responded positively, and four completed the course he ran for them. Roberts subsequently wrote up the experiment in his book *Partners and Ministers*.[19]

If attracting the right numbers of students was one problem, the appointment of the right staff was another. Soon after taking up his appointment both senior members of the academic staff, Taylor and Simpson, informed Wheaton that they hoped to be leaving at the end of the academic year. This posed a dilemma. The concept of APM training, that men should be able to attend whatever course was nearest to their home, meant that certain diocesan authorities were looking rather askance at the idea of a so-called 'party' college teaching men from all the traditions of the Church of England. They therefore wanted Wheaton to appoint staff from a wider range of churchmanship and theological views than had hitherto been the case at Oak Hill. However, he was not only aware of the founder's wishes for the college, which he endorsed, but he also knew that if he were to take this step he would lose the confidence of the evangelical constituency, and especially the former students, on whom the college relied heavily for its supply of ordinands.

The situation was further complicated by the fact that neither Taylor nor Simpson was in a position to hand in his notice immediately. Until either of them could announce his new appointment nothing could be done by way of approaching persons to succeed them. Taylor was finally able to announce his appointment to a parish early in the summer term, and the new principal was then faced with his first appointment. Taylor had more than fulfilled Wood's high expectations as scholar, teacher and pastor, and would go on to have a distinguished career as Archdeacon of West Ham, Bishop of St Albans, and High Almoner. Finding an Old Testament specialist with the stature of a vice-principal was not going to be easy, particularly after the fine work done by Taylor in all respects.

---

[19] Published as a Falcon book by CPAS 1972.

Fortunately the name of Geoffrey Shaw, a teacher in Sheffield, was suggested. He had had a fruitful ministry as an incumbent in Woking and St Leonards-on-Sea, and was also well known for the young people's house parties he had run for a number of years. He was appointed, and for the next seven years he and his wife, Cynthia, played a valuable part in college life. His teaching was greatly appreciated, as well as his musical gifts, and he was greatly used in leading student teams on college missions. When he left in 1979 to take up the principalship of his old college at Wycliffe Hall his teaching gifts were recognized in Oxford University.

Oak Hill was fortunate in that Simpson was appointed to the living of Ridge, near South Mimms, Hertfordshire, and for a further two years continued to come in to the college one day a week to continue his teaching of worship, which he had developed to a high level. His ministry was valued not only for close attention to detail in his teaching, but for the high standard he had set as the first official college chaplain: this stood him in good stead when he, too, achieved high office as Archdeacon and then Dean of Canterbury. The teaching of worship was then taken over by the principal, who felt it important that he should be teaching one of the 'academic' subjects and thereby sharing the pressures experienced by his colleagues.

For the teaching of church history the college secured the services of Tony Lane, who was working for a PhD at Ridley Hall, and came down to Oak Hill for one day a week during the academic year 1972–3. He subsequently followed a career in teaching at LBC.

Wheaton knew from experience that there were clergy whose training had done little to enable them to relate to individuals or to teach the faith effectively. One of his priorities was to develop pastoral training on a systematic basis, and award a Diploma in Pastoral Studies (DPS) on the basis of satisfactory completion of certain requirements. This priority was enthusiastically endorsed by the teaching staff, and the academic year 1972–3 was restructured from the previous pattern of three ten-week terms to one of two eleven-week terms, followed by a summer term of eight weeks. This enabled all the student body to sit the GOE in March (previously, those in their final year had taken the March examination so as to be free to benefit from the pastoral training programme offered in the summer term since Wilkinson's days). The new vice-principal described the development in these terms:

> Pastoralia is at last being taken seriously! It is no longer dealt with by an off-the-syllabus talk scheduled at a time of the day when no-one can keep awake! During the DPS term a careful balance has been sought to find room for a comprehensive training and to allot each topic sufficient time for adequate reading, grass-roots involvement where feasible, and a written project. For instance, in this first year, nearly four weeks will be devoted to sociology consisting of lectures, seminars, a fortnight away from college on field work, reporting and assessment. Areas such as psychology, youth work and education will be covered in a similar way.[20]

The college would then award the DPS to those students who successfully completed two summer terms of this course, and the college ordination hood would in future be awarded only to those who had gained the DPS as well as satisfying their examiners in the GOE. Students would be encouraged to develop a Bible-teaching ministry by the diploma's requirement of a systematic coverage of the Bible to equip them with material for sermons and expositions. The scheme also required at least two weeks to be spent in a designated parish during a student's time at the college, and there would be opportunities to take specialist courses such as urban training schemes, hospital chaplaincy or radio and television courses. At this time the relevant committee of ACCM was also concerned about the proper pastoral training of ordinands, and the Oak Hill scheme in many ways anticipated requirements that were introduced at an official level in the ensuing years.

However, this development was not without its critics. From 12–14 February 1973 the college was once more subject to an inspection by a team appointed by ACCM, who gave careful

---

[20] *The Oak Leaf*, 1973, p. 4.

thought to what the college was about to begin in the following term. They urged the staff to keep the new system under close review, particularly with regard to the separation of the academic year into two 'academic' terms and one 'pastoral' term. Their comment was:

> the students may tackle the pastoral side of their training more seriously if it is separated off, and concentrated in this way; on the other hand it may only encourage the idea that GOE is just an intellectual chore to be got out of the way before getting down to the real (i.e. the pastoral) job. We would prefer to see the two elements more closely related to each other and integrated as much as possible. It seems to us that there must necessarily be overlap if the academic and pastoral aspects of a subject are to be kept so much apart. To postpone consideration of issues as they arise is bad teaching method.[21]

These strictures were not lost on the teaching staff, who were already beginning to explore further developments. In his May 1973 report to the college council (before the inspection report had been received) Wheaton reported that the Middlesex Polytechnic was about to include Trent Park College of Education in its orbit, and locate its administrative headquarters on the old Bohun Lodge site at the corner of Cat Hill. Trent Park was a mansion in hundreds of acres of parkland about a mile north of Oak Hill, opened by Middlesex County Council as a College of Education in the immediate post-war boom. The two colleges had developed friendly relations over the years, with Oak Hill students helping the Christian Union at Trent Park, and members of staff meeting informally. The principal informed the council that he had been unofficially approached by the Trent Park staff to see whether there were any ways in which the two establishments could work together to provide humanities teaching (an area the polytechnic was keen to maintain from the old Trent Park curriculum, but which was unusual in such an institution).

---

[21] Report of 1973 ACCM inspection.

Little did those concerned know it at the time, but Oak Hill was now on the brink of one of the most important developments in its history thus far.

For a long time Wheaton had been concerned that ministerial training had been focusing on the wrong model. Theological colleges had been developed by university-trained men, who had sought to run their colleges as a mini-version of an Oxbridge college, and it was understandable that those colleges in university centres should adhere to this model. But his contention was that ministerial training should be more akin to that of colleges of education, where the emphasis was not just simply on enabling students to gain information and be trained to think with a view to passing examinations or writing essays. He saw its task in terms of passing on the theological tradition to the students in such a way as to equip them to be competent communicators of that tradition not only in the pulpit, but also through the media, in the classroom, in informal group settings and on a one-to-one basis.

For some time the opinion had been voiced in ACCM circles that the standard of GOE was that of a pass degree, but students who had gained this qualification were hampered if they wished to pursue further studies as no university was prepared to give them credit for their achievements. In 1964 the government had set up the Council for National Academic Awards (CNAA) as a validating authority for courses offered by polytechnics, which had previously had to rely on City and Guilds or Higher National Diploma awards. Following this restructuring a Diploma in Higher Education (DipHE) had been introduced as a goal for the two-year student, with the possibility of proceeding to a pass or honours degree in the third year. Such a pattern had two further attractions for Oak Hill staff and students. In the first place, the validating authority was accustomed to looking at courses that included assessment of practical elements as part of the training, and there would be the opportunity of meeting the inspectors' criticism by planning a course which would run the academic and the practical elements together. Provided that the courses planned could be seen by the relevant committee of ACCM to be covering the material required for the GOE, the college would be free to place the emphasis on the practical biblical training for which it had always stood. The other advantage of switching to courses validated by the CNAA was that hitherto many local education authorities had been reluctant to make grants to students for ministerial training, arguing that the courses they took were mainly validated only by the churches. It was hoped, with some degree of justification, that students who could be shown to be studying for a nationally recognized qualification were entitled to be grant maintained. The college found that many more did receive grants, though these always remained within the discretionary category, as it was claimed that mandatory grants were not applicable when the student was at a privately run institution.

For the Oak Hill community this involved learning a whole new language. The three ten-week terms of the traditional academic year were divided into two fifteen-week semesters, so students returned after the Christmas vacation to face a further three weeks of the first semester of the academic year. After a week's break, during which the staff did their marking and met the external examiner(s), the second semester ran from around the beginning of February until mid-June with a break over Easter. A further examinations board meeting would then complete its work in good time to communicate results to bishops prior to ordination dates.

Each student would take three modules per semester, and each module would gain so many credits towards the award of the diploma or degree. A further bonus for students who were fearful of examinations lay in the fact that much of the assessment would be done continuously, on the basis of written work or projects completed during the course, with optional examinations or a major written project at the end of each semester. This system also allowed the staff to design a course that married two 'academic' modules with one 'pastoral' module in each semester. Each subject module was based on the theory that it should provide for four hours' 'contact' time (i.e. spent with the tutor in lectures, seminars or tutorials) and eight hours' 'non-contact' time (i.e. private study, reading or producing the necessary coursework) each week. An encouragement for students wishing to proceed to further studies was that credits gained on CNAA-validated courses were also recognized by the Open University.

The staff had been conscious of their responsibility to look more closely at their teaching methods, especially in the light of advice given in the 1973 inspectors' report:

> The students come from a wide variety of backgrounds, and their different academic abilities make effective teaching in groups extremely difficult. The principal and his staff are fully aware of this, and are giving constant thought as to how these difficulties may be surmounted. They have recently talked this over with the vice-principal of Bishop Lonsdale College of Education [in Derby] who, in a written report, has made a number of valuable suggestions. We would particularly endorse his comments on the need to consider the purpose of lectures and seminars, and the dangers of over lecturing and the value of using a variety of teaching techniques.[22]

The college council gave their support to the idea of approaching the CNAA with a course planned in conjunction with Middlesex Polytechnic, and such an approach was made in September 1975. The proposed course included material equivalent to the requirements of the GOE, together with modules such as drama, social science, education, humanities and psychology offered at the polytechnic. A reciprocal agreement was made, enabling students from either institution to take components from the other's courses.

Validation by the CNAA required a visit from members of their theological and religious studies board to meet with students, view the facilities and discuss the proposals with the academic staff while subjecting them to severe scrutiny. There was also to be a further visit from council officers to assess the administrative structures of the college and adequacy of the ancillary staff. The result of all this was that the college's first

---

[22] Report of 1973 ACCM inspection.

submission was rejected, the visiting chairman's main criticism being that it was too much of a gallimaufry, with little attention apparently being paid to establishing a coherent pattern between the various disciplines. The officers were also concerned about the failure of the college to have a properly constituted academic board, with subordinate boards of studies supervising the different courses. This experience undoubtedly set all the academic staff on a steep learning curve, and enabled them to achieve a degree of professionalism unknown before in the history of the college.

After the rejection of the first submission, a revision was approved for validation only for the DipHE component. For technical reasons the joint element with the polytechnic was not acceptable, though the reciprocal arrangement was allowed to stand. The staff was left to battle on with various submissions for the degree element, and validation for a pass degree was granted in 1978, in time for the first diplomates to transfer to the degree course in their final year. Approval for an honours degree was not gained until 1990, but Oak Hill had become the first Anglican theological college to gain validation from the CNAA.

One requirement was that the college should appoint an external examiner. An extremely happy appointment was that of the Revd Professor James Atkinson from Sheffield University, who not only understood the college's theological position, but also shared many of their concerns and aims in preparing men for ministry. His wise and friendly but strict and penetrating comments proved invaluable to members of the academic staff as they developed the necessary skills and expertise required in monitoring their courses. When the degree course was validated the college was required to appoint a second external examiner of a different theological tradition. Bishop Kenneth Woollcombe was appointed for this task: with his experience as a diocesan bishop and former college principal he proved a valuable and perceptive assessor of the work of the staff as well as of the students.[23] In due course (as examiners were allowed only five years in the post) Dr Brian Johansen, minister of the City

---

[23] He had been Bishop of Oxford 1971–8 and principal of Edinburgh Theological College 1963–71.

Temple, and the Revd Professor Stuart Hall of King's College London, succeeded them, and their input at the examinations board meetings proved very helpful in establishing the courses. A further CNAA requirement was that the college should greatly improve both the stock and facilities of the library. Here once again the trustees proved extremely supportive. The library budget doubled from £750 in 1975–6 to £1,500 in 1976–7 and by 1984–5 had increased to £7,500, while in 1984 a further one-off sum of £5,000 was provided to make up some of the deficiencies.

For various reasons ACCM had not been able to arrange for the college to be inspected after five years, as it should have been, and so the next inspection was held in February 1981. Here they reported:

> We were fully satisfied that a high standard of teaching is being maintained, and that the academic demands of the theological course are suitable to the preparation of ordinands in today's society. The student work which we saw reflects a wide spectrum of ability, as we expected, but the evidence suggests that there is little lacking in application. We would strongly commend the current academic policy of the college in establishing the Diploma of Higher Education and the BA degree, and in using the CNAA as its validating body. The college is to be congratulated on its success thus far, and on the care with which it is planning further developments in its work especially in the field of Pastoral Studies. It is good that thought is being given also to the extension of CNAA validation into courses of part-time study; this would have relevance to the NSM [Non-Stipendary Ministry, as the APM course was renamed in 1977] work and could be extended in the direction of lay-training at some time in the future ... Staff and students are enthusiastic about the current teaching experiment (which is to be reviewed at the end of the academic year). The students obviously find the tutorials very helpful and claim that the new system allows them to read more widely.'[24]

[24] Report of 1981 ACCM inspection. The new system referred to was a programme providing more opportunity for work in seminars and tutorials.

But such developments were not allowed to go unchallenged. There were fears among some of the student body and former students that with all these new courses the principal was losing sight of the founder's vision for the college – helping the less advantaged student. For this reason from time to time student members of the academic board would voice their reservations about the proposals for the honours degree, fearing that it would tempt the staff to concentrate their energies on the more academically promising students rather than helping those who found that side of things harder, and the staff had to face these fears. It was always their concern to enable every student to achieve their full potential in every area of life – academic, pastoral and spiritual.

While Oak Hill was seeking to develop along these lines, the increase of part-time courses along with the dramatic inflation of the early seventies led many to question whether residential theological colleges were not an expensive luxury the church could well do without. Oak Hill, having well below the level of ordinands for which it could cater, was a prime target for the axe. The numbers entering the college had only gradually risen. The 1972–3 academic year saw only thirteen new ordinands to replace the eighteen who had left. The 1973–4 academic year saw the number of ACCM ordinands rise to forty-five, plus one ordinand from each of the Churches of Ireland and in Wales, and the Anglican Church of Canada. With seven A level students and five non-ordinands reading for diploma or degree courses the total was now sixty-one members of the full-time college.[25]

Nor was Oak Hill alone in being below its ordinand quota. The principals' conference in January 1974 produced a memorandum for the ACCM council suggesting further retrenchment, and drew attention to the problem in a letter to *The Times*. The memorandum addressed the two-fold problem faced by the Church of England arising from the dramatic increase in the costs of residential training because of inflation, and the continuing drop

[25] Principal's reports to the college council 24 November 1972 and 7 December 1973.

in the numbers of those being recommended for such training. Attention was drawn to the fact that the present pattern of training had developed during the previous hundred years or so, and so it was time for a fresh appraisal. It also stated that:

> Despite different emphases among principals, the conference was agreed that a case has yet to be proved which would justify a widescale departure from the traditional pattern of residential training. Such training must continue to have its place in the total scheme since it affords an irreplaceable milieu for personal and inter-personal growth in theological understanding, spirituality, and evangelical purpose.[26]

The principals also suggested a further contraction in the numbers of residential colleges, and that, in view of its shortage of ordinands, Oak Hill should consider merging with either St John's, Nottingham (in view of their wartime link), or Wycliffe Hall, Oxford. One of the arguments put forward was that many more students could benefit from having at least part of their training in a university environment, and that the departments of religious studies springing up in some of the new universities could be strengthened by an influx of ordinands. Wheaton was among those who were more cautious about this, as he knew that many religious studies departments were staffed by liberal teachers, and were more interested in promoting comparative religion than confessional Christianity. His fears were justified when within a decade the government cut the budget for the universities, forcing some of the smaller departments to close.

While agreeing with much of the memorandum, he questioned the wisdom of further retrenchment, urging rather the church's need for more ordinands to meet the potential problems in staffing the parishes if the current decline continued. Here he was in a minority, and reluctantly signed the letter. Consultation with

[26] Extracts from the memorandum were printed as Appendix A to a report *Alternative Patterns of Training*, published as GS265 in 1975.

the principals of St John's and Wycliffe quickly established that neither could possibly expand sufficiently to receive Oak Hill's numbers, and the resources of the Kingham Hill Trust were only available for theological education on the Oak Hill site. Furthermore, the two principals approached emphasized that the recent provision of married quarters at Oak Hill was a facility not to be lightly lost. A factor to which the memorandum did not appear to have given sufficient consideration was that closure of Oak Hill would leave no residential theological college in the London area. Consequently, the principals of Trinity College Bristol, Cranmer Hall, St John's Nottingham, Ridley Hall, Wycliffe Hall and Oak Hill sent a further letter to *The Times* urging that the way ahead was not to close down further resources, which could well be a great loss to the church in the future, but rather to follow a policy of diversification. The rapidly changing scene in church and nation suggested that in the future there was likely to be increasing demand for developments in the fields of in-service and lay training, which the colleges would be well equipped to provide.

The review undertaken in the sixties had set a ceiling of seventy-two places for ACCM-sponsored ordinands at Oak Hill. This was in fact the notional capacity of the college, and so no provision was made for other students, such as ordinands from other provinces of the Anglican Communion, or other churches, non-ordinand undergraduates, EFAC (Evangelical Fellowship of the Anglican Communion) bursars or clergy on refresher courses. So Wheaton invited the support of the principals of Trinity and Wycliffe in a joint approach to the House of Bishops to ask that ten places of the Oak Hill ACCM 'quota' might be redistributed, five each to these other two colleges.

The bishops in fact reduced the Oak Hill quota of ordinands by fifteen, as they had had a request for an allocation of further places from Ridley Hall, to whom they allocated a further five. Significantly, the number of ACCM ordinands at Oak Hill went up to fifty-one the following academic year, and reached its ceiling in September 1975. Amusingly, the following term the principal was asked to take an extra ordinand by the Archbishop of York, who subsequently had (with good humour) to reprimand him for being in excess of his quota!

PERSONALITY PROFILE

Jim Tipp was born in London's East End in 1945, the youngest of three sons. He went to St John's Hoxton Church of England School, then to Shoreditch Central. He left in 1960 along with thirty other pupils who had been asked to leave before the school was officially renamed Shoreditch Comprehensive. He had no qualifications whatsoever. After numerous jobs he finished up working in the printing trade.

He was converted in 1966 after a Billy Graham crusade, and by 1967 was running the youth work at Shoreditch Parish Church under Old Oak Richard Thomson. He became a reader in the London diocese in spite of failing all the exams: bishop Trevor Huddleston overruled the board.

In 1973 he came to Oak Hill where he faced major problems in submitting written work, and was subsequently diagnosed as having severe dyslexia. He is able to read and comprehend at a high level, but cannot write or use English grammar, or spell simple words correctly. He spent many hours with Annette Silvester at the end of the day learning to write the alphabet clearly, as his writing then and now consisted of joined-up writing with capital letters and no punctuation. When he returned to his old printing firm for a vacation job he found himself producing the accounts of the Kingham Hill Trust, which in those days not even the principal was allowed to see!

In 1974–5 he was elected senior student by his fellows. He was ordained in the Rochester diocese to St Paulinus and St Mary Cray and in 1978 became curate-in-charge of St Matthew, High Brooms, Southborough, Kent. He moved in 1982 to Snodland, Kent, after receiving a very clear call from God to go there. He began teaching for the diocese in 1981 and was part of the diocesan training team until 1990. In 1991 he went to Heythrop College, London University, to do an MA in Pastoral Studies. He became Rural Dean of Cobham in 1996 and was made a Canon of Rochester Cathedral in 2001. At the time of writing he is serving on the Advisory Council for Mission and Training, the Canterbury and Rochester Board of Studies, the Bishop's Council, the Cathedral Council and the Diocesan Synod.

While the college faced these problems, another important side of the estate was in difficulties of its own. For years the farm had been supplying milk in churns to the local dairy, whose lorries had called daily to collect them from a platform constructed in Farm Lane. The increasing technology in milk production required the college to install machinery for bulk tanker production, which would also involve an increase in the herd. As the farm had consistently shown a loss each year, in spite of the valiant attempts of Farmer Brown to increase the market for farm fresh eggs and vegetables, the decision was reluctantly taken at the council's May meeting in 1973 to close it. Brown remained as estate manager to continue running the market garden side of the business, providing vegetables for the college. Milk production ceased on 20 August and the entire herd, which had been lovingly built up over the years, was transferred to the farm on the Kingham Hill estate. Egg production ceased on 28 August after the farm shop, which had recently taken around £3,000 per annum from sales, closed to the public on July 31. In an effort to avoid redundancy the college was able to offer a post in the kitchen to Joyce Brown, who had served for several years on the dairy side. Regretfully no place could be found for Sid Carrington, who had been on the farm staff for twenty years. He went to work on the domestic staff at Trent Park.

The opening of married quarters in 1969 meant that wives and children living on the campus were now very much part of the community, and in spite of fewer ordinands there were always more applicants for married accommodation than could be housed on the estate. The college had been able to rent a small number of properties in the neighbourhood, but it was realized that rent would be hard to keep at an affordable level for students. In consequence the trustees agreed in 1973 to build a further two houses in Mohan Close. When the farm buildings became redundant they were very imaginatively converted (with plans drawn up by an architect among the student body, Andrew Platt) into maisonettes, known today as The Byre, for student families. This enabled wives on the campus and in the locality to join in the life of the college to a far greater extent. It also meant that the college 'family' was regularly expanding in a particularly noticeable way: the 1974 *Oak Leaf* records nine births to student families. When the principal visited Victoria Maternity Hospital twice in a week, the ward sister mischievously enquired, 'What are you putting in the water at Oak Hill College?'

Wood had told Wheaton on his appointment there were two issues that were hot potatoes in the college – contraception and the charismatic movement. Where a married man with no children was accepted for training, his bishop or director of ordinands usually stated that on no account must he and his wife think of starting a family during the period at college. It was expected that the wife would be working to fund their accommodation and living expenses during that period, and the man would receive a grant as a single student. But the greater freedom for wives to join in college life was frequently a strain for the childless couples, who saw those who already had families living on the campus, and, being provided with a grant for family maintenance, becoming pregnant. In a number of cases the principal saw that this ruling was putting a strain on marriages, and so negotiated from time to time on behalf of those students with their bishops to find funds from diocesan sources to enable them to start a family. When Wheaton was appointed to the ACCM council the chairman introduced him and the grants secretary gave a spontaneous reaction: 'Principal of Oak Hill – he's the man responsible for all those babies!'

Early in Wheaton's principalship a college meeting was held to look at the issue of the charismatic movement. Views for and against the movement were heard, followed by questions and discussion. At the end of the day it was felt there had been a genuine meeting of minds, and those in favour and those with reservations continued to live and work together in harmony. While the college remained as a conservative rather than a charismatic evangelical institution, students with charismatic views were welcomed and shared from time to time in praise and healing services in the chapel, and some members of staff were more sympathetic than others to this developing phenomenon. An article by student Kerry Thorpe, who after ordination became a leader in the movement, in the 1977 *Oak Leaf* is typical of the eirenic approach to the subject that the college fostered.[27]

When Geoffrey Shaw joined the team in 1972 Oak Hill students were encouraged that the staff between them had far more actual parochial and pastoral experience than the staff of any other Anglican college. This bore fruit in the developments in pastoral studies already noted. Writing in the 1976 *Oak Leaf* Shaw quoted a remark made to him by a diocesan bishop: 'What I value in an Oak Hill training is that it produces a good parish man.'[28] However bishops and patrons were aware of the staff's potential, and approaches were made to staff members when key livings became vacant. In 1975 Christopher Byworth was invited to Norwich diocese by his former boss to become rector of the Thetford team. He would be well remembered for the prodigious amount of reading he did in the early mornings, and the extreme care he took to acquaint students with every aspect of a subject. The following year Hugh Silvester was called to the important parish and student work at Holy Trinity, Rusholme, Manchester. By then he had firmly established the APM course and had been a popular contributor both in the lecture room and on the sports field. It was a tragedy for the church when his promising career was cut short by a fatal heart attack in 1980 at the relatively young age of fifty. The quest for John Simpson's successor resulted in the appointment in 1973 of Ian Cundy, who had been

---

[27] See 'The Charismatic Movement and The Church' in *The Oak Leaf*, 1977, p. 24.

[28] See *The Oak Leaf*, 1976, p. 21.

curate to an Old Oak, John Short, in New Malden, in the Southwark diocese. Ian taught church history and some of the doctrine syllabus, but in January 1978 he was wooed back by his former bishop to become team rector of Mortlake. During his time at Oak Hill he and Silvester enjoyed sharpening their minds in theological and philosophical discussions, which proved of great benefit to their students, as both were stimulating teachers as well as caring pastors. Subsequently his career has taken him back to theological college work at Cranmer Hall, and to the episcopate as Bishop of Lewes and then of Peterborough.

The growing numbers at the college and development of the DipHE course enabled the appointment of further academic staff. Following Byworth's departure Michael Shallcross was appointed for one year to teach New Testament. Silvester's leaving in 1976 created a further gap, and the college council gave permission for a new appointment of the first ever director of pastoral training. Peter Pytches was head-hunted from his parish in Parkstone, Dorset, where he had a reputation as a trainer of curates. He had continued his academic interests, gaining both master's and doctor's degrees. The students benefited richly from his knowledge of parochial life, while his eirenic personality, administrative skills and wide knowledge made him an especially valuable member of staff.

For doctrinal teaching Dr Peter Toon was appointed from the staff of Latimer House, and his academic prowess gave greater credibility to the staff in the eyes of the CNAA. He instilled in students his own deep appreciation of the Anglican heritage, and was never satisfied with facile, poorly thought-out answers, challenging his colleagues as well as his students to think more deeply. For the New Testament post Oak Hill strengthened its links with Bristol by appointing Stephen Motyer, son of Alec, the principal of Trinity, who was researching for a master's degree in New Testament studies. He proved to be a stimulating and encouraging teacher of students of all abilities, and a good

---

[29] Canon C5.2.(d).

scholar, having inherited his father's enthusiasm for the Bible. Motyer had been studying at Trinity as an ordinand recommended for training. Under the revised canons[29] it was possible for Bishop Runcie, as episcopal visitor, to ordain him in St Albans Cathedral for his work at the college: previous staff members had had to serve a part-time local curacy on ordination.

Until this time the college had had four episcopal visitors. Their role was technically to keep in touch with the college, represent it in the House of Bishops, and act as intermediary if any conflicts arose between principal and staff or staff and students. They had been the bishops of Norwich (1932–42), Sodor and Man (1943–54), Liverpool (1954–66) and Southwell (1966–70). One of the early items for Wheaton to resolve had been the appointment of a new visitor. In a paper to the college council in November 1972 he suggested that an approach should be made to Robert Runcie of St Albans, who had spoken at that year's garden party and shown himself very favourably disposed to the college. He suggested that it would be valuable to have a visitor who was nearby and who had experience of being a principal (Runcie had been at Cuddesdon from 1960–70), and that it would demonstrate a new openness on the part of the college. The council agreed to the appointment.[30] Runcie accepted and proved a good friend. He stipulated that he wished to be a visitor in the true sense of the word, being allowed to drop in when he was passing, and meet with staff and students informally. Jokingly he said that the one thing he missed about institutional life was custard, so he would be glad to call in for the odd meal! Wheaton found him a ready listener and counsellor as he talked through with him the plans for the change of course and links with the polytechnic: on the latter Runcie had said that the proposed link could make 'a unique contribution for the gospel in North London'.[31] In September 1976 Runcie cemented the relationship between the college

[30] Principal's memorandum to the Kingham Hill trustees, 16 November 1972; minutes of the college council, 24 November 1972.

[31] Principal's memorandum to the Kingham Hill trustees, 26 June 1974.

and the diocese by installing Wheaton as an honorary canon in his cathedral.

The remaining years of Wheaton's principalship saw several further comings and goings among the staff. In November 1977 he reported to the college council that Cundy's place would be taken by the Revd Dr Rudi Heinze, an American Lutheran currently teaching church history at Concordia College in Illinois, but who was a great anglophile and had spent time in Britain on research. Cambridge University Press had recently published his book on Tudor royal proclamations[32] and he was delighted to have the opportunity to teach in Britain, partly for opportunity of further research. Heinze was appointed for two years from September 1978 while on extended sabbatical from Concordia. After he returned to the USA the college's links with Concordia were strengthened by Wes Wilkie, one of his colleagues, who deputized for him in the church history field. Heinze's experience at Oak Hill was so overwhelmingly positive that he returned for a full-time appointment from 1982. This began a long and distinguished period of service to the college on the part of both Rudi and his wife, Mildred, who worked for several years in the bookshop. He was ordained in the Church of England in 1986 to serve in the parish of St Peter, London Colney, Hertfordshire, for over a decade as an NSM curate. He is well remembered by his students for his enthusiasm for Reformation studies, which he taught by means of a board. His colleagues remember Heinze and his wife as good friends and wise counsellors.

In January 1978 the first appointment in social sciences was made when Roger Curl joined the staff from St George's Church in Leeds – a church famous for its social work – where he worked as a lay curate. After a first degree in social sciences at Leicester, Curl had gained an Oxford DPhil for a thesis on charismatic communities, and combined part-time teaching with studies for the London BD. He was also bachelor warden of the single students on the new wing. He continued in this post until leaving for ordi-

---

[32] R.W. Heinze, *The Proclamations of the Tudor Kings*.

nation in 1982. When Shaw was appointed principal of Wycliffe Hall in 1979 Field, who had become senior tutor in place of Simpson in 1972, was appointed vice-principal. The gap in teaching Old Testament was filled by Roger Cowley, who had recently returned from Jerusalem, where he had been teaching at the Anglican School following expulsion from missionary service in Ethiopia. Cowley combined this with a part-time curacy at St Luke's, Watford, and continued to fulfil several roles on the college staff and with the NSM course. From February 1980 the Old Testament department was served by the Revd Mike Butterworth, who had been working as a CMS missionary attached to the Church of South India teaching at the United Theological College in Bangalore. He had been responsible for establishing TAFTEE – the Association for Theological Education by Extension – and his appointment was made in the hope that he would be able to develop similar resources at Oak Hill, distance learning courses being yet another facet of the college's diversification process.

In September 1980 the Revd Dr Gerald Bray came to teach doctrine. A Canadian, he had followed a first degree in that country with a doctorate at the Sorbonne. He was a great linguist, an outstanding teacher and a good scholar. During that academic year Peter Pytches returned to parish life at Christ Church, North Finchley, Greater London and the college appointed Ann Jones, the first female member of the academic staff. With a master's degree in educational psychology from Manchester University and a diploma in pastoral theology from Heythrop College, together with experience of secondary school teaching and lecturing in the School of Education at Reading University, Ann appeared well equipped for the post of tutor and co-ordinator in pastoral studies. This seemed a particularly good appointment: the college was going co-educational and seeking to recruit female students. Unfortunately it was not yet ready for such a development: Ann did not feel she had been given the support she had expected from the students and some of her colleagues, and left after a year.

The well-qualified team of Alan and Elaine Storkey filled the subsequent vacancy. Alan had a MSc in sociology from the London School of Economics as well as a Diploma in Education, while Elaine had added an MA in philosophy from McMaster College in Canada to her Honours degree in the same subject from the University of Wales. Between them they would take over the fields of sociology and co-ordinating pastoral studies, while Tony Rees, the vicar of St Luke's, West Hampstead, in the London diocese, came to teach in the field of homiletics and communication, and to act as college chaplain. This further appointment was made possible as Peter Toon had been invited to combine a parish in the diocese of St Edmondsbury and Ipswich with being director of post-ordination training.

The final academic appointment made by Wheaton was in the New Testament field. Motyer left in 1983 to take up a parochial appointment, and once again the college was fortunate in finding someone who would make an invaluable contribution. Paul Gardner, son of a former student, had been serving a part-time curacy in Cambridge while working on a PhD thesis at Ridley Hall. Prior to this he had gained a degree in Spanish at King's College, London, and an MDiv from the Reformed Seminary at Jackson in the USA. He too brought a fine combination of academic rigour with pastoral insight into the lecture room.

Others served for a short while or as part-timers on the staff. When Motyer went on sabbatical to study at Tübingen in 1982 his workload was taken over by a former student, William Challis, who was able to gain experience before going on to theological teaching in Burundi. For fifteen years until 1977 speech training had been given by Bob Cheeseman, who held a teaching diploma from the Central School of Speech and Drama, with credit in voice training. Bob had been coming down weekly from Manchester where he taught drama at the polytechnic, as well as directing the highly successful production of the musical *Godspell*. When he left, short-term help was given by Pam Shaw and Barbara Houseman, and then in 1981 Christian Lewin took over this brief. Qualifying at the same school as Cheeseman, she had returned there to serve as head of their drama department and supervisor of teaching practice. Since then her contribution has been greatly appreciated by generations of students. A creative and outstanding teacher who sensitively helped students to improve their oral expression, she also directed them in a number of dramas including *The Crucible*, *Threepenny Opera* and *The Imaginary Invalid*, which were greatly appreciated by participants and audience alike.

Over these years the college owed much to those who served faithfully as ancillary staff. When the bursar, Dick Hobson, returned to schoolteaching in 1974, for the first time in its history the college was served by someone trained in accountancy. John Bree had been a company secretary in Northampton, and for the next twenty years he combined the work of the bursar with great entrepreneurial skills. The bookshop, begun as a result of student initiative in 1973, was developed, and with his nose for a bargain many students' curacy houses were carpeted and furnished. He also acquired further properties off campus to house married families, and his wife, Sue, took over the duties of housekeeper, which for some time had been undertaken by Joy Wheaton. When the Wheatons returned to the college Joy had been pleased to resume the leadership of the 'Monday Fellowship' she had founded fifteen years previously. She also started a regular lunchtime meeting for those staff wives who were free, and shared in the pastoral care of the increasing number of wives on and off the campus, including the NSM wives. Experience with the full-time students had taught the value of the annual wives' and fiancées' weekend, and though changing circumstances had made that redundant, it was found valuable to run such a weekend for those on the part-time course.

Reference has been made to the constant demands of caring for the property and those who served as maintenance men. During this period the college was faithfully served by Coleman, who could put his hand to almost anything, and whose knowledge of the inner workings of the internal combustion engine benefited many a student and staff member. He and his wife, Georgie, had moved into the Lodge. When in 1984 the college ran a coach to evangelist Luis Palau's meetings they both came and committed their lives to Christ.

God worked in the lives of those who came to work at Oak Hill. The gardener, Peter Lane, was originally a hairdresser in an exclusive West End shop who normally paid someone else to do his garden at home. In 1981 he had given up his business and was looking for future direction when John Bree asked him to come to the college to help with some decorating. His first job was painting the chapel. He was so overwhelmed by a sense of the presence of God that he decided to stay on. In the year of the silver jubilee he was invited to help in the gardens for three months. He did so well that on being invited to stay on a permanent basis he replied, 'I'm not really a gardener but if you have faith in me, I'll give it a try.'[33] Peter's hairdressing skills were also much appreciated and the appearance of the staff improved dramatically. Most significantly, Peter became a Christian at Earls Court in the 1989 Billy Graham crusade, and his story of how God has worked in his life has been an inspiration to others.

While some met God for the first time while working at college, others met their future spouses. Miriam Cragg, who had served as secretary to Maurice Wood, left the staff on her marriage to Andrew Dow, who had been a student, and her place was taken by Judi Dent, who had been a member of the congregation at St Paul's, Onslow Square. Judi followed the tradition of marrying a student, Barry Brewer, as did the assistant secretary, Gillian Hill, becoming Mrs Stephen Jones. During his fifteen years at Oak Hill Wheaton conducted no fewer than eight weddings of staff members in the college chapel or in their home churches: he joked that he liked to appoint young ladies with potential, which his students were quick to spot. Judi Dent was followed by Joan Atkinson, Linda Vollor (who became Mrs Ginn), Sheila Saunders, Valerie Arnold (who became Mrs Myhill), Christine Money (who became Mrs Cheesman) and Terry Froggatt (who became Mrs Atkins), each of whom shouldered an increasing burden as the volume of secretarial work grew with the requirements of the CNAA. Sue Morley, an

[33] Interview with the Lanes.

answer to prayer in the kitchen, also became the answer to a student's prayers and left the college as Mrs Massey. She was followed by Jean-Anne Bovington, who met her husband, Richard Nagioff, through the young people's group at Christ Church, Cockfosters. Others who kept the college fed during these years were Judith Jamieson, Margaret Duncan, Mary Cumming and Tony Tyler, who will all be remembered with gratitude. An interesting picture of 'life below stairs' (secretaries and cooks had accommodation in the basement of the main house) is given in an article written by 'Les Girls' in the 1973 *Oak Leaf.* They concluded:

> Naturally there are problems living and working in a community, and being conscious of our own failings we have to learn to love and forgive each other. The seven of us find however that despite the diversity of our backgrounds and nationalities we can enjoy a real unity in a common love and faith in the Lord.[34]

Reference to the different nationalities reflects the fact that at this stage the college was still employing au pairs from different European countries to help with domestic and kitchen work. This was phased out in 1973, when the decision was taken to recruit more part-time staff from the locality, and over the years the college built up a faithful band of ladies who came in daily from the neighbourhood. Each day began, as it had from the earliest days of the college, with staff prayers, led by a member of staff or a student, and over the years several came to faith or had their faith strengthened.

In the summer of 1972 the college welcomed possibly its most famous student. Cliff Richard had nailed his Christian colours to the mast and was finding the experience of being quizzed about his faith very draining. In summer 1972 he cleared his diary for two months in order to come to the college and deepen his grasp of doctrinal and ethical issues. Because he only had a limited amount of time the staff decided to give their celebrated student a

---

[34] *The Oak Leaf*, 1973, pp. 10, 19.

series of private tutorials, and a study in the college was put at his disposal. Margie Lane, who at the time was working as a cleaner on that section of the old wing, was teased unmercifully that she would wear out the linoleum outside his study. The college was rewarded when Cliff sang at the following Christmas concert. Summing up the benefit of those weeks Cliff wrote: 'The world thinks that Christianity can't take a deep probe – I know the world is wrong because, if I gained nothing else from Oak Hill, I did gain the knowledge that the deeper one digs the more there is to believe and all the more reasons for believing.'[35]

Robert Runcie introduced another unusual student to the college. He had been asked by the Archbishop of Canterbury to be responsible for building relationships with the Eastern Orthodox churches, and in 1979 he spent part of a sabbatical in Jerusalem and Asia Minor, visiting the Ecumenical Patriarch at Istanbul. The patriarch had expressed the desire that one of his staff, the Great Archdeacon,[36] should spend a year at an Anglican college in order to foster understanding between the two communions. Daringly, Runcie had suggested that he had a theological college in his diocese that might introduce the Orthodox to a side of the Church of England they might not otherwise encounter, and wrote to ask whether Wheaton could take the Great Archdeacon for a special one-year course. When Archdeacon Kyrillos arrived he became a very popular figure among the college body, thoroughly enjoying Oak Hill's emphasis on the Bible and informing the college of Orthodox belief and practice. He explored English idiom and loved quoting sayings, telling the principal that he could not stop to talk as he had 'the other fish to fry'. The mind boggled as members of the college foresaw a future ecumenical version of the Lord's Prayer ending with 'for the kingdom, the power and the glory are yours until the cows come home'! The experiment

---

[35] *The Oak Leaf*, 1973, pp. 7, 8.

[36] In the Orthodox tradition bishops are appointed direct from among the deacons, and the Great Archdeacon is the next in line waiting to be appointed to a bishopric.

was a success. The next year the patriarch sent Dimitrios, the next senior of his deacons, to Oak Hill for two terms.

Subsequently, through the offices of the Dean of St Albans, Peter Moore, the college was able to widen its ecumenical contacts with continental Christians. Moore had visited former Czechoslovakia during the days of communist rule, and had arranged that a pastor in the Moravian church should be allowed to come for three months to study at an Anglican college. He approached Oak Hill, who once again welcomed this further contact. The dean explained to Wheaton that before the arrangement could be finalized, the college would have to be visited by two cultural attaches from the Czech embassy, who would in fact be agents of the KGB. The principal was in a quandary: he wanted the visit to be totally spontaneous and natural. However, he feared that if he simply introduced the visitors as members of the Czech embassy making arrangements for a pastor from their country to study, some students might assume that they would be Christian and zealously attempt to get them to smuggle some Bibles back with them. So he warned the college about the true situation, and lunchtime passed without any untoward happenings. However, when it came to showing the visitors what sort of facilities the college could offer, the principal found that an additional letter had been added to the signs of all the men's lavatories to read 'AGENTS'! The college benefited from this contact with a church under oppression when Bohumil Kejr, the pastor in question, was able to give his peers an insight into what it was like to be a Christian minister under communist oppression. He also reminded them how privileged they were to have opportunities to serve in chaplaincies in the forces, hospitals and prisons, all denied in his country.

Throughout this period the college continued to welcome EFAC bursars and other clergy from the Third World, many of whom returned to theological teaching or senior positions in their own churches. Isaac Namango, Stanley Kashillingi, Daniel Zindo and Samson Mwaluda all became bishops, and Silvanus Wani was elected as Archbishop of Uganda.

PERSONALITY PROFILE

Alphaeus Ndebele is a clergyman in the diocese of Zululand, whose bishop sent him to Oak Hill in 1973 to be 'evangelicalized' following his experience of conversion. In an article in the 1974 *Oak Leaf* Alphaeus describes how he was attracted to ordination by the splendid dignity of the fine vestments and liturgies, but throughout his five years of training found nothing he could do about the burden of his sins.

In his first parochial charge he was afflicted with a paralysis down one side, and a member of a prayer group challenged him to reject formal, empty Christianity and claim the promise of 1 John 5:13: 'I write these things to you who believe in the name of the Son of God so that you may know that you have eternal life.' As Alphaeus broke down and confessed his sins with tears he found that his disability disappeared and he was whole again – more so than he had ever been before. He concluded, 'Now I just thank the Lord that I am a free pastor: free from the burden of my sins because of what Jesus did on the cross: free from the torment of paralysis, and free from the trappings of a dead religiosity. Free to preach the gospel of Jesus Christ.'

With so many wives living on campus, coming into lectures and joining in activities it was inevitable that the question of opening the college to female students should arise. In previous decades women training for parish ministry as deaconesses had been catered for at separate institutions, but the establishment of Trinity College had seen the bringing together of men and women for co-education, while Cranmer Hall had been co-educational for some years. ACCM appeared to be in favour of this development, and the CNAA was firmly of the opinion that the college must offer equal opportunities if it was to gain recognition by them.

A report of a working party under the chairmanship of the Bishop of Guildford[37] had favoured the establishment of regional

[37] *Theological Training: A Policy for the Future*, 1977 (GS Misc 57).

theological institutes that should serve the church in a number of ways, including ensuring 'that men and women in every diocese can be offered the opportunity to train for their appropriate form of ministry, whether as lay persons or clergy'. At their meeting the following May the college council passed a resolution 'That the council asks the trustees to accept in principle the admission of women students to the college courses.' In prior debate some of the members present wished it to be made plain that female students should not be accepted for ordination training (at that stage this was not possible anyway), but the college was keen to be on the same footing as the other colleges training women for work as deaconesses and accredited lay ministers. However, the trust deed allowed the principal to admit only male students up to the age of thirty-five. An approach was made to the trustees, who agreed that they would apply to the Charity Commissioners to have the relevant clause in the foundation document defining the trustees' powers amended. The trustees were subsequently allowed:

> To found and endow control and carry on or permit to be carried on upon any convenient part or parts of the landed property of the Trust in England Theological Training Schools and Theological Colleges for the purpose of training *men and women (of any age)* for ordination *or other ministry* in the Church of England *or other Protestant denominations who* are without adequate means of paying the expenses of their training *(whether or not receiving or being qualified to receive grants or other assistance from other sources).*[38]

A further requirement laid down before the college was allowed to admit ACCM-sponsored women was that there should be a female member of staff available for their pastoral needs. An arrangement was made whereby Anne Waghorn, secretary in the CPAS Vocation and Ministry Department, who lived locally, would become an associate staff member, sharing on a regular basis in teaching and chapel and pastoral ministry.

[38] Kingham Hill trust deed as revised March 1984.

When Anne moved on, her place was taken by Deaconess Jean Howard, who came into residence while studying for her London BD.

One of the first female students was Jeanette Power, who studied as a non-ordinand alongside her ordinand husband: she went on to be made deaconess and has since been ordained. The first woman officially sponsored by ACCM was Mary Abbott, who had spinal problems, and often spent time on the floor during lectures. She remembers the debate within the student body over female students:

> David Wheaton chaired a long, and rather stormy, meeting, at which many of the arguments I had heard advanced in nursing as to why men should not come into the profession were being advanced in slightly more theological garb against women coming to study alongside the men. After some time David gently pointed out that they already had three women working with them, but they ignored him and carried on until some time later one student remarked that 'we already have Jeanette and Mary and one other student' (whose name I cannot recall),[39] adding words to the effect 'but they don't count'. And so, after some further discussion, thankfully for women now, they agreed to have us.[40]

Four years later Mary returned to the college as tutor for female students.

The college was gaining a reputation as a place for married students only, making it quite hard to attract a proper balance of single and married students as well as women and men. Writing in the 1979 *Oak Leaf* vice-senior student Roger Dixon charted that the ratio of married to single students was 3:1. Dixon commented:

> Oak Hill's reputation in this respect has been responsible for a number of single men avoiding the college. There is no need for such

---

[39] Probably Jane Blakely.
[40] Account written by Mary Abbott, April 2001.

> action. The accommodation for single men is excellent. Graduates need not fear that the courses at Oak Hill are too non-academic. The new degree course is evidence that the college seeks to maintain good academic standards while still catering for the needs of those with less background of study. The truth is that married and single ordinands can benefit from living alongside one another, learning from one another's experiences. As a recent graduate I have benefited enormously from fellowship with older, married men from a wide variety of backgrounds.[41]

Sport drew single and married students together – rugby, soccer, tennis, cricket, hockey, squash, table-tennis and croquet were enjoyed. The 1974 and 1975 seasons saw the Oak Hill soccer team victorious – it had the advantage of ex-professional John Kilford (Derby County and Leeds United) playing in the team.

A number of significant changes occurred in the chapel during the Wheaton years. In their report the 1973 inspectors made the comment that 'in this very united community it seemed contrary to the ethos of the college that the old hierarchical practice is retained in chapel of the separation of staff and students, with the staff reserved seats at the back'.[42] This practice had enabled successive principals to keep an eye on who wasn't in chapel. By this time compulsory attendance had been replaced by a system whereby each student discussed and agreed with his personal tutor what rule of life he would follow in this respect, and in regular sessions with his tutor he would review how well or otherwise the rule was being kept.

Perhaps the most obvious change was the provision of the tapestry hanging for the east wall of the chapel. Hugh Dibbens, a former student and part-time tutor, had come back to preach and commented that the college might be the headquarters of the League of Empire Loyalists (a reference to the coronation wall-hanging in the chapel and the portrait of the Queen that Wood had introduced in the staffroom). Inspectors had previously

---

[41] *The Oak Leaf*, 1979, pp. 16–17.

[42] 1973 ACCM inspection report.

commented on the lack of any distinctively Christian symbolism in the chapel. The college community decided to raise the funds for a suitable hanging. The Benedictine sisters at Vita et Pax were asked if they could produce something based on the college's motto (2 Cor. 4:5). The tapestry, based on the cross in the form of the water welling up to eternal life, and with the early Christian creed of 'Jesus Christ is Lord' at its centre, all in a blaze of colour, was hung in the chapel in 1975, and dedicated by the Archbishop of York during the course of the quiet weekend with which each term traditionally began. The sisters from the priory were invited to the ceremony, thus strengthening a friendship. Their prior, Dom Edmund Jones, was a regular contributor to the liturgical studies course, where he spoke on modern developments in Roman Catholic liturgy. He and the principal each knew where they stood, and respected each other's views without being able to agree, making for a good and frank interchange.

This period also saw the introduction first of the Series 3 of Alternative Services and in 1980 the *Alternative Service Book*. The staff were keen to encourage students to use these new services in creative and imaginative ways. The chapel furniture lent itself to being re-arranged so that the community could experience worship in the round. Provision was made for experimental as well as informal worship (the 1973 inspectors found the community using forms from the Church of South India during their visit), while there was still regular use of the *Book of Common Prayer*. Some members of General Synod had been complaining that the colleges were producing ordinands who had little experience of the church's liturgical heritage, but Oak Hill recognized the importance of maintaining its use alongside the more modern forms.

In 1982 morning worship was moved from the traditional 7.20 a.m. slot to 8.30 a.m. to allow married men with families to breakfast at home and help get the children to school. Many feared that the time for quiet between chapel and breakfast would be lost, but it was felt that it was more realistic to let students create their own discipline of private prayer and Bible reading, as they would have to in a parish.

An example of Oxbridge influence on the college had been the requirement for staff and students to wear gowns for lectures, meals and chapel. This, coupled with the honours boards, tended to give the wrong impression to potential students who feared that the college would be far too formal and 'prep-schooly'. Therefore in the mid-seventies the boards disappeared and gowns were no longer required except for the one formal academic occasion of the year when degrees and diplomas were conferred. Similarly, whereas previously formalities were observed in addressing staff, Christian names became familiar. In an increasingly egalitarian age it was felt that the awarding of prizes, particularly for homiletics, was somewhat invidious. One of the prizes displaced was that for reading. The competition had been used as an opportunity to invite a celebrity judge. In the final year of the competition comedienne Joyce Grenfell acted as judge and was so amusing that many found it hard to keep a straight face in her company. Later in the year *The Oak Leaf* published her moving testimony about the place of prayer in her life.[43]

In Wheaton's early days the college had had a number of A level students. As the demand for places for ordinands and students on the diploma and degree course grew, it proved less easy to cater for them. Staff also had less time for teaching at A level, and needed help from outside, which was not economical. A level students were directed to Romsey House in Cambridge, where one of the college council, Canon Mark Ruston, could exercise a pastoral ministry over them.

A popular innovation was the introduction of an 'Incumbents' Day' each summer term. Those incumbents who would be receiving curates later in the year could visit the college to meet their prospective colleague. They would be told about the training their new curate had been receiving, and sample something of the community in which they had been living.

---

[43] *The Oak Leaf*, 1974, pp. 8–10.

During the mid-seventies the garden party had been replaced by an annual open day to which visitors were invited, and displays of work and activities were arranged for them. Following CNAA validation it was recognized that the big public occasion each year should now be a graduation ceremony. This began in January 1979 when the first diplomas were presented by Archbishop Coggan. 'The practice also began of an annual evening lecture or lectures open to the public and given by a scholar who would live in the college for a week. The first of these was given in December 1980 by the external examiner, Professor James Atkinson, entitled 'Justification by Faith: A Truth for our Times'.[44] Subsequent lecturers included Dr Peter Kuzmič, Director/President of the Biblical Theological Institute in Zagreb, and Professor James Torrance.

Successive inspectors had drawn attention to the lack of a centrally placed common room. Wheaton had on several occasions brought the matter to the college council. They finally agreed that a purpose-built common room linking the student wings with the main building should be explored, but that the members of the college should be responsible for some of the fundraising. It was agreed that this would be a suitable way of commemorating the college's golden jubilee in 1982. The community responded to the challenge, and the new facilities were dedicated by the Archbishop of Canterbury. A commemorative plaque had been commissioned. However, the archbishop's name had been spelt as if it was ROBERTA KRUNCIE instead of Robert A.K. Runcie! Fortunately it was possible to do the necessary doctoring in time. On this day the college was able to announce a first – former student Michael Baughen had been appointed Bishop of Chester, thereby becoming the first Old Oak to become an English diocesan bishop.

Unlike the silver jubilee, the whole day's proceedings were held on the campus. A marquee was erected on the front field, and after dedicating the new premises the archbishop conducted the conferment ceremony. A buffet lunch was then provided in the dining hall for the 600 guests. After lunch a thanksgiving

---

[44] Published as chapter 3 of J.I. Packer (ed.), *Here We Stand.*

service of Holy Communion was held in the marquee. Former principal Maurice Wood presided and former vice-principal and now visitor, John Taylor (who had taken over that function when succeeding Runcie as Bishop of St Albans) preached, and members of the college past and present who wished to do so renewed their ordination vows or commitment to Christian service. True to their tradition, the members of the college used the opportunity of having the marquee in the grounds to lay on an evangelistic concert on the evening of the jubilee.

As far back as the silver jubilee Stibbs had expressed the idea of the staff producing a symposium of essays that reflected the college's stance and concern. Much to his disappointment that never materialized, but the staff rose to the idea of such a venture for the golden jubilee. Hodder and Stoughton were willing to commission such a publication, and James Packer, who had begun his teaching career at Oak Hill, agreed to contribute a chapter, as did George Carey, who was at that time principal of Trinity College, Bristol. The first public lecture given by Professor Atkinson was included, and other contributions came from the current teaching staff.[45]

Like his predecessors, the principal received considerable support and encouragement from the members of the college council, and especially from G.F. Rocke and Douglas Scott, who chaired it during these years. Rocke retired when taking over the chairmanship of the Kingham Hill trustees from the Hon. T.G. Roche, and served the college faithfully in that further capacity. It was appropriate that after his death a thanksgiving service was held in the college chapel in January 1997. Scott had been introduced to the trust and college council initially for his farming expertise, so it must have been galling for him that one of his first actions on the council was to agree to the closure of the farm. However, with his keen Christian commitment and involvement as a member of the General Synod he quickly gained a grasp of the technicalities of a theological college.

---

[45] Published as Packer (ed.), *Here We Stand*.

From past experience Wheaton knew that tensions and problems could arise between the staff and students of the college and their governing body when decisions were taken at a distance by people who did not appear to be familiar with the situation on the ground. It was agreed that the summer term meeting of the council, which had for some years been held at the college, should take the form of an overnight residential occasion, thereby enabling council members to join the college in worship and meals, meet staff and students informally, and think about future developments without being under pressure for time.

At the meeting of 1973 the council considered a paper on their constitution. This suggested that the senior and vice-senior student in each year should become *ex officio* members of the college council. This possibility had been discussed the previous term with the visiting ACCM inspectors, who were to comment in their report:

> This [student representation] seemed to us a natural development in a community in which there is fullest consultation between staff and students on every aspect of their common life and work. Since there is, at present, no pressure from the student body for such representation, it seemed to us an appropriate time for the council to consider the possibility.[46]

Many of the older students currently in training had been in business or the professions and were the sort of people who, in other circumstances, were likely to have been invited to become council members or trustees. The council agreed to invite the senior and vice-senior students to be in attendance as non-voting members (as at that stage were the vice-principal and bursar), with the proviso that they could be requested to withdraw when any confidential matters concerning staff or students came up for discussion. Following the reorganization of the colleges in the late sixties it had been felt by ACCM and the colleges that it would be helpful if an ACCM staff member were to be in attendance at each

[46] 1973 ACCM inspection report.

governing body. Accordingly the Oak Hill council had had John Reading OBE from the ACCM staff attending, and over the years he was of great help in explaining the implications of various ACCM reports to his colleagues on the council. As the links with Trent Park College and then Middlesex Polytechnic developed first of all David Lovatt, senior tutor of Trent Park, and subsequently Michael Edwards, deputy director of the polytechnic, were also invited to join the council.

It was seen as important that there be at least one female member of the council. In 1976 Annette Farrer joined, making a most helpful contribution as an incumbent's wife and formerly a staff wife at Clifton Theological College. For some time she was the sole female member, but in 1980 the General Synod determined that in view of the large proportion of its budget spent on ministerial training it should appoint two of its members to each of the college councils. Accordingly, in 1981 Pat Nappin and Daphne Wales (members from Chelmsford and St Albans dioceses respectively) were welcomed to the council as appointees.

With the resignation of Peter Johnston and Douglas Clark, two Old Oaks who had faithfully served from the days of the management committee, it was agreed that the Old Oaks should be invited to elect two of their number to the council. A request was made in 1981 for all the members of staff to be granted membership of the body, arguing that there should be scope for the expression of differing views on matters where the staff were divided. This would have been in line with what had been the practice at St John's, Nottingham, but the ACCM representative pointed out that they had been criticized for having an imbalance of membership. After debate it was agreed that two members of the academic staff should attend each council meeting, to be nominated for each occasion by their colleagues in the light of any particular matters on the agenda. In every two-year period each member should have been able to attend at least one meeting. A further development at the same time dispensed with the distinction between voting and non-voting membership, though the previously agreed proviso for students to withdraw when required was maintained. The verdict of the 1981 inspectors was:

> The widened membership of the council is already proving of great value. We were impressed by the way in which student members have been integrated into the governing body. It is obvious that the council goes out of its way to be supportive of the college, and there is ample evidence of good personal relationships between council members and staff of the college. We particularly commend the annual residential meeting of the council at the college in this respect; also for the opportunity it gives to consider the more long-term aspects of the college's development. It is clear that the whole development policy of the college is a joint exercise in which the governing body, college staff and academic board are working in fruitful partnership.[47]

One other structural innovation introduced was a college committee. Its brief was to look at all aspects of community life, and it brought in representative members of the ancillary staff, staff and student wives living on the campus, and any others who were involved in the corporate aspects of college life. This proved a valuable forum for the expression of ideas and bringing into the open any frustrations felt about the whole experience of community living.

During this time the APM course had also been making steady progress. In 1971 there were just two participants: Stanley Smerdon, headmaster of a school in Bournemouth, who expected to exercise his ministry mainly in the parish at weekends; and Fred Williams, taking the course with a view to retiring to the west country and exercising a post-retirement ministry. One stipulation for the course was that it should have a steering committee to act as its governing body. After consultation the bishops of London, Chelmsford and St Albans (whose dioceses would provide the main catchment area for the course) approved a constitution whereby they each appointed two clergy representatives from each of their dioceses, together with a representative nominated by Southwark diocese. These would join with the moderator, principal and registrar to form the committee.

---

[47] 1981 ACCM inspection report.

The steering committee met at Oak Hill for the first time on 4 July 1972. In his concern to put everyone at ease the chairman (Frank Chadwick, Bishop of Barking) greeted the principal with the words 'Don't worry, Wheatflake, we're on your side.' Discussion then centred on how far it would be possible for a course centred on Oak Hill to cater for all traditions, and members looked to the principal to see how far he would be prepared to broaden his staff. Help came from an unexpected quarter, in that a St Albans representative, Director of Education Geoffrey Lang, said that he knew his bishop would not wish Oak Hill to be anything other than what it had always stood for. It was agreed that while it would not be reasonable to require the college to alter its own tradition the hope was expressed that it might be possible to set up the kind of course that would appeal to a wider range of people. Further thought was given to the function of the committee in the light of its relation to the college council and to the trust, and in the light of the parameters imposed by using the college's facilities it was decided to adopt the title of the 'Oak Hill Auxiliary Pastoral Ministry Course Steering Committee'.[48] It was also decided that the chairman should always be one of the diocesan representatives, rotating between the dioceses on a two-yearly basis.

A further requirement for such courses was that each should have a moderator responsible for interviewing the candidates on their progress and conducting an annual assessment board, which would include course staff and the director of ordinands of each candidate's diocese. Oak Hill was fortunate in that before his departure Wood had arranged for the appointment of Canon Frank Colquhoun to this post. Colquhoun was a clear evangelical who had been the first principal of the Southwark Ordination Course, an appointment designed by the bishop (Mervyn Stockwood) to gain the confidence of evangelicals in the diocese, and was to bring the benefit of his experience gained in training men on a part-time course. As well as conducting the annual

---

[48] This title was subsequently changed to Advisory Committee and then Management Committee.

assessment board, the moderator visited the course two or three times each year during the residential weekends, sitting in on sessions with the students, and making time to see each one individually. This gave those from other traditions opportunity to say frankly how they found the experience, and their views could be communicated to the principal and staff.

The students were expected to submit essays and achieve a standard comparable to those written by full-time students on the essay scheme. Students came to the college one evening a week during term time and were expected to attend eight residential weekends per year together with an annual summer school, usually timetabled during the school half-term for the benefit of teachers attending the course. While some of those training were hoping to use their ministry mainly in the workplace, most were expecting to be assisting in parishes, and subsequent history has shown that a significant number have transferred to full-time ministry and become incumbents. So the home parish was seen as a key factor in the overall pattern of training, and the course sought to enter into a partnership with the clergy of those parishes, who were appointed in most cases as pastoral supervisors. Regular meetings were arranged for these supervisors to visit the college and discuss progress.

By 1977 there were twenty men on the course, and following discussion in official circles it had been decided to rename the course NSM (Non-Stipendiary Ministry). Pytches had replaced Silvester as registrar, and the moderator was Canon Gordon Hewitt of Chelmsford cathedral. In his 1977 report the moderator spoke of the gratitude to members of Oak Hill for acceptance of NSM candidates into their fellowship; of pride of achievement in an unfamiliar learning situation on the part of first-year candidates; and of continuing progress on the part of those in the second and third years. He also stated that several of the first-year students from churches of different worship traditions seemed to be thoroughly at home in the services in the college chapel, and there was no evidence in his interviews of anyone feeling out of place on the course on grounds of churchmanship. The meeting that received that report also noted the mutual benefits of NSM training being carried out at a theological college where there was a worshipping community of full-time ordinands.[49]

When Hewitt retired in 1979 the Bishop of Bedford (Alec Graham, who had been warden of Lincoln Theological College) followed him in the role, as a deliberate move to involve someone from a clearly different tradition. On Graham's move to Newcastle upon Tyne the Bishop of Kensington, Mark Santer, formerly the principal of Westcott House, became moderator, and when he moved to Birmingham he was followed by Dr David Hope, formerly principal of St Stephen's House, Oxford, and later to become Archbishop of York.

In its early days the course was used as a resource by dioceses where there was as yet no convenient local facility. In 1973 Glyn Morgan from Peterborough joined the course, travelling in weekly from Barton Seagrave, near Kettering, Northamptonshire. Recognizing the problems for people living at such a distance, in 1975 the course approached the bishops of Chelmsford and St Albans about the possibility of an extension course in the Chelmsford or Bedford area. St Albans was in fact beginning to explore the possibility of setting up his own ministerial training course, but Chelmsford expressed great interest in view of the fact that there was a number of potential candidates in the Colchester area of his diocese. A Colchester extension was set up. Oak Hill staff travelled there each week to give lectures, and the students concerned came to college for the residential periods. Unfortunately the supply of candidates did not last for long, and the extension was terminated by the end of the seventies.

The course gained an ecumenical dimension by training candidates for the ministry of the United Reformed Church (Michael Hensman and Jim Gascoigne), and became co-educational with the arrival of Doreen Fossett, who trained to become a Baptist minister. As the course grew and developed it was felt that the principal should not carry so much of the responsibility for it, and

[49] Minutes of Oak Hill NSM advisory committee, 24 June 1977.

a recommendation to this effect was made by the moderator in 1982, and underlined by the inspection team in the same year. Accordingly Roger Cowley was appointed NSM course leader, and proved to be most assiduous in his new duties, particularly in visiting the candidates in their homes and meeting their PCCs to explain their particular position and the pressures they would be facing. Links between the college and the course were further strengthened by the appointment of a member of the college council to the advisory committee, and a reciprocal arrangement whereby a member of the committee was co-opted to the council. Strangely enough, although throughout the 1970s there had been a representative from ACCM on the college council, it was not until 1980 that they were invited to nominate a representative to the committee, and that was at the committee's initiative.

The golden jubilee was a forceful reminder to the principal that he had been in the driving seat for eleven years. He was approaching his mid-fifties, beyond which he was not likely to be considered for another post, and knew that it would not be good for him or the college if he were to stay on until retirement. Having introduced more changes into the college than he had ever envisaged, he found that he was becoming resistant to further suggestions for improvements being put forward by his colleagues, and he knew that was a danger sign.

In 1985 he was offered the living of Christ Church, Ware, Hertfordshire, and arranged to leave in February 1986. Thus ended twenty-three years of service to the college, eight as junior tutor and fifteen as principal. His final report to the college council recorded that during his principalship 425 men and women had left the college for a variety of Christian ministries. They comprised 407 men and 18 women, 356 from the full-time college and 69 from the NSM course: 400 went into Anglican ministry and 25 into other forms of Christian ministry, 107 with the Oak Hill degree and 86 with the diploma.

7

New Priorities and New Directions (1986–1991)

> We were pleased to meet with the principal elect, and welcome the gifts, particularly those deriving from extensive parochial experience, which he will bring to the college ... The college is at present developing thoughts concerning 'mixed mode' training and is awaiting the arrival of [the] new principal who will bring to the college new priorities and new direction.[1]

So reported the inspection team that visited the college a month after Gordon Bridger was nominated as the fifth principal. The Bridger years were indeed a time when the college was blessed with 'new priorities and new direction'. There were new buildings, new staff members, new modules, a new validation, new programmes and some creative new approaches to training. However, it was also a time of challenges and controversies: the existence of the college was threatened and the principal had to deal with a series of controversial matters that threatened to divide the community. Two of the major achievements of the previous administration, the relationship with CNAA and the part-time course, came to an end, so the college was faced with the challenge of finding a replacement for CNAA validation and establishing a working relationship with the new North Thames Ministerial Training Course (NTMTC).

---

[1] ACCM inspection report, February 1986.

Because there was such a dramatic difference between two halves of what might be called the Bridger decade his principalship is covered in two chapters. The first examines the busy but successful first five years, while the second describes the challenges and controversies that plagued the college in the last half of the Bridger decade, and the way in which the college met those challenges.

When Bridger was asked to apply for the principalship he was, according to his own statement, very surprised, because he did not feel his previous background qualified him for the post. He had been a parish minister since his ordination in 1956 and had no experience either as a teacher or as an administrator in higher education. After curacies under Wood at Islington and at the Round Church in Cambridge he had held incumbencies at St Mary's Church, West Kensington, and St Thomas's Episcopal Church in Edinburgh, and was rector of Holy Trinity, Norwich, when invited to apply for the post. According to his own testimony he was nonplussed: 'To be honest, I hadn't thought at all about being a principal ... I loved preaching and teaching in the local church. I wasn't interested in leaving it, but I thought it was a serious enough question to consider.'[2] But complications regarding a new curate and his daughter's education stood in the way of Bridger leaving Holy Trinity, and so 'the whole idea of being a principal was put completely out of my mind'.[3]

A number of other qualified candidates had applied for the post and five were shortlisted. On 18 October 1985, after meeting all the candidates, the staff could not agree as to whom they would recommend to the selection committee of the college council. Eventually they recommended a candidate to the trustees. When in due course the trustees met, they did not appoint the recommended candidate. The search began anew and Timothy Dudley-Smith, the Bishop of Thetford, who initially encouraged Bridger to apply, now asked him to reconsider. Bridger reminded him of all the things that stood in the way of his applying in the first

---

[2] Interview with the Bridgers, 14 May 1999.

[3] Ibid.

place, and pointed out that he could not possibly come for a year. However, he was persuaded to come for interview and was surprised to find out that he was the only candidate. Bridger left the interview conscious that if he were to be called to the post it must be with the unanimous support of both the staff and the college council. On 10 January 1986 the trustees also 'resolved unanimously to offer the appointment of principal of Oak Hill College to the Reverend Canon Gordon Bridger such appointment to take effect on 1 February 1987'. During the ensuing year Field agreed to serve as acting principal and Heinze as acting vice-principal. Bridger was to be available one day a week for college business and requested a month's sabbatical in the spring of 1986 to prepare himself for his future responsibilities.[4]

Although happy with the outcome, not everybody was pleased with the way the appointment had been made. In a special meeting held a week later the college council expressed its concerns about the procedures followed and presented a number of suggestions for the future. The bishops' inspectors who visited the college in February 1986 also expressed concern that the relationship between the council and the trust needed clarification. In May 1987 the House of Bishops asked the council 'to look again at their relationship with the trustees with a view to drawing up a formal constitution'.[5] It was agreed that while the trustees had the sole right of appointing any new principal, the council was charged with appointing the selection panel, shortlisting and interviewing candidates, and presenting to the trust their advice on which candidates 'would be acceptable and which would be unacceptable'. If the trustees declined to appoint, the panel was to begin a new search.[6] In October 1988 a draft constitution describing the procedure was presented to the college council with a covering letter explaining that 'while the trust deed allows delegation by the trustees, the trustees must retain ultimate control both under

---

[4] Minutes of Kingham Hill trust, 10 January 1986.

[5] ACCM inspection report, February 1986; minutes of college council, 20 May 1987.

[6] Ibid., 21 October 1986.

the general law and because of certain entrenched provisions of the trust deed'. It was also pointed out that 'though the trustees have the right (and in some cases the duty) of veto, the decision (e.g. on appointment of principal) must be the result of consideration and choice by the council and not primarily by the trustees'.[7]

There were still some church officials who were not satisfied, objecting particularly to the provision that the trustees might make an appointment 'other than the council's recommended candidate' if the normal procedure did not produce results 'within a time scale convenient for the proper and effective running of the college'. This was, of course, precisely what had happened in Bridger's case. At the council meeting in February 1989 the chief secretary of ACCM pointed out that the bishops would be likely to question that provision. In response it was agreed to amend the wording to make it clear that the trustees would act only to avoid anything prejudicial to the running of the college.[8]

The long debate over the relationship of the trust and the council coincided with major changes in the college community and environment. While Field normally preferred to remain in the background, he proved an exceedingly capable leader and administrator. His year as acting principal began with the inspection, after which a submission had to be prepared for a validation visit by the CNAA, which took place in February 1987. In addition three new staff members were appointed, a new programme begun and a significant amount of building work undertaken.

The inspectors were very thorough in their task, perceptive in their recommendations, and sensitive to the fact that the college was in a period of transition. They were impressed with many aspects of college life, and complimented the 'highly competent and approachable staff' as well as the excellent teaching they observed, which included the use of video, extensive handouts and visiting lecturers. They were pleased with both the CNAA link and the association with Middlesex Polytechnic, but they

---

[7] Ibid., 11 October 1988.
[8] Ibid., 5 February 1989.

were concerned that the administrative load on staff members resulting from the requirements of CNAA was particularly heavy. They commented favourably on the quality of the written work submitted by students, and they interviewed or spoke informally to a number of students who provided them with some very honest reactions, which also found their way into the report. Finally, they commented positively on chapel worship, which they found 'impressive, well planned and well conducted'.[9]

However, the inspectors were also perceptive in noting weaknesses. In addition to the recommendation that the relationship between the trust and the council be clarified, the report contained seven other recommendations. Although chapel attendance was considered adequate at the morning service, the inspectors noted that only 'about ten students' attended the prayer meeting, so they recommended that 'an internal review of the pattern of corporate worship be undertaken, considering both its timing and its nature to ensure a more full participation by the college body'. The concern about the heavy administrative responsibilities carried by the staff led them to call for an administrative review and consideration of 'whether the functioning of the college would be improved by the appointment of a person with professional skills in academic administration'. The tutorial system, about which the 1981 inspectors had expressed concern, was criticized for a somewhat 'haphazard' approach, and they repeated the recommendation from that report that a part-time librarian be appointed. They also believed that the pastoral training offered by the college needed some reconsideration and reform, calling for 'a thorough re-appraisal of the pastoral component in training', and that the role of pastoral supervisors be defined more clearly, 'giving them clear aims and objectives for their task'. The inspectors also noted in their conversations with students that there was a lack of 'concerned theological argument', so they recommended that 'steps be taken to encourage more self-criticism and critical reflection in the college'. In encouraging student wives to be more involved in college life it was suggested that 'soundings be taken as to the appropriateness of

---

[9] ACCM inspection report, February 1986.

having some formal sessions for wives and crèche facilities provided for the children'.[10] In less than two years most of the matters had been dealt with effectively. In November 1987 the chairman of the inspectors, Brian Smith, in a follow-up visit, congratulated the college 'on the way in which it has addressed itself to the recommendations of our report'.[11] Each one had been satisfactorily met.

Newly appointed members of staff were very much involved in meeting the concerns expressed in the recommendations. In the twenty-one months between the inspection and the return visit three members left and six new staff were appointed. Jean Howard finished her course and was replaced by Mary Abbott as women's tutor. She knew well the challenges of a largely male environment. The women found in Mary a sympathetic, wise and strong person who was a great help to those who found the Oak Hill environment particularly difficult. She was also the first female staff member to be ordained priest and the first to preside at communion in the chapel. Mary was especially helpful to both male and female students when they faced problems. She was also a patient and able teacher who helped many students complete the Greek requirement for ordinands. Claire Hendry was appointed to teach pastoral counselling in June 1986.[12] Hitherto a part-time tutor had taught pastoral counselling, therefore when students really needed someone to talk to the tutor was often not available.

Although the above two new female members of staff were appointed during the interregnum, the college suffered a major loss when Elaine Storkey left to take up a position on the Open University staff. Elaine was to become an international spokesperson on women's issues, appearing regularly on radio and television, publishing extensively, and playing an important role in advising the leadership of the Church of England.

---

[10] Ibid.

[11] Brian A. Smith, report on follow-up visit to Oak Hill, 10 November 1987.

[12] At the time of appointment she was Clare Woodhouse.

Another loss was the departure of Tony Rees to become vicar of Christ Church, Cockfosters, after serving the college well as chaplain and pastoral studies lecturer. He was an outstanding preacher and his wonderful Welsh sense of humour as well his remarkable command of the English language were greatly missed by students and staff alike.

A new chaplain was needed, as was a lecturer in liturgical studies, which Wheaton had covered. Dick Hines was reluctant to apply because his highest qualification in theology was a DipHE, although he did have a doctorate in science. However, he was encouraged by Bridger, who knew him from Norwich, and Heinze, who had been his tutor in his student days. Bridger's appointment of Hines as chaplain and tutor in liturgical studies was a very courageous decision. However, those who knew Hines were well aware of his many gifts and the potential he had to master any subject. He obtained an MTh in Liturgical Studies with distinction from King's College, London, within two years, and became an excellent teacher and one of the founding members of the liturgical study group Praxis. He was also responsible for a major reorganization of the placement system and changes in chapel worship that met the concerns expressed in the visitation report. Hines was to be an especially valuable member of staff in the difficult times ahead and his balanced, thoroughly Anglican, perspective would be valued when the college was under threat. He would later play a major role in the transition from the Oak Hill Ministerial Training Course (OHMTC) to the NTMTC.

Changes also took place in the leadership of the trust. In June 1986 Rocke, who had served as chairman for eleven years and as a trustee for some thirty years, announced that he would be turning over the chairmanship to Peter Dale. In his final report to the annual general meeting of the Kingham Hill Trust Corporation he could hardly have been more enthusiastic or optimistic about the future of the college:

> The most exciting news is that the college is fuller than it has ever been in its existence. There are now 101 full time students booked for the September term. In all the years I have been associated with the

> college, I have never known such a position ... Today there are more men seeking ordination from the evangelical wing of the church than for many years. All the evangelical colleges are full, and it looks as if this situation will continue. In conjunction with the college council, we have been preparing plans and starting new building projects at the college, all aimed at improving the facilities at the college.[13]

The building projects would result in a house for the principal, thereby freeing part of the principal's old flat for expansion of the library, a flat for the Kingham Hill Fellow,[14] a significant addition to student housing, two new staff houses and a block linking the old and new wings.[15] This was a massive achievement financed by the generosity of the trust and made possible by some very intelligent management of the trust funds.[16] It would, however, be dwarfed by the building that would take place at the end of the century under the leadership of Rocke's successor.

The college community over which Bridger came to preside had become a good deal more diverse and considerably younger! In September 1986 ten students from two American Lutheran colleges and their professor, Dr William Lehmann, joined the college community to initiate a new programme that had been under consideration for some time. In 1982, when he returned to

---

[13] Minutes of annual general meeting of Kingham Hill Trust Corporation, 27 June 1986.

[14] See p. 229 for details of this appointment.

[15] Much of the construction work began during the interregnum. The six additional student homes were begun in March 1986, followed by the principal's house in August 1986 and the link block in February 1987. The new staff houses were begun in April 1987, the library addition and the Fellow's flat in August 1987.

[16] The sale of the farm at Kingham 'helped to replenish the depleted endowment at the very start of the best two decades of investment performance in living history. £3 million in 1980 turned into £18 million in 2000 and that was after having spent an enormous amount on capital projects at both Kingham and Oak Hill and also after supporting both establishments through difficult times'. Interview with Peter Dale, 15 August 2001.

the Oak Hill staff after two years teaching at Concordia College in River Forest, Illinois, Heinze had an idea. In 1982 only one new full-time female student entered the college. In addition the overall number of students in residence was low and there were not enough single students to fill the rooms in the new wing. It was thought that the presence in the student body of young, single students, including, hopefully, a number of women, might encourage other female and single students. In 1984 negotiations began to establish a semester abroad programme for students from Concordia. However, formidable difficulties stood in the way. The Concordia faculty and administration had to be convinced that the programme would be beneficial to their students, and that students coming from a conservative Lutheran background would feel comfortable and accepted in an Anglican environment. Oak Hill had also to be convinced that bringing in young students from a foreign country would benefit them. Negotiations lasted over two years, during which time a second Lutheran foundation, Concordia College, Ann Arbor, Michigan, became involved. By February 1986 the college council and both American colleges had given their approval.

By this time the original reason for introducing the programme no longer applied. In his acting principal's report in October 1986 Field was able to report 'a record-breaking intake' with 112 full-time students in total.[17] This resulted in a new problem – there were no longer unfilled single rooms. When the American students arrived two weeks before term began, all the college accommodation was taken up by conferences. In order to find affordable accommodation for two weeks the American students were booked on a tour to visit the historic Lutheran sites in East Germany. In addition, because they were to be housed in the NSM rooms, occupied by the NSM students on residential weekends, three weekend trips were made a part of the programme.

[17] In September 1985 a record number of fifty-three new students joined the college. Eleven of them were women and there were at least fifteen single students in the new intake. In September 1986 forty new students joined the college.

In both cases the need of finding solutions to practical problems resulted in valuable and much-appreciated additions to the programme.

The American students integrated quickly and were readily accepted. Lehmann was especially popular for his preaching in chapel and taking Bible analysis during the term. He returned in 1993 as visiting scholar to teach philosophy and, when Field left the staff in 1994, Lehmann took his place for a semester teaching ethics until a replacement could be found. One of the highlights of the first term, to become a continuing tradition, was the Thanksgiving celebration. It included a chapel service led by the American students, a Thanksgiving meal in which the American students provided the entertainment, and an American football game, the Americans playing Oak Hill.

The programme was expanded in future years to include eight additional Lutheran colleges and universities.[18] In April 1987 Professor Norman Schmaltz from Concordia College, Ann Arbor, took over the direction from the American side. His organizational gifts and ability to relate to the people on both sides of the Atlantic was instrumental in its success. In 1989 a second semester programme involving Calvin College in Grand Rapids, Michigan, was introduced. Professor Ron Wells played a major role in its initiation. During the Bridger decade at least 233 students participated and 15 staff members from 8 different colleges and universities were involved. The students benefited greatly from their time at Oak Hill. Many testified that the experience had changed their life. One student became a Christian and was baptized in the chapel. Regular evaluations were held and the Oak Hill students and staff were consistently strongly in favour of

---

[18] The institutions and the year they joined the programme are: Concordia College, Portland, Oregon (1987); Concordia University, Mequon, Wisconsin (1988); Concordia College, Bronxville, New York (1988); Concordia College, St Paul, Minnesota (1988); Concordia College, Seward, Nebraska (1990); Valparaiso University, Valparaiso, Indiana (1992); Concordia College, Irvine, California (1996); Concordia College, Austin, Texas (1997).

continuing the programme. Exchange programmes with Calvin College and Concordia College, Ann Arbor, were added in 1990. Since neither Calvin nor Concordia was a seminary, ordinands could not be sent on these exchanges, so in order to make provision for them a programme was arranged with Trinity Lutheran Seminary in Columbus, Ohio, and approved by ACCM. The relationship with Trinity had begun when they granted generous scholarships to Oak Hill African students for postgraduate study.

In February 1987 the college council welcomed Bridger to his first meeting as principal, thanked Field for his work as acting principal during the previous year, and 'expressed relief and gratitude that the college had not experienced the usual symptoms of an interregnum'.[19] Bridger would be the first to live in the new principal's house at the end of Farm Lane. He and his wife, Elizabeth, opened their home to the community in many ways. Both students and staff benefited from their hospitality. Elizabeth added a special new dimension. A gifted teacher, she taught the advanced Greek module ably for a number of years. Her creative leadership in the wives' fellowship and her overall contribution to the community were greatly appreciated.

Bridger compensated for his lack of academic experience by having a great heart for the parochial ministry. The bishops' inspectors had noted his extensive parish experience and pointed out that this met a real need: 'if there is a weakness in the staff as at present constituted it lies in this area'.[20] From the beginning he stated that his objectives for the college would be based on the three principles that had undergirded his parochial ministry: prayer, preaching and people. A week after he arrived, CNAA visited the college. The submission for this combined institutional and course review was produced during the interregnum. The visiting party was obviously impressed both with the submission and their observations. Their report was largely positive, and 'indefinite approval' was granted to the DipHE and the BA in theological and pastoral studies.

---

[19] Minutes of college council, 11 February 1987.

[20] ACCM inspection report, February 1986.

The visitors had only two reservations. The first was that the library provision should be expanded and restructured along the lines suggested by a consultant. The second concern dealt with what they called 'critical awareness'. Although they were pleased that lecturers confronted the students with differing points of view in both doctrine and philosophy, they stressed the need 'to heighten the degree of critical awareness within the course'. They also stated that 'the assessment pattern should be monitored'.[21] This was probably the most positive report the college had ever received from them. Bridger had met his first challenge very effectively.

The reference in the report to the recommendations of a library consultant referred to the work of Miss Brenda Gooday. She had been appointed in response to the concerns expressed by the bishops' inspectors to study the library facilities and make suggestions as to how they might be upgraded. Although the library had continued to grow in the number of books[22] a great deal needed to be done in order for it to reach the standard expected by both CNAA and the inspectors. Her report stated that it was necessary:

> 1. To adopt a complete change in philosophy, attitude and approach. 2. To upgrade and develop the stock and services, especially in light of advanced courses. 3. To appoint a professional librarian with experience of running such a library. 4. To consider alternative and larger space and accommodation possibly a purpose built library. 5. To consider library computerisation (but with some caution).[23]

All of these suggestions were eventually adopted; however, in 1987 the trustees did not feel a separate building was necessary

---

[21] CNAA joint institutional and course review visit report, 17 February 1987.

[22] In 1985 the collection was augmented by a gift of some 500 books from Kenneth Schueler, who had been the dean of Concordia College, River Forest, Illinois, and a colleague of Heinze when he was on that faculty.

[23] Report on Oak Hill library by Brenda Gooday, 25 February 1987.

and computerization would come later. In October 1987 interviews were held and Wendy Bell was appointed as the first full-time librarian. She proved to be an excellent choice. Her competence and vast knowledge of resources as well as her readiness to give her time to help both staff and students made the staff wonder how they had managed previously.

Bridger proved able to learn what he needed to know about the academic world quickly. He also had the capacity to work under intense pressure and in the face of enormous challenges without becoming emotionally or spiritually drained. He had that wonderful ability to give things to his Lord and leave them there so that even after the most tension-filled days he could go home and relax. His eirenic spirit helped to hold the college community together at a time when the debate over women's ordination was dividing the church, and maintained unity in a staff divided over issues in the wider church. Although a man of peace, he was also a man of principle and, when he needed to take a strong stand, he showed courage and foresight in the decisions he made. While the procedures of his appointment could rightly be called into question, there is no doubt that once again the Lord had provided the right man to lead the college during an especially turbulent time.

The concerns of the college community and the divisions experienced in the Bridger decade reflected to some degree events in the wider world. It was firstly a period of answered prayer both in international relations and in the church. With the rest of the free world, the Oak Hill community rejoiced in the ending of the cold war, and this was an encouragement to continuing praying for the alleviating of injustice and tyranny in the world. Some students became involved in the relief efforts in the newly liberated countries of Eastern Europe. The principal-elect of the new Institute of Biblical Studies in Romania, Paul Negrut, preached in the chapel in 1994. He needed faculty members with postgraduate experience, who were in short supply in Romania. As a result an appeal was begun at Oak Hill to provide bursaries for Romanian students to undertake postgraduate work in the college, using its links with Middlesex Polytechnic and London

University.[24] National politics were the source of a good deal of discussion. Alan Storkey regularly challenged students on economic and social justice in his classes. He was also involved in the establishment of a Christian Socialist party – in the 1997 election he ran as a Social Democratic candidate for the Southgate seat held by Michael Portillo.

The Bridger decade was a time when conservative evangelicals obtained positions of power in the Church of England. This could not have been imagined by the men who founded Oak Hill in the 1930s:

> In 1993, 56 per cent of ordinands were training in evangelical colleges, 27 per cent in 'central' colleges and 17 percent in anglo-catholic colleges. In 1967 only a very small number of evangelicals occupied senior positions in the Church of England hierarchy. By 1993 there were thirteen evangelical diocesan bishops, thirteen suffragans, eight deans and twenty archdeacons.[25]

In 1992 George Carey became Archbishop of Canterbury. Although Carey no longer identified himself solely with the 'evangelical' label, he maintained 'I have not left behind any of the great truths of an evangelical faith.'[26]

However, although there were many positive and hopeful developments in these years, the Church of England was also plagued by a serious of divisive controversies. The first concerned a new phase of charismatic renewal. John Wimber, the founder of the Association of Vineyard Churches, published a book in 1986

---

[24] *Oak Hill Newsfax*, Issue 1, has an article on Negrut's visit and the bursary appeal.

[25] Roger Steer, *Church on Fire: The Story of Anglican Evangelicalism*, p. 290.

[26] Ibid., p. 329. Carey stated: 'My own unwillingness to use the label evangelical of myself ... is because I owe so much to other traditions in the church that a simple designation does not do justice now to my theology. I am a Christian before I am Anglican and I am an Anglican before I am an evangelical.'

entitled *Power Evangelism: Signs and Wonders Today*[27] in which he made a distinction between the traditional 'programmatic evangelism' and 'power evangelism'. Whereas the former relied on rational argument to present the Christian message, 'power evangelism' presented the message accompanied by demonstrations of God's power in spiritual gifts such as 'words of knowledge', healing or discernment of spirits. Wimber's teaching affected a significant number of churches including St Andrews, Chorleywood, whose services were sometimes attended by Oak Hill students and staff.

Even more controversial was a new emphasis on 'prophecy' connected with the so-called 'Kansas City Prophets'. In the late eighties and early nineties the prophetic ministry of three members of the Kansas City Fellowship was being promoted by John Wimber. He and many others were originally convinced that their prophecies were inspired by the Holy Spirit. Others, including some people who had been fully involved in charismatic renewal, were extremely suspicious of them from the beginning. This led to division among many who were associated with the charismatic movement: in the end Wimber recognized the mistake in his uncritical acceptance of the Prophets and the issue was quickly forgotten. However, by then an even more divisive issue had arisen connected with the 'Toronto Blessing'. In January 1994, at the Airport Vineyard Church in Toronto, strange manifestations began to occur, including falling, trembling, twitching, bodily convulsions of various types, uncontrollable laughter, weeping and animal sounds. News of the phenomena spread quickly as some 4,000 pastors and church leaders including some Oak Hill students visited the church and brought the 'blessing' back to their congregations. By October 1994 it is estimated that some 3,000 churches were affected and it was difficult to discuss the movement objectively as people felt so strongly that it was either a great work of God, or a clever trick of Satan.

Each of these movements had some impact on Oak Hill. A number of the staff were very committed to charismatic renewal,

[27] London: Hodder & Stoughton, 1985.

including Roger Cowley, probably the most impressive scholar on the staff. He was a world-renowned expert in his field and had a Cambridge University DD. Cowley began a study group at his house that included representatives from various theological colleges to investigate and discuss the new phenomena. He believed in power evangelism and was convinced that rational discussion, although necessary, was not sufficient. Discussion must be accompanied by demonstrations. In the last months of Wheaton's principalship tensions were already beginning to develop between those staff members and students who were sympathetic to this position and those who were strongly opposed to it.

In February 1986 a team from St Andrews, Chorleywood, including David Pytches (brother of Peter, and at that time vicar of St Andrew's), led a quiet day at Oak Hill. During the day there were some very dramatic manifestations. Several people 'rested in the Spirit', there were a number of 'words of knowledge' that seemed to be accurate, and one person claimed to have been healed. This led to a major controversy. Those who supported power evangelism believed the manifestations were proof of God's power at work. Those who were opposed to it questioned seriously whether these manifestations were of God. In April a forum on 'Signs and Wonders' was held. Cowley and Butterworth produced papers in support of Wimber's position while Gardner and Bray presented an opposing position. The debate was, to a large extent, on a high level, and, although no agreement was reached, the issues had been presented fairly and students expressed their sincere appreciation for the forum.[28] In the mid-nineties, when the controversy over the Toronto Blessing was at a high point, the college held another forum with two external speakers. Sandy Miller from Holy Trinity, Brompton, South

---

[28] At the house committee meeting the following month David Gardner, the senior student, expressed the gratitude of the student body 'for the pastoral concern shown in addressing the Quiet Day' and reported that the student committee felt the day 'had been one of positive bridge building'. Minutes of house committee meeting, 9 March 1986.

Kensington and Wallace Benn from Harold Wood in Essex presented opposing positions and held a very rational debate. Although they differed strongly, they treated each other as Christian brothers who were seeking to understand God's truth on the basis of his Word, but who had arrived at differing opinions.

The other two issues that divided evangelicals in the nineties concerned women priests and homosexuality. In 1986 synod had enacted the Deacon's Measure, admitting women to the diaconate, and six years later it passed, by a small margin, the Priests' (Ordination of Women) Measure, permitting admission of women to the priesthood. Because the church was so divided on this issue the synod accepted that two positions could be held on the question with equal integrity. Parishes that found woman priests unacceptable and that would have difficulty in being under the authority of a bishop who had ordained women were allowed to opt for the oversight of a bishop who supported their position. Despite the generous provisions of the act, many were uncomfortable with the concept of 'two integrities'. Evangelicals were divided over the issue and those divisions were reflected at Oak Hill.

There was considerably less division on questions involving sexuality. In 1991 the House of Bishops issued a report entitled *Issues in Human Sexuality*.[29] It began by summarizing biblical teaching on sex outside marriage and homosexual practice and concluded that in the Bible 'sexual activity of any kind outside marriage comes to be seen as sinful, and homosexual practice as especially dishonourable'. The report also stated that 'in our considered judgement the clergy cannot claim the liberty to enter into sexually active homophile relationships'. However, it was less clear on whether the same standards applied to the laity. The sentence in the report that spoke of having 'an open and welcoming place in the Christian community' both for 'those homophiles who follow the way of abstinence' as well as 'those

---

[29] *Issues in Human Sexuality: A Report by the House of Bishops* (London: Church House, 1991).

who are conscientiously convinced that a faithful, sexually active relationship with one other person, aimed at helping both partners to grown in discipleship in the way of life God wills for them' was of particular concern to many at Oak Hill.[30]

These were just some of the issues that Bridger had to confront as leader of the most conservative evangelical college. His philosophy of leadership was expressed in an interview published in the *Church of England Newspaper* shortly after his appointment. He described the function of the principal as 'being pastor in a real community serving and caring for a very able staff, listening and discerning priorities and leading a team'.[31] He also commented that 'the secret of administration is good secretaries',[32] and in the second year of his principalship he was blessed by the appointment of Cilla Tracy, an outstanding secretary who was at his side throughout his principalship and who was responsible for organizing one of the most creative going-away parties in Oak Hill history when Bridger retired in 1996. One of his great strengths was in appointing the people who made up the team he was called to lead. A number of appointments were made in his first year.

In February 1987 Field noted that recruitment for the coming year was so good that 'we had, in fact, to stop interviewing prospective students as a temporary measure in the autumn, pending results from selection conferences'.[33] The large number of students had justified the addition of another staff member. The greatest need was in biblical studies, so the college advertised

---

[30] *Issues in Human Sexuality*, pp. 18, 45, 47. George Carey clearly did not feel the report was ambiguous. He told the Anglican Evangelical Assembly in May 1995 that it 'recognised two options as being in full accord with the bible and the church's tradition, namely heterosexual marriage and celibacy. It underlines that there's a particular requirement on the clergy to follow those patterns as examples to their flocks, but it does not thereby judge them to be matters which can be treated with indifference by the laity.' Steer, *Church on Fire*, p. 395.

[31] *Church of England Newspaper*, 27 March 1986.

[32] Ibid.

[33] Acting principal's report, February 1987.

for a tutor. Twenty-two people applied and four were eventually shortlisted. Paul Woodbridge, who had been working as a staff member for UCCF (Universities and Colleges Christian Fellowship), was unanimously recommended by the staff and appointed in October 1987. Paul was to prove an outstanding teacher who related extremely well to students and would also serve the college in an administrative capacity as academic dean. John Stibbs was also appointed assistant academic registrar. The appointment of Tony Archer as assistant cook was to prove a great blessing.

In 1987 the trustees selected Ian Bunting as the first Kingham Hill Fellow. The idea of such a fellowship had been mooted as far back as the golden jubilee, and the trustees and principal had been waiting for the right purpose and person for such an appointment. Ian had been vicar of Chester-le-Street in the Durham diocese and his appointment indicated the sensitivity of the college to growing concern about urban ministry. He brought with him the practical experience of a successful ministry in an urban priority parish, and was asked 'to research the training of ordinands and lay Christians for ministry in Urban Priority Areas [UPAs] as defined by the Report *Faith in the City*'. He was also to 'identify achievable objectives which would enable the Church of England to equip her members for effective mission and ministry in Urban Priority Areas'.[34] In May 1988 he produced an interim report, containing some radical but intriguing suggestions as to how Oak Hill might better serve the UPA at its doorstep. He proposed that the college establish a training centre in Holloway or Islington where students would spend a semester studying and working in a UPA. The proposal was discussed extensively in staff meetings as well as the college council and a good deal of support was expressed. However it was felt that more work needed to be done before 'a firm proposal' could be made to the trustees.[35]

---

[34] Minutes of the Kingham Hill Trust, 2 February 1987.

[35] Quotation taken from the November 1988 progress report on staff–student discussion on Ian Bunting's recommendations. The council minutes of 11 October 1988 record the discussion in great detail.

Although Bunting's proposal was not accepted, a series of other new programmes were introduced and during the first five years of Bridger's time the college was blessed with one success after another. Student numbers also continued to be high. In 1988 forty-four new students entered the residential course. Recruitment was so successful that the ACCM representative on the council expressed concern that the college had exceeded its quota of ordinands. Forty new students entered the college in 1989. Although the number of new students dropped slightly to twenty-five in 1990, in the following year it was back up to forty-four and in 1992 to forty-two. In addition the NSM course thrived under Cowley's leadership. Since this course drew students from all Anglican traditions he and the staff were concerned that all positions were fairly presented. Questions were regularly asked at NSM advisory committee meetings about the degree to which the course catered 'for the full range of churchmanship'. Since there was some concern about the limitations of the trust deed, after examining it, Bridger explained that he understood the requirement that instruction should be 'Protestant and Evangelical' to be governed primarily by the prior statement that it is to be 'Biblical'. The course leader also pointed out that worship on the course had been diversified, and pastoral supervisors provided 'instruction in the conduct of worship of various traditions and denominations'.[36]

In April 1988 the college and the course suffered a grievous loss when Cowley died of bone marrow cancer. It was a terrible shock to both students and staff. He had been on the staff for eight years and had served in a variety of capacities. Bridger paid him a fitting tribute in his May 1988 principal's report:

> Tributes have been paid elsewhere to his many gifts. These include his outstanding scholarship in the field of Ethiopic Studies, his ability as a teacher, his efficiency and eye for detail in his academic and administrative work, and his pastoral care for many, especially his NSM

---

[36] Minutes of the NSM advisory committee, 17 March 1987.

> students. Roger was sometimes an uncomfortable person to work with – he demanded high standards for himself and others. Sometimes he sought to lead us in areas of Christian spirituality where some of us were unable to follow. But as Dr. Gerald Bray wrote in the obituary in the *Church Times* 'he was never afraid to explore new areas of thought, and always tried to do so with the greatest fairness and dedication to his subject'.[37]

Field was asked to take Cowley's place as NSM course leader and he proved a worthy successor. When in 1989 it was no longer limited to training for NSM its title was changed to the Oak Hill Ministerial Training Course (OHMTC) and Field was given the title of dean. Numbers of new students reached record levels before it was terminated in 1994.[38]

Meanwhile, on the regular course, Gardner and Bridger began the development of a homiletics module for CNAA approval. Although one would expect a module on preaching to be regarded as a necessary component of a course designed for future ministers, CNAA was always very suspicious of what they considered 'how-to-do-it' modules, which they did not consider academic. It was a challenging task to convince them that the module was academically respectable. In February 1989 CNAA accepted the new module with the proviso that it be taught for two years and then reviewed. Gardner and Bridger taught the module, and it was very popular among students. In May 1989 Paul Weston was appointed as next Kingham Hill Fellow. Although his brief was to teach evangelism and to lead students on missions, he was also to become involved in teaching the homiletics module after Gardner left Oak Hill the following year. The module, taught by Bridger, Weston and Christian Lewin for many years, was to be one of the best-designed, well-taught and popular modules in the course. Weston also introduced a module in evangelism and his overall contributions to the college were so significant that his

---

[37] Principal's report, May 1988.

[38] In 1991 there were twenty-six new students and in the final two years of the course there were twenty new students in each year.

appointment as Kingham Hill Fellow, originally for three years, was extended to six years in February 1991.

Butterworth's faithful promoting of extension education finally received the support it deserved from both the staff and the trust, and introduced another new direction. In the October 1987 council meeting Butterworth was able to report that future plans had received the 'unanimous support' of the staff. This was a source of great satisfaction. The trust also made a significant financial commitment to the programme and the Oak Hill Extension College (OHEC) was launched, with former student Ambrose Mason subsequently appointed as field officer. His brief was to aid the development of new courses and the revision of existing ones, as well as to publicize and promote the courses where extension education might meet a need in the church. His enthusiasm and commitment as well as his willingness to travel throughout the country resulted in OHEC growing both in the number of courses and the number of people taking them. In February 1991 Douglas Scott reported to the council that 'the trustees were very encouraged with progress since Mason had started', and they extended his appointment to three years 'with a possibility of five'.[39] Not only was OHEC succeeding, but Butterworth's vision for extension education became one of the major factors in the founding of the Open Theological College.

Another new direction was the link with the Uganda Martyrs Seminary in Namugongo. On the same day as the trust announced that they were prepared to spend more money on the library, Bridger received a letter from Uganda asking for prayer for the Namugongo seminary because soldiers had killed their principal and seventeen students and destroyed their library. Bridger explained:

> I read extracts from these two letters at lunch one day and then made a simple comment that we needed to pray about this and do something about it. Here we've got all these riches and here are people training for ministry in Uganda with nothing. And very quickly, and it was

[39] Minutes of college council, February 1991.

> student initiative, a few students came and said we must set up a group to raise money to provide books and to help Namugongo in any way possible.[40]

The response from the college was remarkable. Within a year £10,000 was raised, beginning an ongoing link. Over the years students and staff have gone to Namagongo to teach and aid in the building projects. Each year there were drives to raise money for new projects, and new buildings were added. The most recent addition was the Cecily Kirkaldy conference hall, built with money given in memory of an Oak Hill student who died of cancer in 1999.

The college also received positive publicity in the media. A reporter from the *Church Times*, who described herself as 'a broad church Catholic', visited the college in January 1989 and her article appeared in the paper on 14 April, giving a very a fair picture. She commented on the efforts 'made to give the students experience of other forms of churchmanship', called Bridger and Field 'tolerant men who are concerned to broaden the experience of their students', and noted that 'in the NSM course there are men and women of every shade of churchmanship'.[41] In addition in 1988 Heinze wrote and presented three programmes on the early church, part of a series aired by the BBC on Sunday mornings.

PERSONALITY PROFILE

Angela Butler joined the OHMTC in 1987. She had left school after A levels and had worked for the Department of Social Security for about twenty years.

Starting the course with twenty-three others from all walks of life, she writes: 'We embarked on what was to be one of the most enriching periods of my life. On Tuesday evenings and weekends over three years we delved deeply into the wonders of our faith, and, led by wonderful

[40] Interview with the Bridgers.

[41] *Church Times*, 14 April 1989. She was, however, more critical of the church history lecture, which she seems to have misunderstood.

tutors, grew in knowledge and faith as we prepared for ministry in a whole host of different ways. In my final year I had the privilege of being elected one of two senior students.'

Ordained in 1990 as a deacon in St Albans diocese and licensed as an NSM to St Paul's, Chipperfield, Angela continued to work, now with the employment service. Over the next three years she reduced her hours to half, and from 1993–6 returned to work at Oak Hill as part-time academic registrar, admissions officer and general administrator. This coincided with her being asked to take over as deacon-in-charge at Chipperfield, Hertfordshire, prior to being priested in 1994. On leaving Oak Hill in 1996 she was invited to work nationally in evangelism as a member of the archbishops' Springboard team. This was combined with parish work at Chipperfield until 2001, when she moved to Gloucester diocese to be Springboard Missioner and priest-in-charge of Hempsted.

Angela concludes: 'In my years in ministry I thank God time and again for Oak Hill, for its inspired and sound teaching, for its willingness to grapple sensitively with the difficult questions about life, churchmanship, ministry and not least for its continued teaching for Old Oaks.'

It is remarkable that the staff found time for outside activities considering that between 1989–91 they had to prepare four submissions – two for ACCM and two for CNAA. In response to a paper known as 'ACCM 22' all colleges were asked to respond to three questions:

1. What ordained ministry does the Church of England require?
2. What is the shape of the educational programme best suited for people to exercise this ministry?
3. What are the appropriate means to assess suitability for the exercise of ministry?

The staff devoted a great deal of time to preparing a carefully thought out submission and ACCM responded positively, though requiring further information. However, there were still three more submissions to be made in the following two years. The first involved the most detailed and sophisticated submission ever made to CNAA as the college applied for validation of an honours degree after the previously abortive attempts. A central argument in the proposal was the improved facilities especially in the library, and most significantly that a full-time librarian had been appointed. In addition the quality of the faculty was stressed. Five staff members now had doctoral degrees and Alan Storkey was close to completing his doctorate. The staff had also grown in size, as in May 1989 Michael Peat, who was studying for a doctorate at Westminster Theological Seminary, was appointed lecturer in doctrine and philosophy. It was also stressed that for the first time the college had a tutor with an advanced degree in liturgical studies – Hines had been awarded his MTh with distinction in September 1989.

The proposal described a particularly demanding course. Modules were grouped in three areas of biblical, theological and historical, and pastoral studies. Honours students were required to select at least one module from each of the three subject areas and two of those modules were to be at the advanced level. In addition they must complete a 12,000-word dissertation in one of the areas.

A CNAA visiting party in December 1990 was very thorough in its investigation and approved the BA honours degree in theological and pastoral studies for an initial period of five years. Although they felt 'the college was a bit insular' and stressed that 'the issue of awareness and openness to other world views and views of education should continue to be addressed', the overall tone of the report was very positive. The visiting party were especially pleased with the 'contacts and exchanges with American colleges', which were 'considered to be of great importance to the college'. They also thought that the 'appointment of a new college academic dean' was a positive step. They concluded: 'there was unanimous agreement that the honours degree will provide an important extra dimension to the student profile of the college'. Their only further requirement was that the college should present a single document describing all three courses, the DipHE, BA pass and BA honours degree, and demonstrating 'routes by which various students may make their way through the particular courses'.[42] When that was met the college received a letter stating that the condition had been met satisfactorily and the course was officially approved for a five-year period, with Oak Hill also being recognized for post-graduate study. The first review was scheduled for 1995–6.

There was not much time for rejoicing. A month later the staff had to prepare for another bishops' inspection. As usual the documentation had to be prepared well before the visit and was quite lengthy, but the result more than justified the time spent preparing it. The report of the visiting party was one of the most positive the college had ever received. It began:

> A great deal has happened since the last inspection and action has been taken on all of the recommendations made at that time. We were generally impressed by the way in which the college is managed; the supportive and unstinting dedication of the staff in all parts of the college; the care and attention to detail of all connected with chapel and worship; the clear sense of respect and affection for the college and staff by its many different kinds of students; the understanding of what is meant by academic standards ... and the clear sense of direction and development that the college continues to identify.[43]

The inspectors 'were generally impressed with the openness that now appears to characterise together the teaching and the way of life at the college'. They found that 'alternative views are expressed' and they 'came to the conclusion that the overall outlook was not particularly narrow'.[44] There were inevitably a number of recommendations, the two most significant dealing

---

[42] Report of course review visit of the CNAA to Oak Hill, 13 December 1990.

[43] ACCM inspection report, October 1991.

[44] Ibid.

with the large percentage of non-ordinands[45] and the small number of women in the student body. They recommended first that 'more systematic, sustained and targeted guidance and support for ordinands needed to be provided'. In addition since there were only seven women among the fifty-five ordinands the report recommended that 'the college give urgent consideration to increasing the number of women in training', and 'ensure they are fully integrated into the college way of life'. In addition the college was asked to raise 'the profile of issues concerning women's ministry' and to implement in full 'the Bishops' Guidelines for Colleges and Courses Training Women'.[46] The college responded to all of the recommendations in an effective and constructive manner. When the chairman of the inspectors, Peter Toyne, revisited the college he reported that 'Oak Hill is in good shape' and 'has already responded sensibly and with alacrity to our recommendations in a way which should give us all confidence in its ability to train ordinands properly, and to run its affairs effectively, efficiently and dynamically'.[47]

During this period there were staff changes. Gardner left in 1990 to take a parish in the Chester diocese. He had been on the college staff for seven years and had made vital contributions in many areas. As admissions officer he had rationalized the procedure to make it more effective and attractive to applicants – this must have been at least partially responsible for the large increase in numbers. Bridger paid him a well-deserved tribute when he announced his leaving to the council:

> He has largely master-minded the new homiletics module taught for the first time this year, and his own preaching in chapel has always

---

[45] They attributed this to the 'great success' of the college in attracting students and the drop in the number of candidates recommended by selection conferences.

[46] Ibid. The other recommendations dealt with reviewing the arrangements for personal tutorials, establishing a Health and Safety Committee and upgrading the student kitchens.

[47] ACCM inspection report of follow-up visit to Oak Hill.

> been greatly appreciated. There are many who will bear witness to his pastoral care for them, and many who have been encouraged by his enthusiasm for the Bible. His colleagues and staff will also miss his administrative ability as he has been an excellent academic registrar and has included amongst his duties visits to America to encourage the American programme. More recently he has willingly accepted the onerous task of drafting and writing up the submission for BA honours. We shall miss Paul's commitment to the college, his warmth and friendship and his teaching, pastoral and administrative gifts.[48]

Gardner's leaving opened the door to appoint a New Testament tutor who would also be the college dean. The dean's role was intended to relieve the principal of academic administration duties. When, after advertisements and interviews, no appointment could be made, it was decided to readvertise in the following year and meanwhile to fill the position of New Testament tutor temporarily. The 'temporary replacement' was Peter Head, a young Australian who had been studying at Tyndale House. The college was quickly introduced to his delightful sense of humour. At his first meal when he was introduced to the community he commented that, although he was happy to be here, he felt a bit insecure because his job was being advertised before he had even delivered his first lecture. However, once the staff became aware of his great gifts in teaching and scholarship as well as the overall contribution that he and his wife Fiona made to the college community, he became a valued permanent member of the staff.

The readvertisement was answered by a very promising candidate from the staff of Moore College, Sydney, who came for interview. Although he had impressive credentials and interviewed well, he would not be able to start as quickly as the college needed him, so he was ruled out. In informing him of this decision Bridger wrote that 'we all felt that much as we would love to have you at Oak Hill', they wondered if this was the best move for him at the present time.[49] The candidate had also had some doubts

---

[48] Principal's report, May 1990.
[49] Letter from Bridger to Peterson, 13 November 1990.

about whether the position was right for him. But this would not be the last the college heard of David Peterson. In the end it was decided to fill the position of dean from within the staff, and Heinze was appointed in May 1991.

In February 1992 Bridger began a well-deserved sabbatical, and Field and Heinze stepped back into the roles of acting principal and acting vice-principal. The principal could look back on five years of great achievement. It had been a busy and successful time. Overall numbers remained high. Consequently Bridger could leave on his sabbatical with a great sense of achievement. He would need a rest before facing the enormous challenges that lay ahead.

8

Challenges and Controversies (1992–1996)

> The Advisory Group concludes that, in the light of the various constraints under which it operates, Oak Hill College is not likely to make the changes that are necessary if it is to continue to prepare candidates for ministry in the Church of England. It therefore recommends that the House of Bishops should withdraw recognition from the College for the training of ordinands.[1]

Of the many challenges that confronted the college in the second half of the Bridger decade none was more serious than that which resulted from the above report of the Steering Committee for Theological Colleges. Bridger first saw the report with the other theological college principals on 27 October 1992. It was to be debated in the General Synod on 11 November. Consequently the college had only two weeks to respond. It met the challenge successfully, as it did a series of other problems during these years. Bridger's first five years had been a time of almost unmitigated blessings and successes, but the next five were to be quite the reverse. Hopeful new directions sadly did not come to fruition.

The first problem was reported to the council meeting (October 1991) that approved Bridger's sabbatical plans. As a result of the recent Higher Education Bill the CNAA would be dissolved by October 1992. The college would need to seek a new validating authority just after the CNAA had granted 'permanent validation' for its courses and approved the honours degree. At

[1] *Theological Training: A Way Ahead*, p. 67.

the same meeting the dean of the OHMTC announced that his course was also under threat. Field reported that a Steering Committee set up in June 1989 under the chairmanship of Robert Hardy, Bishop of Lincoln, had been studying the possibility of uniting non-residential courses, proposing that the Oxford, St Albans and Oak Hill courses be merged. Field had countered with a proposal that there be one course covering the diocese of Oxford and St Albans and a second covering London and Chelmsford dioceses – this would make it possible for the OHMTC to survive as the London/Chelmsford course. Bridger's sabbatical would be spent dealing with these problems.

Paradoxically, the demise of the CNAA was to prove very beneficial. At the council meeting Heinze stated that there were a number of possible options for new validation including Middlesex Polytechnic, the Open University, Cheltenham and Gloucester College of Higher Education (now the University of Gloucestershire) and London University. It was even suggested that a consortium of former CNAA colleges to which Oak Hill had belonged might seek recognition as a university and validate its own courses. Each of these possibilities was considered and in the end it was decided to pursue the Middlesex option. A member of the council who had served with CNAA, Alan Crispin, was especially helpful in providing advice and guidance. Ken Goulding, the deputy vice-chancellor, represented Middlesex in the negotiations. His efficiency, clear perception of the issues and reasonableness in finding compromise solutions when there were differences made it possible to arrive at an agreement in a relatively short period of time. At the May 1992 council meeting Heinze paid tribute to the good working relations the college enjoyed with the authorities at Middlesex University[2] and announced that the academic board had 'recommended the adoption of a Memorandum of Co-operation between the College and Middlesex University, and an Instrument of Accreditation'. A submission was to be presented by 8 June and an accreditation visit was scheduled for July.[3]

---

[2] Middlesex was granted university status in 1992.

[3] College council minutes, 19 May 1992.

This meant, of course, the preparation of yet another submission, but of a different kind. Rather than seeking validation of its courses, as had been the case with CNAA, the college was asking Middlesex to grant it the right to validate its own courses. Therefore it was not necessary to include the details of the courses in the submission since, if the university granted accredited status to the college, it 'would be responsible for the validation, monitoring and progress review' of its own courses leading to the award of the university's diplomas and degrees. In contrast with the 1990 CNAA submission, which ran to 150 pages and 5 appendices, the June 1992 submission to Middlesex was 45 pages long including 4 appendices. The visiting party met with both staff and students and 'unanimously agreed' that 'from September 1992 Oak Hill College should be an accredited institution of the University for the purposes of reviews and validation in theological and pastoral studies for five years'. The approval was subject to three conditions, which were easily met by a minor revision of the submission.[4] On 2 October 1992 the Instrument of Accreditation and a Memorandum of Co-operation between Middlesex University and Oak Hill College was signed.

This was the beginning of a new relationship between the university and the college, which in the next five years was to lead to a series of new programmes that benefited students of both institutions. A joint management committee was set up to deal with problems that arose in the relationship and to recommend new areas of co-operation. In 1994 Oak Hill developed an even closer relationship by becoming an associate college of the university. Joint faculty seminars were held to discuss topics of mutual interest and Oak Hill students became full members of the university and were able to use all its facilities. American students were able to benefit from Middlesex modules and the university generously made allowances for the fact that the Lutheran students were not able to stay for the full semester.

---

[4] They involved changing the composition of the review and validation panels, clarifying the role of the ABM external examiner and agreeing upon a date for the next review of the Oak Hill courses.

Middlesex's Religious Studies department also added a new Christian Studies option, combining Middlesex and Oak Hill modules in a single programme. An Old Oak on the Middlesex staff, Gary Gibson, was largely responsible for developing the programme, working in co-operation with the Oak Hill dean. Since Middlesex students were eligible for a full grant, those who could not afford the Oak Hill fees could benefit from the financial aid available to Middlesex students and still do a major part of their studies at Oak Hill. This was especially attractive to Christian students and a substantial number of the students taking the course were committed Christians. Initially it proved very popular, reaching a high point in the second semester of 1997, when twenty-six Middlesex students were taking modules at Oak Hill. Although complications arose from trying to integrate a substantial number of part-time students, they were effectively dealt with by the joint management committee and by the patient and efficient new Oak Hill academic registrar, Claire Osborne.

In 1995 a Master of Arts degree in theology was validated. It included both a dissertation and advanced modules taught by Oak Hill staff. A number of new modules at postgraduate level were developed and were taught on a single day of the week (usually Wednesday) so that part-time students, especially busy parish ministers, could participate. Students interested in pursuing research degrees could register for a PhD, MPhil or BPhil at the university and be supervized partly by the Oak Hill faculty. In 1996 Colin Weale, a Hertfordshire incumbent, became the first Oak Hill PhD.[5]

The successful new relationship with Middlesex was, unfortunately, not matched by developments affecting the OHMTC. In the 1990s the course had record enrolments and was praised

[5] Weale was awarded the degree at a Middlesex University conferment in July 1996 for a dissertation, supervised by Heinze, entitled *Patronage, Priest and Parish in the Archdeaconry of Huntingdon 1109–1547*.

by all participants and visitors. In 1992 the course's external examiner,[6] Canon Alistair Redfern, reported:

> The course maintains a high standard and an impressive openness to learning and changing. Much is gained by the close link with the theological college. The calibre of teaching staff is very high ... Further, the resources of the college, in terms of library and facilities are a great benefit. I have been impressed by the range of churchmanship amongst the students and the sensitivity of the course ethos and content to those from such a variety of traditions – including students who come to Oak Hill MTC with a degree of nervousness about an 'evangelical line' and have found that their fears are not justified and that a very positive and broad experience has awaited them.[7]

Despite all the strong reasons for continuing the course it was to be terminated and replaced. The note in the official register of Oak Hill students for the year 1994 simply reads 'From lst September 1993 the Oak Hill Ministerial Course ceased to exist. On that date, the North Thames Ministerial Training Course began.' It was sad that something that had worked so well had ended. The new course was a partnership between the Kingham Hill Trust and the dioceses of Chelmsford and London. Field's proposal that there be one course covering the dioceses of Oxford and St Albans and a second covering London and Chelmsford dioceses had won the day, but his objective in making that proposal was not to be achieved. In an interview he commented: 'The course had grown to a reasonable size and we didn't want to lose it because we felt that we were able to help students from different traditions to get training for ministry that had the gospel at its heart.'[8] The story of the establishing of the NTMTC is told later. Before its inception the college suffered two traumatic

---

[6] The title of moderator was changed to external examiner to fall into line with the college's other courses.

[7] Alistair Redfern, Oak Hill MTC, annual report of the external examiner 1992.

[8] Interview with Field.

experiences. The first involved the loss of one of its very gifted and popular lecturers, while the second posed a threat to the continued existence of both the course and the college.

In his report in October 1992 Bridger informed the council of a very difficult problem that confronted him at the end of his sabbatical:

> The last month of my sabbatical ... was taken up with the circumstances that surrounded the resignation of Dr. Gerald Bray. I took no pleasure in asking Gerald to resign as I regard him not only as a friend but a very gifted teacher. As you know the reasons for his resignation were not doctrinal but professional and Oak Hill has lost an outstanding lecturer. We are grateful for the quality of his teaching, his hard work and his concern for many students during his twelve years at Oak Hill.[9]

At the same meeting Douglas Scott, the chairman, referred to the situation as 'sad and traumatic for both staff and students' and he assured the council 'it had not been a decision taken lightly'. He also emphasized that Bray's 'resignation was due to irreconcilable difficulties in professional relations and not for theological reasons'.[10] The staff had had a series of unsuccessful meetings while Bridger was on sabbatical in an effort to resolve the problems that had arisen between Bray and other staff members. The 'irreconcilable difficulties in professional relations' were again mentioned in the official public statement, on whose wording Bridger maintained he and Bray had agreed. It read:

> Dr. Gerald Bray has resigned from the staff of Oak Hill College after twelve years as tutor in doctrine. His resignation is due to irreconcilable difficulties in professional relationship with other members of staff. The college wishes to express its appreciation for his hard work and the quality of his teaching during those years. He will take up

[9] Principal's report, October 1992.
[10] College council minutes, October 1992.

residence at Tyndale House, Cambridge, the Biblical Research Centre, from the beginning of September.[11]

Bray clearly did not accept this explanation. He distributed a letter dated 31 August 1992 to the student body stating 'my resignation was not voluntary – far from it! When I returned from my language course in Poland on 11 August I was summoned into the principal's study and given a choice between immediate resignation or dismissal.'[12] Bray was to take a position in an American college and in the years since he left Oak Hill he has been an especially productive scholar.

The college was to go on to face its greatest test three months later with the publication of the so-called 'Lincoln Report', to which reference was made at the beginning of this chapter.[13] Entitled *Theological Training: A Way Ahead*,[14] it comprised two committee reports, both chaired by the Bishop of Lincoln, and included representatives from the Advisory Board for Ministry

---

[11] Letter from Bridger to staff, 12 August 1992.

[12] Letter from Bray beginning 'Dear Friends', 31 August 1992.

[13] Clearly there was no connection between the resignation of Bray and the survival of the college, as he seemed to imply in an editorial in *Churchman* (vol. 107, no. 4, pp. 291–3) in 1993, which is quoted by Iain Murray. The editorial read. 'Of the six Evangelical training colleges, it was the one which was perceived to be the least 'open' which was slated for closure, and the response of the college authorities was both quick and revealing. Elements suspected of being resistant to 'openness' were purged in a particularly nasty and brutal manner, and when Church authorities took a second look they gratefully announced that the teaching of the college was not as 'narrow' as they had been led to believe'. Murray, *Evangelicalism Divided*, p. 128. Since the report in which the college was 'slated for closure' was published over three months after Bray's resignation clearly Bray's leaving did not help the college to survive. It may, in fact, have made survival more difficult as it cost the support of some evangelicals who believed the rumours about his resignation being due to theological differences.

[14] ACCM report, 1992.

(ABM).[15] One committee dealt with courses. A number of MTC courses were having serious financial problems and some were clearly not viable as they had few participants and were on too small a scale. Most of the recommendations contained in the report did not seem to be particularly threatening to the OHMTC since it was one of the larger courses and was financially solvent.

The committee reacted to the concerns about financial viability and size of courses by suggesting that they be reorganized on a regional basis with a core teaching staff of four or five. The Oak Hill course was to be combined with the St Albans and Oxford courses in a single unit. The steering group was unwilling to give serious consideration to Field's alternative proposal or even to discuss a study of cost effectiveness the trust had commissioned from the accountants Robson Rhodes.[16] In July 1992 Field reported to the trust:

> It is hard to escape the conclusion that the Lincoln group's insistence on keeping to its own plan is based on ideological not educational or economic considerations. It just does not want an evangelical college to have a prominent role in the future of part-time ordination training. This impression is reinforced by ... [the group's] unwillingness to debate our alternative proposal [or discuss the Robson Rhodes document] with us.[17]

The fact that theological concerns played a major role in the decision to end the Oak Hill course is evident from the report of the steering group five months later. In commenting on the reluctance of Oak Hill to join the proposed regional course they stated that Oak Hill proposed to offer its own course to the

---

[15] In April 1991 ACCM's name was changed to ABM.

[16] The study, made in April 1992, revealed that the cost per student on the Oak Hill MTC was £1,929. This was well below the average cost on the other courses, which was £2,500 per student. Only one course had a lower cost per student than Oak Hill. 'An Examination of the Cost Effectiveness of Part Time training at Oak Hill' (April 1992), p. 7.

[17] Field, Report to Kingham Hill trustees, 3 June 1992.

dioceses of London and Chelmsford, but added that 'because of its *particular theological stance* it would however be unworkable for OHMTC to have exclusive responsibility for a geographical area' (emphasis added).[18] The fact that the Oak Hill course had been acceptable to people from other Anglican traditions for twenty years seemed to have been ignored.

The second committee chaired by the Bishop of Lincoln, called the Advisory Group on Full-Time Theological Training, had been set up in April 1991 in response to the worrying drop in the number of full-time students training and the serious financial implications of the decline in numbers. It was 'to recommend a plan to the house of bishops by the summer of 1992' that would match 'the capacity of theological colleges to the numbers of clergy required for the future ... taking into account also the likely flow of ordination candidates'.[19] Although the concerns about numbers and finances the committee was asked to address did not seem to pose a serious threat to Oak Hill throughout the period when the report was being compiled, there were rumours that Oak Hill might well be targeted for closure.

Bridger had only one meeting with the Lincoln committee. Although there were no indications of serious problems he recalls that they asked questions about the number of female ordinands training at the college and 'seemed to probe us quite a lot about how much we were prepared to work with people of other traditions'.[20] A more substantial indication that the college was in trouble came in an undated confidential memo sent to the chairs of the trust and the council, Bridger and Field, which was probably written shortly before the report was published. It pointed out that since no evangelical colleges had been closed following the de Bunsen report and since there were now proportionally more evangelical colleges than before 1972 it was likely that one of them would be closed. All the other evangelical colleges had close links with universities with theology

[18] *Theological Training: A Way Ahead*, p. 18.
[19] Ibid, p. 33.
[20] Interview with Bridger.

departments, which the committee considered important, so Oak Hill might well be the one selected for closure.[21] As the time for the publication of the report approached, the college had already begun to prepare its defences in case its worst fears were realized. On 6 October 1992 a mailing was sent out to evangelical members of synod with a briefing paper, which Bridger pointed out in his covering letter 'could be useful if Oak Hill is under any kind of threat from the Lincoln Report, when it is published'.[22]

When Bridger received the report on 27 October he turned immediately to the section dealing with Oak Hill. He must have been surprised to read first that Oak Hill was 'the most expensive theological college in total terms' and that it had recently been operating at a £50,000 loss per year. Although he might have been encouraged by the second comment, which pointed out that it was the only Anglican theological college in the Greater London area and that it had 'an admirable record of offering training to less academically able ordination candidates', he would have been astounded by the next paragraph:

> Oak Hill College is however too constrained by its circumstances and, in particular, by its trust deed with which the staff are expected to comply. This undoubtedly has restrictive effects on the educational programme and means that it does not benefit satisfactorily from the considerable local resources of theological education. For example, no

---

[21] An article in the *Church of England Newspaper* stated that three colleges were likely to be closed as the number of ordinands in full-time training had fallen from 900–760 in the previous five years. The author speculated on the basis of enrolments that Chichester, Queen's and Lincoln seemed most vulnerable, but also noted: 'There is increasing speculation that if it is decided to close an evangelical college, then Oak Hill is most vulnerable.' *Church of England Newspaper*, 11 September 1992.

[22] Letter from Bridger to synod members, 6 October 1992. The same letter included the following comment on Bray's resignation: 'Some of you have heard that Dr. Gerald Bray has been asked to resign from the staff of Oak Hill. This is true; but I would like to assure you that it is not for doctrinal reasons and that I have every intention of seeking to appoint someone in the same classical evangelical tradition.'

> one may give religious teaching unless prepared to sign a declaration that 'he is a Protestant and Evangelical in the strictest sense of the terms'.[23]

He also read that the college 'despite being pressed by ABM under the ACCM 22 procedure' still did 'not provide sufficient opportunities for contemporary methodology or integrative approaches to training and links between practice and theology (especially as regards placements) have not been satisfactorily developed'. In addition he would have been amazed by the criticism of the link with Middlesex University, 'which has no theology department', and failure to benefit from 'the rich teaching resources available in the London area'. As he read on he should not have found it surprising that the report singled out the college's record on training female ordinands as a subject for criticism, but he would have had difficulty recognizing that they were talking about Oak Hill when he read:

> The Advisory Group is concerned at the college's inadequate response to the training requirements for women set out in the House of Bishop's Guidelines. The college has attracted only a low proportion of women ordinands. There is no evidence that women's perspectives in theology are appreciated and the woman part-time staff member is used as a tutor for women only.[24]

Having read thus far he should not have been surprised by paragraph 185, which recommended that 'the House of Bishops ... withdraw recognition from the college for the training of ordinands'. Bridger's own account confirms many of the suppositions we have made about his reactions:

> I remember quickly looking at the relevant paragraphs and my first reaction was not horror, although I could see it was recommended that they would close Oak Hill and Mirfield and Salisbury, but actually a quiet sort of confidence that it wouldn't be as bad as I had

[23] *Theological Training: A Way Ahead*, p. 67.
[24] Ibid.

> thought, because some of the things I read were clearly inaccurate and I immediately saw, without looking at it very carefully, that there were a number of things we could immediately answer and rebut.[25]

In the discussion that followed Bridger came to realize that the commitee wanted to be even-handed and close one college from each of the Anglican traditions. Although he recognized that it would be considerably more difficult to win the fight on that issue, he remained confident.

The documents in the college archives relating to the events following the publication of the Lincoln report are so numerous that one can hardly do justice to them in a few pages.[26] The overwhelming support that the college received from people of all traditions is documented by a huge file of letters sent to the principal as well as copies of letters sent to bishops. More letters were sent to the editors of both the church and national newspapers supporting the college than could be published. Two in particular, one by three women students on behalf of the female students at the college, and one by the ABM external examiner, Francis Bridger, sought to correct the 'inaccuracies' and the 'misleading impressions' given in the report.[27] Oak Hill students also rose to the challenge – the student leadership wrote a letter,

---

[25] Interview with Bridger.

[26] Most were originally stored in a 2' × 1' × 1 1/2' box that was completely full. In addition there were a number of other files that could not fit into the box. There are, of course, also substantial materials in the Church of England archives. Although the Bishop of Lincoln responded to our request and sent us material from his files and a member of the advisory group was willing to be interviewed, we have decided to limit our coverage to the college's reaction and how the report affected the college. Hopefully others will one day write a broader study, which will consider the perspective of the advisory group, the way in which other colleges were affected and reacted, as well as the long-term impact on the Church of England.

[27] *Church of England Newspaper*, 6 November 1992. The students were Alison Le Cornu, Cathy Pullinger and Sarah Wood. In addition Graham Davies, one of the college's external examiners, wrote to the

sent to all bishops, and individual students were encouraged to write their bishops personal letters. Gardner organized a meeting of concerned evangelical clergy. Over 100 busy clergymen took a day to come to the college for a meeting held on 14 November. At that meeting Prebendary John Pearce was able to report the first victory in the struggle for survival as he reviewed the debate in the General Synod two days earlier which had voted overwhelmingly 'not to take note' of the report.[28]

Many people contributed to the victory, but special credit must be given to those who devoted long hours to writing letters, making contacts, and helping the college's supporters in synod to prepare for the debate. In two days Field produced an eighteen-page document pointing out the inaccuracies and misleading statements in the report. This was then discussed and revised by the staff and subsequently by Peter Dale and David Monro (now chairman of the council). A nine-point critique of the process behind the report's preparation was also produced, including the fact that no member of the committee had visited Oak Hill in person, that the information supplied by the college for the report had not been used, and that inadequate time had been allowed for a response.

Further investigation revealed that the report's compilers had never carefully checked the accuracy of the information they included, and had totally ignored the fact that the college clearly

---

27 (*continued*) *Church of England Newspaper* the week after Francis Bridger's letter, endorsing his remarks and commending the academic excellence of the students and staff at the college.

28 One of the results of the clergy meeting was an advertisement that appeared in the *Church of England Newspaper* on 4 December 1992 entitled 'Oak Hill College Southgate, London is Alive and Well'. It stated 'We were thrilled that the General Synod ... refused even to "take note" of the Report' and it recommended ordinands to apply to Oak Hill. It was signed by the members of the steering group appointed at the meeting: Wallace Benn, Richard Bewes, Paul Gardner, Philip Hacking, Tony Higton, David Holloway, Dick Lucas and Melvin Tinker.

met the criteria listed in the first part of the report. In addition they had not taken into consideration the statements of people like the ABM external examiner, whose comments were directly at variance with the report's criticism of the college's placement scheme. A number of glaring inaccuracies or particularly misleading statements made it easy for Field to point out weaknesses in the report.[29] For example, no staff member had ever been asked to sign his or her assent to the trust deed – the committee could easily have known this if they had asked. In addition the statement that the college was the most expensive college and had recently been operating at a £50,000 annual loss was countered by statistical evidence, showing the loss had occurred only in the 1990–91 academic year due to some extraordinary expenses. In the two previous years Oak Hill had been the only college to show a profit. A statement in the report about 'the woman part-time staff member' who was 'used as tutor for women only' was also clearly incorrect since Mary Abbott was neither part-time nor a 'women only' tutor. In addition the committee had overlooked two other women on the teaching staff who were clearly listed in the information sent to them.

Although the critique of the report was comprehensive, it would do the college little good unless the people who would make the decision received it in the limited time left before the scheduled synodical debate. Aided by students the secretaries duplicated the response and mailed it to every member of synod. Copies were also sent to all Old Oaks and a number of other people who had requested it, encouraging them to write letters to their bishops and synodical representatives. A separate letter was sent to students who had studied on the OHMTC containing the section of the response dealing with the course and the resolutions

[29] Field commented in interview 'I must confess that I was never really worried by the Lincoln report because when I read it, I realised that it was such a bad report. It was factually wrong and statistically wrong. Its conclusions were based on no foundations at all and therefore writing the college's response to that was one of the easiest things I have ever done in my life.'

passed unanimously by the course management committee at its meeting on 3 November.[30] Oak Hill ordinands also wrote their own reply to the report in which they commented on the contrasts between the positive statements about the college made by the bishops' inspectors who had spent time at the college and the negative statements of the advisory group who had never visited.

Meanwhile personal letters were written to people who might influence the decision. The day after the report was given to the principals Dale wrote to the Bishop of Lincoln asking him to stay its publication because it was 'likely to be inaccurate' and 'misrepresent the position of the college'. A 'misleading report', he pointed out, might damage the church and have 'severe financial consequences' for the college.[31] He was correct in both assumptions, but unfortunately his advice was ignored. On 3 November he and Scott wrote to the Archbishop of Canterbury. Pointing out that the 'report is fatally flawed; in the process with which it was undertaken, in the facts presented, which in Oak Hill's case are both wrong and misleading, and in the conclusions it reaches', they asked that the recommendations be withdrawn before it was presented to the synod.[32] On the same day Dale wrote the Bishop of Lincoln a second letter, and on the following day he wrote to a

---

[30] It affirmed the educational principles in the report, but regretted 'the errors which have formed the basis of the steering group's conclusions'. It asked the bishops to 'reappraise' the conclusions and affirmed the 'negotiations currently being conducted to secure validation of the curriculum for a new London/Oak Hill/Chelmsford Regional Course'. Minutes of management committee (formerly the steering committee, and subsequently advisory committee), 3 November 1991.

[31] Letter from Dale to the Bishop of Lincoln, 28 October 1992. Before the report was published he had also written to the Bishop of London, David Hope, providing him with important information concerning the trust deed and the 'ecumenical nature of Oak Hill', which the bishop had requested. He used the opportunity to add a good deal of additional information that the bishop could use in defending the college. Hope's support of the college was to prove vital in the struggle for survival. Letter from Dale to the Bishop of London, 19 October 1992.

[32] Letter from Dale and Scott to Archbishop Carey, 3 November 1992.

member of synod asking her to speak on behalf of Oak Hill in the debate. Meanwhile Bishop Dudley-Smith wrote personal letters to a number of bishops stating the case for the college. In addition Bridger wrote to both church and national newspapers pointing out that despite the confusion caused by the Lincoln report Oak Hill was alive and well. He stated that the college would certainly remain open and there was good reason to be hopeful that when the bishops objectively considered the report they would support continuing recognition of the college.

On 11 November Scott called an extraordinary meeting of the college council. The members unanimously expressed their 'indignation over the inaccuracies, omissions, misrepresentations and misleading statements', their 'dissatisfaction with the process leading to the compilation and publication of the report' as well as their 'disagreement with the conclusions and recommendations of the report'. They also expressed their support for the response, the letters written by Dale and Scott to the Bishop of Lincoln and the archbishop as well as the critique of the process.[33] On the same day synod debated and passed the Priests' (Ordination of Women) Measure. On the following day the same members, who must have been exhausted by the emotions raised in the previous day's debate, turned to the Lincoln report. By that time every member had received the college's documentation. The college's future rested on a single morning's debate.

Bridger had been encouraged when David Edwards, the Provost of Southwark, stated in a letter that he wished to speak in opposition to the motion that the synod 'take note' of the report. He thought it his 'duty as an ex-Oxbridge theologian who is not identified with either the Catholic or evangelical party, or with any college or course' to speak against the motion.[34] The debate began at 10.00 a.m. on 12 November with a motion by the Bishop of Bristol, Barry Rogerson, 'that the Synod do take note of this Report'. He learned that this would not be an easy motion to carry when Edwards spoke. Edwards reminded synod that those

---

[33] College council minutes, 11 November 1992.

[34] Letter from Edwards to Mawer (synod secretary), 6 November 1992.

who had opposed women's priesting were assured that they had 'a protected and honoured place in the church'. He then urged the members to 'refrain from any action which might add to the hurt and anxiety felt by those who were in the minority yesterday, as I was not'. He also commented on the 'evident injustice' done to both Mirfield and Oak Hill:

> I have never seen Mirfield, and when I was invited to Oak Hill some years ago I felt a bit like a moth-eaten old lion in a den of Daniels! However, the whole Church is, I believe, committed to the defence of those traditionalists who may now feel insecure or marginalised and, if I may say so, this is an opportunity for us liberals to show that we are indeed liberal.[35]

Although the Bishop of Lincoln defended the report and a few others spoke in its favour, most speakers were opposed to it.[36] The Bishop of London convincingly defended Oak Hill and the plan for a London/Chelmsford/Oak Hill course, commenting: 'many students from a variety of backgrounds have appreciated the clear evangelical stance which is to be found at Oak Hill but which is in no way closed'. The Kingham Hill trustees, he said, 'have a fairly restricted trust deed, but ... the trustees are aware of that, have tried to be sensitive to it, and are working to interpret it in as positive and generous a light as possible'.[37] The factual errors were mentioned by a number of speakers. Field, who was in

---

[35] The General Synod of the Church of England, *Report of Proceedings*, vol. 23, no. 3, p. 785.

[36] An argument for accepting the report's recommendation on Oak Hill was made by one of the members of the advisory group, who pointed out that some colleges would have to close and 'if these colleges do not close, we have a duty to say which will close instead. If not Oak Hill, then which evangelical colleges?' Ibid., p. 804. This was the same argument that bishops who were not sympathetic to Oak Hill made in their responses to the student letters they received.

[37] The full debate is reported in General Synod, *Report of Proceedings*, vol. 23, no. 3, pp. 779–820.

the gallery, commented that most delegates had copies of the response. 'The debate', he observed, 'went almost totally in our favour. There were just one or two speeches out of a couple of dozen made in favour of the report and the rest were heavily critical of it.'[38] The vote was taken and by an overwhelming majority the synod refused to 'take note' of the report. The first battle had been won, but the war was far from over.[39]

The relief quickly abated when it became evident how many more battles needed to be fought. Dale commented that success in the synod was the result of 'a wonderful team effort'. However he continued, 'we have managed to jump Beechers Brook the first time round but there is a round still to go'.[40] Actually there were still several rounds to go. The final decision on the report rested with the House of Bishops. The college had to wait two months before they met.

Those months were filled with meetings and production of documents, while the college continued to receive support. On the 20 November the college and course principals met and asked the House of Bishops to withdraw 'immediately and publicly' the portion of the Lincoln report recommending the closure of the three colleges.[41] In December the vice-chancellor of Middlesex University, David Melville, wrote to the Bishop of Bristol in response to the criticism of Oak Hill's association with them, and Heinze wrote a lengthy document explaining in great detail the

---

[38] Interview with Field.

[39] In an interview Elizabeth Bridger described the attitude at the college during the struggle as positive throughout. 'There was a total lack of vindictiveness and there was a real spirit of charity. Prayers would be asking for God's wisdom and God's will to be done, rather than that those who made the report would be overthrown or put to shame. The only time I did actually detect a little tiny spirit of vindictiveness was on 5 November when there was a college bonfire party and I did spot that around the neck of the guy on top of the bonfire, was a little label Lincoln.'

[40] Letter from Dale to trustee Sir Timothy Hoare, 19 November 1992.

[41] Letter from Parsons to the Archbishop of York, 20 November 1992.

history, advantages and the potential benefits of the relationship. Following correspondence from Bridger, Hugh Marshall, the chief secretary of ABM, came to Oak Hill on 9 December to meet with Bridger, Field and Heinze in an effort to correct errors in the report. The meeting, however, failed to clear up the misunderstandings. On 7 December Dale wrote a nine-page letter to the Bishop of Bristol in response to questions concerning the relationship of the Kingham Hill Trust to the college. Included in the questions was one dealing with how the principal was appointed. In his response Dale referred again to Bridger's appointment and the eventual resolution of that question mentioned earlier. He also pointed out that the trust deed simply required:

> teaching which is in full accord with the Church of England's ecclesiastical and doctrinal stance as expressed in the Ordinal. Its objective, as the staff understand it, is to enable ordinands to give full and informed assent to the Bishop's questions 'Do you accept the holy Scriptures as revealing all things necessary for eternal salvation through faith in Jesus Christ?' and 'do you believe the doctrine of the Christian faith as the Church of England has received it, and in your ministry will you expound and teach it?[42]

On 12 January 1993 the House of Bishops met, but did not arrive at a final decision. The bishops affirmed the section of the report dealing with setting up part-time courses on a regional basis, but set up a new committee to examine the assessment of all colleges and to make new recommendations. The final decision was scheduled for June 1993. The Archbishop of York wrote to the principals on 14 January that 'the period of uncertainty must now extend longer than had been hoped and will cover a wider range of colleges staff and students than might otherwise have been the case'.[43] On 21 January Scott wrote to the archbishop expressing the concern felt by the college council. The 'period

---

[42] Letter from Dale to the Bishop of Bristol, 7 December 1992.
[43] Letter from the Archbishop of York to principals of theological colleges and courses, 14 January 1993.

of uncertainty', he stated, would make it very difficult for colleges and courses 'to plan and budget effectively' and would be particularly hard on potential students. Although the archbishop responded with an understanding letter and promised to bring those concerns to the standing committee of the House of Bishops, he warned that 'I think it unlikely that the committee will want to reverse a quite hard won decision by the whole house.'[44]

The new committee was chaired by the Bishop of Hereford, John Oliver, and included an impressive group of educators, with one college and one course principal nominated by the principals of the theological colleges and courses. Both conservative evangelicals and conservative Anglo-Catholics were represented, and each college was to be visited. On 11–12 May the Bishop of Hereford, the principal of the Oxford Ministerial Training Course, Vincent Strudwick, and Geoffrey Rowell, chaplain of Keble College, visited Oak Hill. Although they represented different traditions from Oak Hill they were scrupulously fair and objective, visiting classes, interviewing both students and staff, and asking some very hard questions. The written material preparatory to the visit was fairly minimal in comparison with what the previous committee had requested. Each college was asked to respond to six questions, to which Oak Hill was able to respond in two pages. A number were concerned with the links with Middlesex, so the college also included Heinze's detailed statement defending the Middlesex link. Middlesex also provided impressive support during the visit. On the first night of the visit David Melville, Ken Goulding and Gary Gibson from their staff came to Oak Hill voluntarily after a long session of their board of governors to meet the visiting party and state their case supporting the college. Goulding also sent a detailed letter to both archbishops summarizing the points made in that meeting, ending with a telling point: 'A church which produced *Faith in the City* should strongly support one of its own theological colleges which wishes to associate with a university which is seeking to teach that

[44] Letter from the Archbishop of York to Scott, 1 February 1993.

very sector of the population which the Church of England has, by its own admission, tended to neglect.'[45]

The bishops did not meet until 13 July to make their final decision but the committee's report was published in June under the title *Theological Colleges: The Next Steps*.[46] The comments on Oak Hill were in marked contrast to those in the Lincoln report. The report stated that although Oak Hill was 'perceived by some and criticised in *A Way Ahead* as being theologically narrow on account of its strictly evangelical foundation, we were pleased to find a greater breadth than we had expected. A range of traditions is represented amongst students and staff.' The link with Middlesex was commended as was the support of the Kingham Hill Trust, and it was also mentioned that the college was working with the dioceses of London and Chelmsford to develop a new part-time ministerial training course. The paragraph at the end was read with a sigh of relief:

> WE RECOMMEND that Oak Hill College should continue to be recognised for the training of ordination candidates provided that it can attract a higher proportion of sponsored candidates and that it should continue to develop creative links with London and Middlesex Universities.[47]

Although Mirfield received a positive recommendation in the report, Salisbury and Wells did not. Chichester was also selected for closure. On 2 July Philip Crowe, now the principal of Salisbury and Wells, wrote to Bridger informing him that the governors had decided to accept the committee's recommendation and close the college, adding a meaningful brief note at the end: 'I am very delighted for you all, and sorry that you've had to go through so much for so long and so unnecessarily.'[48] Ian Cundy, who was

---

[45] Letter from Goulding to the Archbishops of Canterbury and York, 11 June 1993.
[46] *Theological Colleges: The Next Steps* (London: Church House, 1993).
[47] Ibid., p. 26.
[48] Letter from Crowe to Bridger, 2 July 1993.

now Bishop of Lewes, was appointed to monitor the implementation of the recommendations relating to Oak Hill. He visited the college in March and November of 1994 and at the end of the year he wrote a very positive report to the Bishop of Hereford. In it he stated that that the college 'had taken on board all the points in the Lincoln and Hereford Reports and was addressing those which need to be addressed'.[49]

The cost of victory was high. The financial cost was immense, and the college never received an apology or financial compensation for the false and damaging information that had been published and widely publicized in the media. As it was not known until 25 June whether the college would be allowed to continue to train ordinands, relatively few had applied. Bridger reported to the trust in June 1993 that 'in view of the damage caused by the Bishop of Lincoln's report, enquiries and interviews have been at a level of only 50% compared with previous years'.[50] Fortunately the college was able to attract a number of independent students who made their decisions later than the ordinands, so in September 1993 thirty-seven new students joined the college, but only twelve were ordinands, representing a drop of almost fifty per cent from the previous year. Relatively few were willing to risk committing themselves to a college whose future was so uncertain.[51] Ambrose Mason was taken from his OHEC work to help promote the college by preparing new publicity material, writing a new prospectus and sending out the *Oak Hill Newsfax* twice a year. In the long run diverting Mason's attention from OHEC affected the expansion of that programme

[49] Letter from the Bishop of Lewes to the Bishop of Hereford, 6 December 1994.

[50] Minutes of the Kingham Hill trust, 25 June 1993.

[51] Typical of the letters the college received from potential students was one written on 30 November 1992 by a student who had been offered a place. It read: 'we both really enjoyed ourselves at Oak Hill, but with the uncertainty over the Bishop of Lincoln's report we have decided to accept elsewhere.' Letter from Rowe to the admissions office, 30 November 1992.

negatively. In April 1993 Angela Butler was appointed as a part-time member of staff to serve as academic registrar and development officer in an effort to promote the programmes of the college in neighbouring dioceses and to see how the college might provide additional services to them.

A number of staff changes took place during the spring of 1993. Interviews were held for Bray's position as doctrine lecturer, but the college was unsuccessful in finding the qualified, ordained Anglican they were seeking. The position was offered to Martin Davie for a year and readvertised, since he was not ordained. Again, an intended one-year appointment became permanent as Davie proved ideal. An outstanding teacher and a gifted scholar, he also served the college ably as an administrator of the postgraduate programme. In addition his wife, Alyson, who was ordained, served as a part-time tutor in pastoral studies.

The college lost of one of its most valuable staff members when Field announced that he had accepted a position as director of professional ministry with CPAS. Field had been at Oak Hill for twenty-five years, and the college without him seemed inconceivable. Bridger reported to the council 'we are all rather stunned by the news that David Field is leaving', adding that he and his wife Margaret would be greatly missed.[52] At that same meeting Douglas Scott handed over the chair of the council to David Monro after seventeen eventful years:

> Under his chairmanship the college and course have grown in numbers. There have also been significant developments in the validation of diplomas and degrees, first with CNAA and now with Middlesex University. New houses, the new link block and more recently the new tennis courts have been provided for students and their families. Playground and crèche facilities have been provided for children. The library has expanded and a full-time librarian and two Kingham Hill Fellows and the extension field officer have been appointed. In all this

[52] Principal's report, May 1993.

> Douglas has been unfailingly courteous and generous with his time, energy and wisdom.[53]

Field's position as dean of the OHMTC was taken over by Hines. He ably led the course in its final semester, and made a major contribution to the establishment of the new NTMTC. At the May 1993 council meeting Field presented a prospectus for the new London/Chelmsford/Oak Hill ministerial training course. It aimed to develop on and use the resources and experience of the OHMTC and to 'offer opportunity for mixed-mode training' – a mix of part- and full-time training.

The same council meeting received a proposal for mixed-mode training, which had been previously accepted by the Oak Hill academic board. In 1984 Heinze had presented a document outlining the possibility of a mixed-mode course to an informal gathering of council and staff. In October 1990 a proposal was presented to the college strategy review group, and included a contextualized learning approach proposed by Ian Bunting. An appendix to the Lincoln report by Joy Tetley provided further impetus for this approach, and the proposal combined some of her ideas with the previous thinking of the college and Bunting's plans. It suggested a five-year programme including non-residential part-time training while based in a parish, distance-learning courses utilizing the OHEC materials, a year in full-time residential studies and two years of post-ordination training during which the candidate could complete a BA through summer school and distance learning.[54]

This proposal included a major role for OHEC. A report written by an outside advisor, Michael Bulman, who had been asked to review OHEC and make recommendations on mixed-mode training, was presented to the February 1994 council meeting. Entitled 'Mixed-Mode Training for Ordinands', Bulman's

---

53 Ibid.

54 Both the prospectus for the new MTC and the proposal for mixed-mode training are included in the attachments to the minutes of 25 May 1993 council meeting.

proposal laid out in some detail the advantages of this type of training and the role of OHEC. He commented favourably on both the Tetley plan and the Heinze proposal and proposed that Oak Hill should negotiate with adjacent dioceses and begin mixed-mode training 'as soon as practical'.[55] The council also proposed that the trust be asked to appoint a full-time director for OHEC who would also aid in the development of mixed-mode training. The same council meeting received a report that the House of Bishops had formally endorsed the establishment of the NTMTC. A principal would be appointed by June. Tim Thornton, the chaplain to the Bishop of London, a great friend of the college in the difficult months following the Lincoln report, was appointed and Hines became vice-principal. In October 1994 Thornton reported to the college council that progress was being made in the development of a syllabus for the new course, which it was hoped would be introduced within the year. It was also announced that Alan Palmer had been appointed full-time director of OHEC. Mike Butterworth, who had been appointed college dean on Heinze's becoming vice-principal, was thanked for his contribution and the council paid tribute to him, saying that 'it should not be forgotten that the vision for extension training was brought here by Dr Butterworth'.[56]

In October 1994 the future looked extremely hopeful for OHEC, for a mutually beneficial relationship between the college and the NTMTC and for the introduction of mixed-mode training, which would tie the three courses together. In a letter to ABM in July 1994 Bridger pointed out that Oak Hill was in an ideal position to develop mixed-mode training:

> As a college which has full-time, part-time and extension education, which is also in partnership with NTMTC, an associate college of Middlesex University (who advocate mixed-mode vocational courses

---

[55] '*Mixed-mode Training for Ordinands: A Report for Oak Hill College* by the Rev Michael Bulman', December 1993, p. 22.

[56] College council minutes, 19 October 1994.

> themselves), and a founder college of the Open Theological College, we are in a unique position to develop mixed-mode training.[57]

Unfortunately the hopes expressed in that letter were never realized. The relationship with the NTMTC became weaker in the years that followed. A radically different syllabus from the college's was developed and NTMTC sought to establish its independence from the college rather than working to establish joint programmes. Oak Hill staff became less and less involved in teaching on the NTMTC, and efforts to bridge the growing gap between the course and the college were unsuccessful. Even though a development group including both principals, the director of OHEC, the college dean and the development officer was set up and met regularly it was never able to achieve the desired co-operation. A mixed-mode working party with two representatives from the college and two from the NTMTC met regularly until February 1996. Although the members devoted a good deal of time to writing proposals and discussing them, the working party was never able to agree on any specific way forward. In February 1996 Bridger and Thornton dissolved the working party. The two principals expressed their continuing 'commitment to the principle of mixed-mode training' and thanked the working party.[58] This was the end of the bright hope for mixed-mode training and the plans for meaningful co-operation between the college and the NTMTC.

While the college was fighting for survival, seeking to introduce new programmes and establishing a relationship with the NTMTC it also had to deal with developments in the wider church (partly discussed in the previous chapter). The first of these was the passing of the Priests' (Ordination of Women) Measure. Bridger knew this would be a sensitive issue at the college, as it was throughout the church, and despite the pressures he was facing concerning the future of the college, he did not

[57] Letter from Bridger to David Way, 29 July 1994.

[58] Notice from Bridger and Thornton to members of the mixed-mode working group, 27 February 1996.

neglect the needs of Oak Hill's female students. Sensitive to the pressures they would be facing during the debate and after the decision, he and Elizabeth invited the female students to spend the day at their house watching the debate on television. They felt that, away from the other students, women could express their emotions more freely and support each other whatever the outcome of the debate. When the vote went in favour of women's priesting, there were mixed emotions in the group: 'Some women had tears of relief that they were going to be able to be ordained, and there were others who knew that it would produce tensions within their own marriages.'[59] Although there were clearly divisions both on the staff and among the students, the college community, except for a tiny minority who reacted in an emotional and immature way, dealt with the differences in a compassionate and understanding manner.

In the months following the vote Bridger never neglected to provide both male and female students with the support they needed at this time. He stated:

> I kept my study door very open to anyone who wanted to come and talk and a lot of people did. Some people wrote to me and then I'd get them in and we'd talk through some of the issues. I tried to argue for the genuineness of the position of two integrities which some people couldn't accept. I encouraged people to talk to one another. I set out some kind of statement that argued for a two integrity position ... Some people found it very hard on both sides and I think it was an agony reflected in the whole of the church at the time and, to some extent, still is.[60]

On 23 April 1994 three women on the Oak Hill staff, Mary Abbott, Angela Butler and Alyson Davie, were ordained at St Albans Abbey. Bridger reported to the trustees in May 1994:

---

[59] Interview with the Bridgers.
[60] Ibid.

> In college and on the course we represent the 'two integrities', and are seeking to work this out with sensitivity in Oak Hill as a whole. There has been considerable discussion and debate which mostly continues to be constructive, and hopefully models critical thought but not a critical or divisive spirit. Working through this issue in our community has been an important aspect of training for future ministry.[61]

At the same meeting he announced the appointment of Moira Hansen as the new chaplain. It was both a courageous move and a very wise appointment. By appointing a female chaplain Bridger was, according to his own statement, affirming women's ministry and making a statement to the wider church confronting the 'prejudice that Oak Hill devalued women's ministry'.[62]

More significantly, Bridger was committed to appointing the right person for the position regardless of gender. It would take an especially gifted, creative and strong person both to continue the tradition that Hines had begun as well as to supervise a number of new programmes which the next principal would introduce. In addition, the appointee needed to be an excellent teacher, because he or she would be lecturing in ethics, which had been so ably taught for many years by Field. Hansen had all these qualities and the staff were well aware of her gifts – she had been a student at the college. Previously, she had taught at King's College, London, in the area of human environmental studies, and subsequently had served in two parishes as parish deacon. She joined the college staff in summer 1994 as chaplain and co-ordinator of placements with Alyson Davie continuing to give her support as part-time chaplain.[63] Although Hansen would meet with some opposition, overall her appointment was well accepted by the student body

---

[61] Principal's report, May 1994.

[62] Interview with the Bridgers.

[63] Ambrose Mason had served the college in still another role as interim chaplain during the previous semester before Hanson came. In the summer of 1994 he left the staff to become European Development Officer for the Intercontinental Church Society.

and the staff. Those who had doubts were quickly convinced by her able handling of a number of problems that arose. Her honesty and balanced approach won over those who had originally questioned the appointment. In April 1996 she was ordained priest in the chapel by the Bishop of Willesden, Graham Dow. Bridger commented: 'This gives Moira an extended chaplaincy role in the college, and it gives me the opportunity to say how much we appreciate both her teaching and pastoral skills.'[64]

Bridger's position on women's ministry was clearly stated in a letter he wrote to a former student who felt he could no longer in good conscience remain in the Church of England's ministry after the ordination of women. Responding to the student he expressed his regret that the man had felt it necessary to leave on this issue, but he clearly appreciated the former student's concerns. Despite the other pressures he took the time to write in detail examining the relevant biblical texts and presenting his own understanding of them. He concluded that although he was fully committed to the authority of Scripture 'in matters of church government and order, Christian people have often not been united in agreeing on what His Word says about these matters'. He described his position as 'in essentials – unity, in non-essentials – diversity, and in all things – charity', which he maintained 'is still a wise path for the Christian to follow'. Bridger certainly understood and sympathized with the concerns of those who opposed women priests, but he did not agree with their application of Scripture that led them to hold that position. In his letter he stated:

> The ordination of women is never mentioned in the New Testament. The headship of man, and the distinctiveness, quality and complementarity of men and women certainly are. In my view, it is possible for a woman to exercise a presbyteral ministry as part of a team of elders ... without infringing any of these principles.[65]

---

[64] Principal's report, May 1996.
[65] Letter from Bridger to Tannett, 13 July 1994.

He also understood concerns about the danger of dismissing some Scriptures by limiting them to a first-century cultural application. He understood that this position could be applied to the area of homosexuality and could be 'the beginning of a slippery slope on which the church would lose its mooring on moral matters'.[66] However, he clearly knew where to draw the line, as is evident from the college's response to the homosexuality debate.

On 15 May 1995 the Oak Hill council devoted a part of its annual evening discussion with staff and student representatives to what was identified in the agenda as 'The Homosexual Issue'. This issue had recently received a great deal of attention in the press. Part of that publicity had been the result of a statement an Old Oak and a good friend of the college during the Lincoln debate had made when interviewed on BBC Radio 4. Roy Williamson, Bishop of Southwark, had been asked whether he would be happy to ordain a homosexual priest who was not celibate. He replied, 'I would be happy, if his life was a life of holiness and godliness and acceptability, in terms of Scripture and tradition and the present teaching of the church.' This led to a major outcry and the bishop issued a statement making it clear that he would certainly not act in opposition to the church's position: 'As a bishop I am bound by, and totally loyal to, the current teaching of the church contained in the house of bishops' Statement on Human Sexuality.'[67] Bridger wrote to the bishop, who had been a member of the college council, asking for clarification of his position and Williamson responded with a detailed letter explaining his struggles over the issue and expressing his gratitude to Bridger for his letter. Bridger clearly did not identify

---

[66] In interview Bridger stated his view on headship as 'carrying with it the sense of responsibility for women. Therefore that responsibility could be exercised by a team rector (where a woman is a team vicar), or rural dean or even a bishop. So, in my view, it would infringe the principle of headship if a woman became a bishop, but it would not necessarily do so if she became a vicar.'.

[67] Statement issued by the Bishop of Southwark, 17 March 1995.

with the bishop's position, but he was able to state his concerns in a gracious manner.

The issue was brought to the attention of the council as students were concerned 'about the ambiguous statements of certain bishops with respect to the church's attitude, and even to some extent the ambiguity of the document affirmed by the house of bishops, namely *Issues in Human Sexuality*'. They were concerned 'that if the Church of England was not speaking clearly on these issues, perhaps Oak Hill needed to in order to reassure present and future students about the clear biblical position of the college'.[68] The staff shared those concerns and so after considerable discussion and revision by staff and students a statement entitled 'Pastoral Norms for Sexual Morality' was presented to the council in February 1996. It set out in clear terms the scriptural teaching on sexual morality beginning with a statement on the authority of Scripture:

> We, as a college community, seek to submit our lives to the Lord Jesus Christ and thus to the teaching of the Scriptures ... We affirm the divine authority of the Scriptures; we affirm that the Scriptures teach what is necessary for salvation, that the Scriptures are clear in relation to salvation, and that, regarding moral conduct, including sexual morality, the Scriptural teaching is sufficient for us clearly to know the will of God ... Scripture sets the place for sexual intercourse solely within the heterosexual marriage union. Other relationships, whilst meaningful, are to be celibate.

It also stated without any ambiguity that 'adultery, pre-marital sexual intercourse, same-gender sexual intercourse, and sexual harassment are morally wrong. They are matters of discipline within the Christian community; such discipline seeks to bring about repentance and restoration.' The statement also expressed regret for 'past and present failures within the Christian church and in dealing with those who found this teaching difficult

---

68 Council discussion on the issue of homosexuality: some background notes, 15 May 1995.

and painful'. It also affirmed 'the need for understanding, and for offering appropriate pastoral care and concern in all such situations'.[69] The council discussed the statement, raised some questions and 'it was left to the principal and the college to make use of the document appropriately'.[70] The college community had taken a clear and carefully thought out scriptural stance on one of the very controversial questions confronting the church.

PERSONALITY PROFILE

Tim Ward was converted in his last year at school, through the witness of a friend and the youth group in a church near his home in Solihull, West Midlands. He left there for Oxford University in 1986, from where he went in 1990 to work as lay assistant at Christ Church, Fulwood, in Sheffield. This was a privileged time, working under Old Oak Philip Hacking and Gavin McGrath.

While in Sheffield Tim went forward for ordained ministry, and in 1992 came to Oak Hill to begin training. Halfway through his time there it was suggested to him that he pursue postgraduate study. He postponed seeking a curacy, and in 1995 moved to Edinburgh to begin a PhD at the university on the doctrine of scripture. Tim's sponsoring diocese (Sheffield) were very supportive, as were the staff at Oak Hill – Tim remained officially an Oak Hill student all through his time in Edinburgh. In particular, the Kingham Hill Trust provided a very generous financial grant towards the cost of studying and living in Edinburgh. Other friends from Oak Hill also gave regularly and generously.

Tim asked the principal, Gordon Bridger, if he knew of a good church in Edinburgh. Gordon suggested that St Thomas, Corstorphine, might be a good place, adding that he had previously been rector there for ten years! The current rector, Mike Parker, provided great opportunities in

[69] 'Pastoral norms for sexual morality: attachment to college council minutes', 7 February 1996.

[70] College council minutes, 7 February 1996.

> ministry to keep Tim's feet on the ground. The PhD topic developed into a study of the sufficiency of Scripture in the modern world, and is being published in revised form by Oxford University Press in 2002. Tim's PhD was awarded in 1999, and he moved straight into a curacy at the other end of the country, at All Saints, Crowborough, in East Sussex.

In his October 1994 principal's report Bridger reported a number of staff changes. After noting that two secretaries, Carrie Field and Lynette Hamilton, were leaving, he reported that the trustees had decided upon a major reorganization of the bursarial department, which would result in John Bree being made redundant. The trustees had decided to create a new position of trust director of administration, responsible for the administration of Oak Hill, Kingham Hill school and other trust matters, and taking over many of the functions of the present Oak Hill bursar. A college bursar with diminished responsibilities would be appointed in place of the existing bursar and assistant bursar positions. This meant that both John Bree's and Tom Hendry's positions would in effect be eliminated. At a leaving party held for the Brees, past and present members of the Oak Hill community expressed their appreciation to them. Bridger paid them the following tribute:

> John and Sue Bree left Oak Hill on January 31 after over twenty years of hard work and committed service to the college. Many tributes were paid to them in the sermon in chapel by Canon David Wheaton and in speeches afterwards during the buffet meal ... John and Sue's commitment to the job has grown and developed over the years, John's entrepreneurial skills, and the way in which both John and Sue have gone the extra mile at times to get a job completed or to help an individual were all mentioned in the tributes. The gratitude and affection of past and present members of the college and course were

[71] Principal's report, February 1995.

> clearly signalled by the size of the cheque which was presented to John and Sue as their farewell gift.[71]

A new bursarial team, consisting of Brian Martin as the trust's director of administration and Allan Brown as bursar, took over in 1995. Carol Forman, an Old Oak who had been minding the crèche, replaced Sue Bree temporarily in the role of domestic bursar. Helen Archer took over six weeks later, and brought to the post the same efficiency and dedication as Sue Bree had shown.

In his February 1995 principal's report Bridger stated that he would like to hand over the principalship to a successor by July 1996. He encouraged the council to set 'in motion, as soon as possible, the procedure to find a new principal'.[72] In view of the criticisms over his appointment, the council carefully laid out the procedure to be followed, which would give them the predominant role. They set up a selection panel to review applications and arrive at a shortlist. The council would then meet to approve or change the list and make arrangements for interviews. A substantial number of candidates applied and five were shortlisted. The candidates met with the staff before formal interviews were held by the council on 12 June. All were well qualified and the decision was extremely difficult, but at the end of an open evening of discussion weighing the merits of each candidate David Peterson was recommended. No one could have raised questions about this appointment as after carefully following the specified procedures the trustees appointed the candidate recommended by the council. Both trustees and council were convinced that he was the man best qualified to lead the college into the new century.

Peterson was appointed in June 1995, but Bridger would stay in office for another year. During that time he contributed significantly to helping his successor make the transition. Many of the programmes Peterson wished to introduce, discussed in the next chapter, were developed in that year. In addition a visiting scholar programme supported by the trust was introduced and another

---

[72] Ibid.

Australian, Bishop Paul Barnett, gave a series of lectures and biblical expositions that were extremely well received. During Bridger's final year he and the staff also prepared the documents for another bishops' inspection, to take place in February 1997. Bridger, who had begun his term of office with a CNAA visit, now ended it by preparing for yet another inspection.

Bridger delivered his final sermon in chapel at the Commissioning Service on 9 June 1996. After he had commissioned the leaving students the vice-principal commissioned him and Elizabeth to go forward to their new ministries in retirement. Bridger's principalship was concluded – no one could deny that it had been an exciting decade, and a creative one, resulting in new programmes and new directions. Bridger had led the college ably through some of the most difficult years in its history. In the final two years of his principalship the trustees utilized the services of an independent consultant, Alan Riley, to promote the college. In December 1994 he produced an audit of attitudes towards the college. The seventy-eight-page report revealed a great many different attitudes and some continuing misunderstanding; however, the overall impression was quite positive. Riley summed up his findings in the following way:

> What is very clear from the audit is that Oak Hill is perceived as being at a critical period in its life, a pivotal time in its development. The audit reveals a sense of expectation of movement or transition for Oak Hill. There is a distinct sense of a bigger potential waiting to be achieved, of a destiny to be grasped. The college is seen by all respondents ... as having a future and a role.[73]

Bridger had carried the college through the greatest crisis in its history. Peterson would now lead it into the new century and seek to realize the 'potential waiting to be achieved'.

---

[73] Alan Riley, audit undertaken for Oak Hill College, October–December 1994, p. 75.

9

A New College for a New Century? (1996–2000)

> Oak Hill Theological College has announced the appointment of Rev. Dr. David Peterson to succeed Canon Gordon Bridger ... David Peterson is an evangelical scholar and pastor of international standing. He is currently head of the Department of Ministry at Moore Theological College, where he has worked full-time for 11 years, and lectures in New Testament, Christian worship, and pastoral studies. He was previously Rector and Senior Canon at St. Michael's Cathedral, Wollongong.[1]

So ran the press release in June 1995 announcing the appointment of David Peterson as the new principal of Oak Hill. His qualifications for the post were excellent. Having been in his present post since 1984, he had written or edited five books, published a substantial number of scholarly articles and was engaged in writing a commentary on Acts. Australian by birth, he had lived in Manchester for three years while completing his PhD and for two six-month periods of study leave at Tyndale House in Cambridge. He also had experience in English parish ministry, having assisted in the parish of St Mary's, Cheadle, Cheshire, while completing his PhD. Like Bridger before him, he had to leave his wife, Lesley, behind until the youngest of their three sons had completed his education.

[1] Press release, 'Oak Hill College announces new principal', 30 June 1995.

Although highly qualified for the position, his appointment was viewed with suspicion by some who thought he was 'reactionary, closed-minded', and opposed to women's ministry.[2] In the effort to dispel false stereotypes Peterson made several visits before he officially took office in September 1996. In August 1995 he met some members of ABM and the NTMTC. During his second visit in January 1996 he held a one-day theology school at Westminster Central Hall based on his book *Possessed by God*.[3] He also met with directors of ordinands and ministry advisors from various dioceses. In addition, the spring 1996 *News Fax* devoted its first two pages to a recording of an interview with him shortly before he returned to Australia. His view of Scripture indicated a commitment to careful scholarship. He also should have dispelled the fears of those who believed he was opposed to women's ministry:

> I want women to come to Oak Hill and be comfortable and appreciated. We want to help them search out in the context of Christian fellowship the most helpful vocation and service for them. On the other hand, we want to help those who have doubts about women's ministry to think through their own position so that in fellowship together we can help women move forward in ministry and encourage them in it.[4]

Peterson brought a new vision to the college, based on his previous experience at Moore College. Building on the tradition established at the college by his predecessors he was committed to a course based on thorough biblical study with good theological foundations combined with practical training to prepare men and women fully for ministry in the Church of England. He

---

[2] Riley produced some guidelines for responding to questions people were asking about Peterson's appointment, see letter to members of council and trust, 30 June 1996. Heinze recalls having a serious discussion with a senior official in the Church of England who misunderstood Peterson's position on a number of issues.

[3] Leicester: IVP, 1995.

[4] *News Fax*, Issue 4, Spring 1996, p. 2.

introduced a number of new approaches to achieve those objectives even before he officially took office. In January 1996 he and the faculty spent two days together at a retreat centre to work out the details of a new course. Building on the solid basis of the former course, a number of innovations were introduced. The new course would be 'more prescriptive' and would spread the Old and New Testament modules over a two-year period, 'with a set book in each semester to focus attention on exegesis, and to teach biblical theology through exegesis'. Peterson recalls those initial meetings with the faculty as 'a very invigorating time'. Although 'some had to give way in areas of teaching to accommodate others', there 'was an enthusiasm to get it right, to get a new balance and to work with a new vision'.[5]

A particularly creative innovation was the introduction of a Certificate of Ministry course. This ran alongside the other courses and focused on preparation for ordination. Based on the Moore College model, it took many of the subjects that had been covered in what were termed leavers' lectures, designed to prepare students for the parish but which were never officially assessed, and made them a part of a validated course. Peterson commented, 'it seemed to me to be a very valuable way of putting the focus on ministry strategies and perspectives and skills for ministry. It also provided the opportunity for the ordinands to be together for two hours a week for two years of their training, focusing on specifically Anglican issues.'[6] Another particularly innovative feature of the new course was a provision for 'integrated seminars'. The idea was based partly on an article by Francis Bridger, entitled 'The Problem of Integration in Theological Education'. He described integration as 'the bringing together and interweaving of various strands of theological education', and called it 'an exercise in synthesis'.[7] The Oak Hill

---

[5] Peterson's account.

[6] Ibid.

[7] Francis Bridger, 'The Problem of Integration in Theological Education', *British Journal of Theological Education*, vol 4, no. 3 (Winter 1991/92), p. 23.

plan was to hold fortnightly seminars combining two disciplines, designed to help the student recognize the unique contributions of each discipline and to integrate academic training with practical parish experience.

During the spring and summer of 1996 the staff were once again busy preparing submissions. First they were required to prepare another ABM 22 submission, which would include the new Certificate of Ministry course. The submission, completed in March, was 130 pages long plus 2 appendices. The visiting team came to the college on 3 April. They reacted very favourably to what they read in the submission and what they observed at the college. They commented particularly on 'the progress made in developing a series of interconnected awards from Certificate to MA level, the projected integrative seminars and the new Certificate of Ministry'. This was accepted following a supplementary submission to provide clarification on some points and additional information on others.[8]

However, the staff also had to arrange for Middlesex to validate the new certificate of ministry. The submission presented for this was considerably shorter and required a good deal less work than the ABM 22 submission. The validation panel was particularly helpful when they met with the college staff and selected students on 5 June, and the following day the chairman of the four-person panel informed them that the certificate had been validated for five years. He also congratulated the college on 'the work they have done on this submission' and spoke highly of its potential benefits stating that it offered 'a coherent package, which works hard at integration of the very broad range of objectives and learning experiences. It would appear to be a very positive development of the existing training programme.'[9] Five recommendations in their report asked for clarification of a number of matters and more information: this was supplied and by September 1996 the Certificate of Ministry became the first

---

[8] Letter from David Way to Bridger, 24 April 1996.
[9] Letter from S.E. Alsford to Butterworth, 6 June 1996.

validated professional qualification to be offered in Church of England theological colleges and courses.

The Bishop of London, Richard Chartres, licensed David Peterson in the college chapel on 27 September 1996. Fortunately, Peterson was full of energy and enthusiasm, as he was immediately confronted with a number of problems. The first and most serious was the decline in student numbers. There were forty-five leavers in June 1995 and twenty-six new students, including only eleven ordinands, joined the college in the new academic year. The after-effects of the Lincoln report were still very much evident. Staff and students alike frequently ran into people who were surprised to learn that Oak Hill was still operating.[10] The trustees realized the seriousness of the problem and they decided to employ a commercial manager to publicize the college. Peter Wood, who had twenty-two years of experience in marketing with British Gas, became the first commercial manager and he has proved an excellent choice. In the autumn 1996 *News Fax* he commented on the need to change the inaccurate perception of the college that many held: 'What Oak Hill now offers is very impressive ... The problem we have is that many do not clearly understand what the college is actually like. There is much hard work to be done to begin to change these perceptions.'[11] In his first report to the college council Peterson stated that the new commercial manager had already begun promotional work by producing a new Oak Hill video for recruitment purposes and a number of new pamphlets advertising the college. This was the beginning of a brilliant campaign.

Another effort to publicize the college were the so-called 'road shows'. Although Peterson probably did not realize at the time, these were similar to the 'Opportunity Knocks' weekends introduced by Wood in 1966. Peterson and other staff members went

---

[10] Dale estimated that the Lincoln report 'had probably cost the trust between £1/2 and £1 million', college council minutes, 10 February 1999.

[11] *News Fax*, Issue 6 (Autumn 1996), p. 4.

out with groups of students to key churches and invited clergy in the region to come with potential theological students. They gave a presentation on Saturday morning and 'invited potential students to ask questions and explore with us the possibility of coming to college'.[12] In addition a group of clergy founded an organization called 9:38, after Matthew 9:38: 'Ask the Lord of the harvest, therefore, to send out workers into his harvest field.' The plan was to hold an annual conference for people who were interested in training for ministry and to provide an apprenticeship scheme where they could serve in local churches. They would also take part in regional conferences focusing on biblical, theological and pastoral issues so that, when they went to selection conferences and afterwards to theological college, they would have the advantage of having had ministerial experience and a certain amount of training.

Peterson also tried to correct the negative image of the college by inviting bishops and directors of ordinands (DDOs) to visit the college so that they could see how inaccurate the image was. Peterson described the problem and his solution to it in the following way:

> I discovered that the prejudice against the college was keeping students from joining us. Some were being told by bishops and DDOs that they simply were not permitted to come to Oak Hill as an option. Others were being strongly urged to go elsewhere. It has therefore been my policy from the very beginning to try and invite as many sponsoring bishops to the college to preach as possible, and to invite DDOs to come on a regular basis to get to know us and get their questions answered. We have been encouraged by the positive responses that we have received from those who have visited us. It is wonderful to see people's attitudes changed by meeting the staff and students, and experiencing a few hours with us at chapel or in lectures.[13]

---

[12] Peterson's account.

[13] Ibid.

The recruitment effort bore fruit almost immediately. The *News Fax* announced 'an encouraging increase on last year's figures' in 1997 and in winter 1998 it was announced that 'with the arrival of 22 new ordinands, we are now close to our current quota of 55 preparing for the Anglican ministry'. Hopes for the future were so high that the college applied for an increase in the quota of ordinands 'to the level applying before the Lincoln Report'.[14] The new century began with the largest intake since before the publication of the Lincoln report as thirty-eight new students, including three female ordinands, joined the college in September 2000. Hopefully the effects of the Lincoln report had finally been overcome.

Another major problem that Peterson faced was the need to build a new staff. He came to lead one of the best-qualified staffs in the Church of England. The August 1996 submission revealed that seven of the ten full-time staff members held doctorates. In addition, their CVs listed an impressive number of publications, including major scholarly works published by Oxford and Cambridge University presses.[15] Although he was fortunate to inherit such a staff, their qualifications resulted in their being sought after for other positions. The first to leave was Mike Butterworth, who in September 1996 was offered the principalship of the St Albans and Oxford Ministerial Training Course. It is hard to imagine a more serious loss to the college at the beginning of a new principal's term. Butterworth was one of the longest-serving members of staff. He was an excellent teacher and a good administrator who had served in a variety of administrative posts including the crucial dean's position. He was also a recognized scholar, having published a major work on Zechariah, and he was the originator of OHEC. Throughout his time at Oak Hill he had never lost contact with the parish and served the parish of St James, New Barnet, in a variety of ministerial roles. Butterworth was important to the college in many ways. His good

---

[14] *News Fax*, Issue 8 (Winter 1997), p. 1 and Issue 10 (Winter 1998), p. 1.
[15] Submission for ministry division inspection, August 1996.

friend and colleague of fourteen years, Alan Storkey, expressed this very well in the tribute he wrote:

> There is a level of commitment to individuals, through the time at Oak Hill and many years beyond, in phone calls, letters, prayer and visits. There is a commitment to the institution of Oak Hill and the community – through committees and prayer, through administration and worship, through reviews and submissions. In all of these Mike has contributed richly to the ethos and efficiency of the place with patience, love and a keen concern for all. There is a level of biblical commitment – to an accurate understanding of what the Scriptures say linguistically, structurally and in terms of ways to address us, to good scholarship which handles arguments thoroughly and fairly. But further, there is the submission and self-examination which this provokes – thoughtful, reflective and life-changing, which should be the real dynamic of Christian living and which Mike is.[16]

Replacing Butterworth was not easy. Initially the position was filled temporarily as the college waited for the person they had in mind to become available. As in the case of Head and Davie, Thomas Renz, who was initially appointed for only a year, became a long-term member of staff when his outstanding gifts in teaching and administration became evident. He and his wife Gabi had grown up in Germany, and he came to Britain to study for his PhD under Gordon Wenham at Cheltenham and Gloucester College of Higher Education. He completed his dissertation on the prophecy of Ezekiel before joining the staff in September 1997.

In the same year the college was also fortunate in finding the right man to replace Allan Brown when Adrian White was appointed as the new bursar. During his tenure, as will be explained later, the college would undertake the largest building project in its history. The heavy burdens of providing for a large entering class and a record number of American students on

[16] *News Fax*, Issue 6 (Autumn 1996), p. 6.

what was literally a building site for over a year would fall on his shoulders. White's placid efficiency was to prove especially important in dealing with the turmoil created by that project. In addition he was asked to take on increased responsibility when Brian Martin resigned at the very time building was beginning.

Another new staff member was Chris Hayward, who joined the staff as an associate member with responsibility for chapel music and teaching Hebrew and Greek. His musical gifts and leadership in establishing a chapel programme that drew on the multiple talents of the student body were to enhance college worship significantly.

The NTMTC suffered a major loss when Hines left to become rector of a number of rural parishes in Norfolk in October 1996. His parting thoughts on leaving summed up in a few words what he had sought to achieve during his time at Oak Hill:

> During my time at the college and, more recently, as vice-principal of the new North Thames Ministerial Training Course, I have sought God's help not only to teach about, but also to model with integrity, what being a Church of England presbyter/priest is all about. I have exhorted hundreds of ordinands both to prepare in all seriousness for the Oaths and Declarations which they would make at their ordination and also to use and appreciate the church's liturgical worship ... I pray that in the coming years many more ordinands will emerge from Oak Hill with full assurance of faith, with their Anglican integrity intact, and ready to co-operate with God in the work of the gospel.[17]

Tim Thornton also wrote a well-deserved tribute to Hines in the same edition of *News Fax*. Thornton would leave the NTMTC within two years to be replaced by David Sceats. Under Sceats's leadership the NTMTC began to mature into an excellent training course and it would begin the new century with great potential for the future and the hope of establishing a closer working relationship with the college.

---

[17] Ibid., pp. 6–7.

At the same time, Peterson introduced another aspect of his vision for the college. As an established biblical scholar it is not surprising that he placed a strong emphasis on serving the wider church by sharing the results of the scholarly work of the Oak Hill staff. An initial step in that direction was a theology school run jointly by the *Church of England Newspaper* and Oak Hill College, launched in January 1997. Two staff members, Mike Peat and Martin Davie, contributed a series of articles on Christian doctrine. Readers could register to receive further material, including a copy of the book *Doctrinal Matters* edited by an Old Oak, Gordon Kurht.[18] By summer 1997 over 700 readers were registered.

Peterson also began a considerably more ambitious project in his first year as principal – the Oak Hill School of Theology. This involved staff members exploring a joint topic from the perspective of their different disciplines and sharing their work in a full-day conference. The first topic was fittingly 'Proclaiming the Resurrection', and it was held on 16 April 1997 with five staff members contributing. Although this added to the pressures of an already overworked staff, they welcomed the opportunity to write scholarly works rather than submissions, and this first School of Theology was a remarkable success. The college had a pleasant surprise when 150 people attended instead of the 30 or so they had anticipated. The feedback from those who attended was enthusiastic about what they had gained from the day and the prospect of further schools. The papers were published in 1998, in a volume edited by Peter Head.[19]

A second school was held in 1998 on the theme 'Witness to the World'. Again, a cross-section of disciplines was represented. Woodbridge, Weston and Storkey contributed papers from the perspective of their disciplines. Andrew Hartropp, an Oak Hill graduate doing doctoral research at King's College, London, and

---

[18] London: Hodder & Stoughton, 1993.

[19] Peter Head (ed.), *Proclaiming the Resurrection* (Carlisle: Paternoster, 1998).

the visiting scholar, Graham Cole, principal of Ridley College, Melbourne, also contributed papers. The volume was edited by David Peterson and published in the following year.[20] The third school in 1999 brought in a well-known evangelical scholar who had begun his teaching career at Oak Hill. James Packer from Regent College, Vancouver, spent a week at the college, giving four lectures on the theme 'The Church, the Churches and Church People'. For the fourth school the staff decided that the topic should be the atonement, since a number of evangelical writers had questioned the penal view or modified it in ways that they felt needed a response. The planned volume also included a reprint of an essay by one of the great men of the college's past, Alan Stibbs. The papers were published in a volume edited by David Peterson entitled *Where Wrath and Mercy Meet: Proclaiming the Atonement Today*.[21] Having established an alternating pattern with a visiting scholar every other year, it was decided to invite Professor Don Carson from Trinity Evangelical Divinity School to lead the school in 2001.

Although preparation for the Oak Hill School of Theology was a welcome diversion, the day of preparing submissions was far from over. Peterson would have his first experience of a bishops' inspection two months before the first School of Theology. The inspectors, led by the Archdeacon of Sudbury, John Cox, were on campus from 10–14 February, and were as perceptive in the questions they asked as in the recommendations they made. They were also fair and quite understanding of some of the difficulties facing the college in a period of transition, as the new principal was only beginning his second semester in residence. In their report they stated:

> We arrived at the college aware that there was a good deal of disquiet in the Church of England about the college, some of it based on direct

[20] David Peterson (ed.), *Witness to the World* (Carlisle: Paternoster, 1999).

[21] Carlisle: Paternoster, 2001.

> knowledge, some of it on hearsay and supposition. Most specifically there was concern about the suitability of the college as a place for the training of women for ordained ministry. We looked into this matter carefully and, as will become evident elsewhere in the report, we discovered that there had been some genuine difficulties, but that these had been tackled in both an open and a sensitive way ... Both among students and the staff there is a broader outlook and sympathy than might have been supposed and in general we found this reassuring.[22]

Of their ten recommendations the first was especially welcome as it stated that 'the college should continue to be recognised by the house of bishops for the training of ordination candidates'. Four of the other recommendations dealt with minor issues that were easy to correct.[23] More substantial concerns expressed were that only one of the staff had experience as an incumbent and 'that there is not currently a woman member of staff who models in herself either the experience or the intention of being an incumbent'. Therefore they recommended that in new staff appointments 'careful consideration be given to the subject balance but also to the need to have a member of staff with recent incumbent experience in the Church of England, preferably a woman'. They also noted that there was within the college 'a strongly articulated viewpoint' that represented a minority position both within the church and 'within the evangelical tradition'. While accepting that this view could legitimately be held, they stated that this 'should not become the only voice nor encourage an exclusive

[22] Report of Ministry Division inspection of Oak Hill College 1997, p. 1.

[23] One recommended that a DDO and 'a person with direct entry into the house of bishops' be added to the membership of the college council. A second asked for a review of assessment board procedures. A third recommendation encouraged the college 'to make every effort to increase the number of men and woman ordinands', which the college was, in fact, already doing. A fourth recommended 'a detailed review of placement assessment and feedback procedures'. This was also already being undertaken.

approach within the college'. Consequently they recommended that 'serious attention be given to the exposure of students to a wider range of Anglican understanding'.[24]

With the exception of the suggestion that a woman with incumbent's experience be appointed[25] the staff were quite committed to putting into practice these recommendations. Efforts had been made to add a staff member with incumbency experience for some time. Peterson stated in his report to the council in October 1997 that he was 'absolutely committed to seeking such incumbency experience if at all possible'. The problem was finding someone who also had the 'academic expertise and experience and who may be able to meet our teaching needs in the particular academic discipline that we may be seeking to develop'.[26] When no suitable qualified candidate applied for the next vacancy, a very experienced incumbent and Old Oak, Alex Ross, the vicar of St James, Muswell Hill, Greater London, was added to the staff as a visiting lecturer for the Certificate of Ministry. The staff were also very committed to exposing students 'to a wider range of Anglican understanding', as the inspectors had recommended. This had been done and would continue to be done by bringing in people from different traditions to speak in chapel, to take part in debates and to contribute to classes as visiting lecturers. In addition students were regularly placed in parishes that represented radically different traditions from that of the college. With the exception of appointing a woman incumbent, none of the recommendations conflicted with any convictions held by the staff.

---

[24] Ibid., pp. 5–6.

[25] In his report to the council after receiving the inspection report Peterson stated that he had 'reservations about the employment of a woman incumbent to the staff'. He explained that his reservations were based on his understanding of 1 Timothy 2:12. He commented: 'it seems to me ... that incumbency or congregational oversight by a woman priest is going beyond the sense of 1 Timothy 2'. Principal's report, October 1997.

[26] Ibid.

The report also drew attention to chapel worship. Evangelicals have always had a deep commitment to preaching and it was not unusual that liturgy was curtailed in order to make more room for it. This pattern had become even more pronounced in the year of the inspection, as every service included at least some comment on the texts. A staff member gave a meditation in the Monday morning service, Tuesday was devoted to Bible exposition, the Thursday communion service included a full-length sermon, and on Friday students were given the opportunity to preach. In commenting on this the inspectors felt the emphasis on preaching was probably too strong and that there was insufficient attention to the liturgy. They were concerned that the college was not giving adequate preparation for Anglican worship. One of their comments was that the college had 'clearly a long way to go before it would be safe to say that the college is helping to inculcate a sense of the continuity, rhythm and discipline of Anglican corporate prayer'. Their first recommendation on worship was, therefore, that 'more attention be given to the formation of a spiritual discipline that will sustain them in their role within the church of the future'. A second urged that 'further attention be given to the pattern, style and conduct of corporate worship' and a third stated that a room 'suitably decorated and furnished' be set aside for private prayer.[27] The last recommendation was by far the easiest to meet and a prayer room furnished with kneelers, bibles, devotional books and music CDs was a welcome addition to the college facilities.

The college took very seriously the need to increase the number of female ordinands and on 28 February 1998 a full-day conference was devoted to the question of women's ministry. Sixty women, lay and ordained, from a large number of different churches attended. After Peterson spoke on 'Prophetic Ministry for All', Christine Farrington, the vicar of St Mark's, Cambridge, who had been one of the inspectors, gave an overview of the situation in the church regarding women's ministry. Three other

[27] Ibid., pp. 15–17.

women spoke on their experiences and frustrations in their particular ministries. Following the day the college agreed on a number of resolutions to encourage women's ministry and training at Oak Hill. The first and clearly determining resolution was that 'the faculty will make every effort to affirm and support women in college whether staff, students or spouses, and in whatever ministry they are pursuing'.[28]

The staff were at this time also preparing another submission. It had been five years since the college had validated its courses, therefore a revalidation exercise had to be undertaken. A document was prepared describing the six courses now taught at the college as well giving the information about the institution and procedures required in CNAA submissions.[29] Organizing this submission and the accreditation visit was to be Heinze's last administrative contribution as academic dean, a post he had resumed on Butterworth's departure. Paul Woodbridge took over from him in September 1997 and Paul Weston became vice-principal. Woodbridge was able to report to the college council in October 1997 that 'the re-validation exercise with Middlesex University had taken place ... with a successful and positive outcome',[30] and Heinze was able to enjoy his final semester at Oak Hill 'just teaching'. He retired at the end of the first semester and returned to the USA. As a statement of the close relationship that had developed between Middlesex University and Oak Hill, vice-chancellor Ken Goulding announced at Heinze's retirement party that the university had bestowed an honorary professorship on him. A year later he returned as visiting scholar to do some teaching and to begin work on this book.[31] In September 1999

---

[28] *News Fax*, Issue 9 (Summer 1998), p. 3.

[29] The courses were Certificate of Ministry, DipHE in theological and pastoral studies, BA in theological and pastoral studies, BA (Hons) in theological and pastoral studies, MA in theology, postgraduate research studies.

[30] College council minutes, 15 October 1997.

[31] The visiting scholar programme continued to add significantly to the college's programme. After Paul Barnett, Colin Buchanan and

Gary Williams joined the staff as the new church historian, bringing scholarly and teaching gifts as well as the creativity, enthusiasm and energy of youth to the college.

During the first years of Peterson's term of office the college was very much affected by a major debate in the Anglican Communion of the question of sexuality and the resolution on that subject passed at the 1998 Lambeth Conference. In November 1996 a service to celebrate the twenty-fifth anniversary of the Lesbian and Gay Christian Movement was held in Southwark Cathedral and addressed by the Bishop of Guildford, John Gladwin. The facts that the bishop spoke at the service and that it was held in the cathedral were controversial, even though the bishop's comments did not endorse the gay lifestyle and in fact pointed out that there was a conflict between how the church had traditionally interpreted the scriptural teachings and the movement's view.

Shortly afterwards Peterson gave a sermon in the chapel in which he presented clearly the biblical view on sexuality. The same view was presented in a statement issued in February 1997 by Anglican leaders from the southern hemisphere meeting at Kuala Lumpur in Malaysia. The churches that the delegates represented contained at least eighty per cent of all the Anglicans in the world and a unanimous statement emerged from the meeting. It contained the following unambiguous statement: 'Holy Scriptures are clear in teaching that all sexual promiscuity is sin. We are convinced that this includes homosexual practices between men or women as well as heterosexual relationships outside marriage.' While the statement expressed compassion for those 'who are trapped in their sexual brokenness', stating 'we wish to stand alongside and welcome them into a process of being whole and restored within our communities of faith', it condemned the 'ordination of practising homosexuals and the blessing of same-sex unions'.[32]

---

[31] (*continued*) Norman Schmaltz, visiting scholars included Dr Graham Cole, Principal of Ridley College, Melbourne, and Dr David Seccombe, Principal of George Whitefield College, Capetown.

[32] Steer, *Church on Fire*, p. 393.

The Kuala Lumpur statement also received support from traditionalists in America who were especially distressed by the direction the Episcopal Church of the USA (ECUSA) had taken on this question. In November 1997 one of the bishops of that church, John Shelby Spong, of the diocese of New Jersey, circulated an open letter to the Anglican primates entitled 'A Message to the Anglican Communion on the Subject of Homosexuality'. It stated in unqualified terms the opposing view to that contained in the Kuala Lumpur statement. It was a confident, threatening letter, showing no sign of anything that might remotely be called a conciliatory attitude on the subject, and Archbishop Carey felt compelled to answer. He reminded the outspoken bishop that the tone of his letter was not particular helpful, and that a large number of bishops throughout the world were in agreement with the Kuala Lumpur statement. He urged him to come to Lambeth 'in peace ... to learn ... to share' and to 'leave behind any campaigning tactics which are inappropriate and unproductive whoever employs them'.[33] Unfortunately, Carey's letter did not have any obvious effect on the bishop and his response was even more vitriolic.

These exchanges set the tone for the Lambeth Conference and assured that, despite all the other questions the bishops had come to discuss, the question of sexuality would receive primary attention in the press. Despite the clamour before and during the meetings, the delegates were remarkably united on the question. The resolution on sexuality was a moderate in tone, but clearly in accord with biblical teaching, showing compassion for those with a homosexual orientation, but rejecting homosexual practice as incompatible with Scripture. It was passed with a final vote of 526 in favour, 70 opposed with 45 abstentions.

A revealing commentary on the conference is contained in an article written by former Oak Hill student Terence Kelshaw, Bishop of the Rio Grande. Continuing the tradition of scriptural gospel ministry, Kelshaw has that deep commitment to evangelism

[33] Ibid., p. 407.

gained at Oak Hill during the Wood years that is sadly not common in ECUSA. He pointed out that:

> I come from a troubled Province in the United States, from a church that is thoroughly enculturated and finds it difficult to separate itself from the culture. It has difficulty in deciding whether it is for the gospel or for the culture, for politics or for prayer. Inevitably, this makes life in the church difficult in many ways. Political correctness is far more significant than the gospel message, and it is more important not to upset anyone than to preach the Truth.[34]

The Lambeth resolution on sexuality was, of course, also very much in accord with the position taken at Oak Hill, and, in fact, it seems that Peterson made a contribution to the Lambeth resolution through an article he wrote in the summer 1997 *News Fax* entitled 'Loving the Homosexual'. It began by reminding his readers of some of the provocative headlines on this subject and then summarized the contents of a book by Marion Soards, a Professor of New Testament studies at an American Presbyterian Seminary. The book, entitled *Scripture and Homosexuality: Biblical Authority and the Church Today*,[35] presented the biblical teaching on homosexuality in a fair and balanced way. Peterson summed up the conclusions of the book in the following words:

> Christians who affirm biblical authority are called to a combination of candour and compassion concerning homosexuality. In candour from a careful study of and reflection on the Scriptures, and with a full measure of humility because we recognise and confess our own sinfulness, we can say that we cannot and do not condone homosexual activity as sexual practice in accordance with the intention of God for humanity. In compassion, we must oppose all mistreatment of homosexuals and any denial of basic civil rights. If there is no

[34] T. Kelshaw, 'Reflections on the Lambeth Conference '98', *Churchman* vol. 113, no. 1 (1999), p. 18.

[35] Louisville, KY: Westminster John Knox Press, 1995.

> demand for approval of homosexual activity, we should welcome into our fellowship anyone who struggles to serve the Lord as a forgiven sinner. With them, we should seek the healing and transforming power of God, acknowledging our brokenness and failure to please him in every area of our lives, not the least in the sexual realm.[36]

Peterson later learned that his article had led the Archbishop of Sydney, Harry Goodhew, to read Soards's book and to use many of the arguments from the book in the debates leading to the Lambeth resolution on sexuality.

The first years of the Peterson administration also witnessed a change in OHEC as in 1996 the name was changed to the Oak Hill Open Learning Centre. The Open Learning Centre expanded its activities to include a series of evening courses for lay people, which began with a course in biblical theology taught by Peterson in February 1997 followed by one in church history taught by Heinze in September 1997. The response exceeded all expectation as eighty-two attended the first course and sixty-five enrolled on the second. In addition a number of new courses were produced and a pastoral counselling course, including two residential schools at the college and six months of distance learning, was planned to begin in September 1997. However, by October 1997 there were serious danger signs. Peterson reported to the council that 'the cost of running the Open Learning Centre and the suitability of our material to meet the needs of churches throughout this land continues to cause concern ... some have been critical of the product that we offer and have pointed to inadequacies at different levels'.[37] At the next council meeting Peterson stated that the Open Learning Centre had become too expensive to continue in its present form. The director, Alan Palmer, left his position and oversight was placed in the hands of the vice-principal with Mary Howard handling the day-to-day operation under the supervision of Peter Wood, who was also asked to conduct a

[36] *News Fax*, Issue 7 (Summer 1997), p. 6.
[37] Principal's report, October 1997.

thorough review of distance learning and to prepare proposals for the future. After completing the review, Wood recommended that the college should form a partnership with LBC, who would administer the courses from September 1999 with both colleges together promoting their combined courses. It was pointed out that this would save approximately £15,000 a year in salaries.[38] Significantly Old Oak Alison Le Cornu, who had made a very important contribution to the development of one OHEC course, was in charge of LBC's extension education programme, and she was sympathetic to the OHEC approach to distance learning.

Although OHEC had failed to realize its potential, plans were already being developed for a new programme. In the council meeting that reported the above changes Wood introduced the possibility of beginning an Oak Hill Christian youth work course. Although a number of similar courses already existed, Wood believed that a course with 'a clear emphasis on biblical grounding'[39] might meet a real need. Planning for this new course had begun in late 1998 when a working party consisting of Wood, Weston and three students who had experience in youth and children's ministry met to consider how Oak Hill might contribute to training in that area. In early 1999 Trevor Archer, the pastor of Chessington Evangelical Church, Surrey, enquired whether Oak Hill might be interested in developing such a course and, working with Ian Fry, the schools worker for the Royal Borough of Kingston, in developing such a programme. This provided the critical contact for bringing into being the new programme. Fry had twenty-five years' experience of working with children and young people and taught the youth work module on the Cornhill Training Course. He proceeded to develop a Diploma in Youth and Children's Ministry. At the time of writing this the new course had received approval from Middlesex on the basis of Oak Hill's position as an associate college of the university. Two colourful brochures advertising the

---

[38] College council minutes, 10 February 1999.
[39] Ibid.

course were sent out and a number of students had already applied to begin study in September 2001.

As the college approached the new millennium the most extensive building project in its history was undertaken. This would be Dale's final legacy to the college as chairman of the trust. Peterson explained how he and Dale came to the decision on this project:

> One of my concerns when I first came to Oak Hill was the inadequacy of the facilities. At Moore College we had the opportunity to build a new academic centre, containing lecture rooms and seminar rooms, which dramatically transformed the teaching and life of the college. When Peter Dale visited me in Sydney he had the opportunity to see this new centre, and was most impressed. He and I decided that we should try and promote such a development at Oak Hill.[40]

The work began with renovation work on the old wing. The size of the faculty studies was increased to provide the staff with sufficient room for their books, files and a comfortable place to meet with their tutees. The renovations also provided the students with new bathrooms, a kitchen, and a general improvement in the quality of their rooms, which would also be beneficial for the NTMTC weekends and conference delegates. At the same time the chapel was refurbished by removing the pews and putting in comfortable chairs and carpeting.

The major project was to be a new academic centre. A number of architects put forward ideas for further development of the college facilities and Sheppard Robson won the competition. It was decided to build the new block on the eastern side of the college and to put more student accommodation upstairs in the old house where the seminar rooms had previously been. A great deal of time was spent in the planning process and negotiating with English Heritage and the local planning authority. From the college's point of view the main concern was to obtain a greatly expanded space for the library, two large lecture rooms,

---

[40] Peterson's account.

three seminar rooms and a postgraduate study area attached to the library. In addition, a large foyer where students could meet for coffee and chat was included in the plans. The building was intended not simply to benefit the college but also the wider church, as it would provide an outstanding conference facility. A design was finally agreed with English Heritage and the London Borough of Barnet, who required that the common room must be replaced by a new link between the original house and the student quarters. The common room was therefore relocated to the room that had housed the old library. At the same time the bookshop was moved into the lobby area of the new link.

Work began in the summer of 1999, and during the next year and a half the college campus became a building site. Teaching and other activities had somehow to be carried on as old facilities were torn down before the new ones had been completed. Contractors failed to meet the promised deadlines and in the course of the renovation new problems were discovered: the dining room floor had to be replaced only a week before the first students were due to return. Peterson's problems became even more severe than those facing Maurice Wood with the building of the dining hall and the new wing. The whole college community rose to the occasion and managed to carry on despite the chaotic environment, but special accolades must go to the principal who somehow surmounted one new problem after another and kept the college running in those difficult circumstances. Adrian White, ably assisted by Helen and Tony Archer, kept the domestic side operating even when it seemed as though there would neither be room nor a place to feed the new students when they arrived. Helen Archer remarkably always managed to provide accommodation and keep the students reasonably happy. A week before he was to feed the largest number of American students ever to participate in the programme Tony Archer still had no kitchen and the dining room floor was being replaced. Somehow, the Archers remained at least outwardly calm and all essential services were maintained.

Simultaneously, Peterson faced the challenging prospect of replacing most of his staff. Between the summers of 1998–2000 five members of staff left. When Mike Peat and his wife, Kathy, who had served in the book room, left in summer 1998 the *NewsFax* published a fitting tribute to them, which included the comments of both colleagues and students.[41] Peat had taught doctrine and philosophy and Mike Ovey, the new Kingham Hill Fellow, joined the staff in the September as lecturer in doctrine. Peter Head left on being appointed research fellow at Tyndale House in the spring of 1999. This position involved supervision and teaching at Cambridge University – he would have the opportunity to exercise both his teaching and research gifts. Those gifts, as well as his unselfish commitment to the community, his wonderful sense of humour and his easy-going nature would be greatly missed. Within six months Peterson announced still another loss as Martin Davie was appointed to the joint post of theological consultant to the house of bishops and theological secretary to the Council for Christian Unity. Davie went to a very influential position and his theological acumen would be invaluable to the church leadership, but his teaching, scholarly and administrative skills would be very difficult to replace.

In less than six months Peterson received the news that two more valued colleagues were leaving. Moira Hanson returned to her first love – parish ministry – being instituted to two benefices with five churches in rural Suffolk. She had been on the staff for six years during a significant and sometimes difficult period of transition and she too would be very hard to replace.

Possibly the greatest blow to Peterson came a few months later when he was informed that Paul Weston had accepted the position of general secretary of UCCF. Weston had been Peterson's great support as vice-principal, also serving ably as acting principal while Peterson was on a three-month study leave in the spring of 1999. His knowledge of the Church of England, his wise counsel, his teaching and evangelistic skills seemed irreplaceable. Peterson had lost a valued colleague and friend.

---

[41] *News Fax*, Issue 9 (Summer 1998), p. 4.

To replace those who had left four gifted new staff members were added. Chris Green, who had served eight years as the minister at Emmanuel, Tolworth, Surbiton, in the diocese of Southwark, who had recently completed a commentary on 2 Peter and was a regular lecturer on the Cornhill Training Course, became the new vice-principal. James Robson, who had been reading for an MPhil in New Testament at Oak Hill and teaching Hebrew was appointed for three years as teaching fellow in biblical studies. A new David Field, who seemed to have many of the gifts of his namesake, was appointed to teach doctrine and ethics and Marion Raikes left parochial ministry to take up Moira Hansen's post with the new title of Dean of Women and Pastoral Studies.

At this time a major administrative change took place and a number of long-term members of staff, who were greatly loved and appreciated, were made redundant. The changes came about as the result an evaluation conducted by the Christian management consultancy, Administry, who were appointed in May 1999 to advise on administrative reorganization. The new structure consisted of three departments. An academic dean's department was headed by Paul Woodbridge. A new finance and administrative department was headed by Adrian White, whose title was now Finance Administration Manager. He was joined by Celal Berker in carrying out the responsibilities of that office. A third department was the development department headed by Peter Wood, who was assisted by Clare Osborne as Development Officer and Val Windsor as a part-time assistant. Although the new administrative scheme brought benefits, the cost of introducing it was high. The college community was deeply pained by the loss of four valued members of the non-academic staff: Margie Lane, Dave Peggs, Phylistina Campbell and Susie Liversidge. In addition the introduction of a new telephone system mean that Myra Mill and Jan Wheeler, who served on reception, were also made redundant. The most emotional departure was that of Margie Lane, who had served in different capacities for thirty-one years, and her leaving was deeply regretted by staff and students alike. She was given one of those marvellous going-away parties that Oak Hill was particularly good at organizing, and Cliff Richard, whose study Margie had once cleaned, sent an autographed picture as a tribute to her.

Two more staff losses were not connected with reorganization. In February 1999 Cecily Kirkaldy, an Oak Hill student, who had also served as assistant registrar, died after a four-month struggle with cancer. Her life was a wonderful witness to the Word, and as she fought her terrible illness she was an inspiration to the community in her calm confident faith. Paul Weston led a very moving service at which a tree was planted in her memory. A final loss was the departure of Cilla Tracy in September 2000 after fourteen years of service as the principal's PA. She was especially valued by students for the assistance she gave them in finding places for a first curacy. Those who served as acting principal especially appreciated her knowledge and skill, as did Peterson, as he became familiar with the demands of the principalship. Fortunately, Peterson found an able replacement in Margaret Jellis.

In the midst of all the changes mentioned above, the college was able to enjoy a day of rejoicing and giving thanks to God when the new academic centre was opened by the Archbishop of Canterbury in September 2000. Although the work on the second stage with the new link and renovations to the old house was not really completed until the following Easter, opening the centre in time to begin teaching there in the new century was a major achievement. In expressing gratitude to the trust whose generous financial support had made the new building possible, Peterson gave special thanks to Peter Dale, who had devoted so much time and effort to the building project. Having served on the trust for thirty years and as chairman for almost thirteen of them he had the great satisfaction of seeing his final and most ambitious project completed before handing over the chair to David Monro. In his speech Dale reminded the archbishop of his time on the staff of Oak Hill and that when Carey moved to St John's, Nottingham, he also moved onto a site where their new college buildings were being completed. He also paid tribute to Charles Baring Young, whose endowment fund, wisely invested over the years, had paid the total cost of the building work, which was in the vicinity of £5 million.

In dedicating the new building the archbishop spoke of his own experience at the college and mentioned some of the great men of God who had been trained there. He specifically named Daniel Zindo, who became Archbishop of the Sudan, whom he called 'one of the great missionary bishops in the Sudanese church'. Carey had met Zindo again at the Lambeth Conference and stated 'I shall never forget Daniel's love of God and neither shall I forget his thirst for God's truth and love of the Scriptures.' He then spoke of his vision for the church:

> The church is not simply to 'tell' a story, but to 'proclaim' – to shout out, to blaze forth, to declare with all boldness – the wonderful love of God in Jesus Christ. And we ourselves are to be witnesses of God's redemptive power. We are to show in our lives, both individual and corporate, that we have been built together into a spiritual house that proclaims God's salvation.[42]

Although he probably was not aware of it, he was echoing the words the founder wrote in his 1922 prayer letter, quoted at the beginning of this history, and he could hardly have described more succinctly what has been the college's tradition for almost seventy years. Through all its vicissitudes the college has faithfully sought to proclaim the gospel of Jesus Christ both in word and deed as well as in its expression of community life, and to carry on the mission of training others to be witnesses to the Word. It has begun the new century with a new building, newly renovated old buildings, new staff, new programmes and new emphases. It is in many ways a new college for a new century, but the important things have not changed. As Oak Hill enters the twenty-first century its basic values remain intact and its commitment to training servants of Jesus Christ who will proclaim his gospel in a needy

[42] Sermon by the Archbishop of Canterbury at Oak Hill, 23 September 2000.

world remains constant. All the newness experienced at the end of the old century will be applied to carrying on the unchanging mission, to which the college has been committed throughout its history, in the new century.

Conclusion

The Past and the Future

In appraising what has been accomplished through the seventy years of the college's history it is fitting to ask how far the founder's vision has been fulfilled. To answer this question adequately would involve visiting countless parishes up and down the dioceses of the Church of England, as well as other situations abroad. Here one could hear many a tale of congregations enlivened, communities evangelized, and individuals whose lives have been transformed by God through the faithful ministry of witnesses to the Word who have been sent out from Oak Hill.

Not all former students have remained faithful; there have been casualties who have had for various reasons to leave the ministry, and this is greatly regretted. However, the vast majority can be found week in and week out pointing to Christ in the ministry of Word and sacrament, or exercising other Christian ministries. For those who have taught in the college there has been the satisfaction of seeing so many men, and latterly women, who have come with grave reservations about their own abilities, but who have discovered that the grace of God extends to equipping them for the academic field. Some indeed have discovered a flair for further academic study, and become high fliers in that world.

As the story has unfolded the keynote of the college's development would appear to be the way it has been able to combine a firm loyalty to its theological principles with a flexibility of approach in facing many changes in church and society during the years of its existence. This narrative has shown how changes have been made in admitting first older men, then graduates, clergy and other students from overseas, and women, developing first a part-time course and then distance learning. Perhaps the most significant change of all was its pioneering role in devising courses in which the academic and pastoral requirements for ministerial formation could be brought together in fruitful juxtaposition and achieving nationally recognized validation for those courses through CNAA and later through Middlesex University.

Comparison of the current prospectus with the early ones would pay tribute to the way in which conservative evangelical scholarship has applied itself to be recognized as rigorous and valid and no longer obscurantist. Today's staff has an academic record and degree of teaching professionalism that would not have been dreamed of in the early days. It is encouraging that teaching in a theological college is no longer thought of as a break from the steady run of parochial ministry, but as a career option to be considered, while the college still benefits from recruiting as a proportion of its staff those who have a proven track record in parochial, evangelistic and pastoral ministry.

The provision by the trustees of so much married accommodation on the campus has created a community of Christian people preparing together for various types of ministry. They have enriched one another with a wide variety of experiences of life, and nowhere is it more true than at Oak Hill that the students stand to gain from their peers no less than from the teaching staff. That in turn has required constant re-evaluation of how best the college can meet so many different needs, serving such a diverse student body, and provide the best kind of preparation for a lifetime of fruitful service.

If the college can respond to whatever challenges the future will produce with the same combination of firmness in adhering to its biblical foundations and flexibility in responding to new developments as it has maintained in the past, then it has every prospect of continuing to fulfil its founder's vision and sending out men and women who will be faithful witnesses to the Word.

Select Bibliography

Anon., *The Canons in the Light of 1927–28: A Story of Truth and Faith* (London: Church Book Room Press, 1957).

Archbishops' Commission on Christian Doctrine, *Doctrine in the Church of England* (London: SPCK, 1938).

—, *Christian Believing: The Nature of Christian Faith and its Expression in Holy Scripture and Creeds* (London: SPCK, 1976).

Archbishops' Commission on Evangelism, *Towards the Conversion of England* (Rochester: Parrett & Neves, 1945).

Arnott, Anne, *Wife to the Archbishop: The Life Story of Jean Coggan* (Oxford: Mowbray, 1976).

Barclay, O.R., *Evangelicalism in Britain 1935–1995* (Leicester: IVP, 1997).

Barr, J., *Fundamentalism* (London: SCM, 1977).

Bebbington, D.W., *Evangelicalism in Modern Britain* (London: Unwin Hyman, 1989).

Bradley, I., *The Call to Seriousness: The Evangelical Impact on the Victorians* (London: Cape, 1976).

Briggs, Asa, *A Social History of England* (Harmondsworth: Penguin, 1985).

Bullock, F.W.B., *A History of Training for the Ministry of the Church of England, vol. 3, 1875–1974* (London: Home Words, 1976).

—, *The History of Ridley Hall Cambridge*, 2 vols (Cambridge: Cambridge University Press, 1953).

Chadwick, Owen, *Michael Ramsey: A Life* (Oxford: Clarendon Press, 1990).

—, *The Victorian Church*, 2 vols. (London: SCM Press, 1971).

Chitty, Susan, *The Beast and the Monk: A Life of Charles Kingsley* (London: Hodder & Stoughton, 1974).

Clements, Keith W., *Lovers of Discord: Twentieth-Century Theological Controversies in England* (London: SPCK, 1988).
Coggan, F.D. (ed.), *Christ and the Colleges* (London: IVF, 1934).
Colloms, Brenda, *Charles Kingsley* (London: Constable, 1975).
Cundy, I. (ed.), *Obeying Christ in a Changing World: The People of God* (vol. 2) (London: Collins, 1977).
Cupitt, Don, 'Four Arguments against the Devil', *Theology* (October 1961), pp. 413ff.
Davie, Grace, *Religion in Britain since 1945* (Oxford: Blackwell, 1996).
Davies, G.C.B. *Men for the Ministry: the History of the London College of Divinity* (London: Hodder & Stoughton, 1963)
Dowland, D., *Nineteenth-Century Anglican Theological Training: The Redbrick Challenge* (Oxford: Oxford University Press, 1997).
Dudley-Smith, T., *John Stott: The Making of a Leader* (Leicester: IVP, 1999)
Ellis, I., *Seven against Christ: A Study of 'Essays and Reviews'* (Leiden, Netherlands: Brill, 1980).
Evangelical Alliance, *On the Other Side* (London: Scripture Union, 1968).
Ferris, P., *The Church of England* (London: Penguin Books, 1962).
Furlong, M., *C. of E.: The State It's In* (London: Hodder & Stoughton, 2000).
Gilbert, A., *The Making of Post-Christian Britain: A History of the Secularization of Modern Society* (London: Longmans, 1980).
Grubb, David, *Beneath the Visiting Moon: An English Childhood* (London: Anthony Mott, 1983).
Hastings, A., *A History of English Christianity 1920–1990* (London: SCM, 3rd edn, 1991).
Head, P. (ed.), *Proclaiming the Resurrection* (Carlisle: Paternoster, 1998).
Heasman, K., *Evangelicals in Action: An Appraisal of their Social Work* (London: Geoffrey Bles, 1962).
Hebert, A.G., *Fundamentalism and the Church of God* (London: SCM, 1957).
Heinze, R.W., *The Proclamations of the Tudor Kings* (Cambridge: Cambridge University Press, 1976).
Hempton, D., *Religion and Political Culture in Britain and Ireland* (Cambridge: Cambridge University Press, 1996).
Hick, J. (ed.), *The Myth of God Incarnate* (London: SCM, 1977).

Hillas, C.E., *Recorded Memories: An Autobiography of Canon Leonard Hickin* (Great Missenden, Buckinghamshire: private publication by C.E. Hillas, 1999).
Hylson-Smith, K., *Evangelicals in the Church of England 1734–1984* (Edinburgh: T. & T. Clark, 1988).
—, *The Churches in England from Elizabeth I to Elizabeth II*, 3 vols (London: SCM, vol.1 [1558–1688], 1996; vol. 2 [1689–1833], 1997; vol. 3 [1833–1998], 1998).
Jarvis, A.F., *Charles Baring Young of Daylesford* (London: Church Book Room Press, 1950).
—, *Fifty Years of Kingham Hill* (Kingham, Oxon: The Kingham Hill Trust, 1936).
Johnson, Paul, *A History of the Modern World from 1917 to the 1990s* (London: Wiedenfeld & Nicolson, 1991).
Joynson-Hicks, W., *The Prayer Book Crisis* (London: Pitmans, 1928).
Kaye, B. (ed.), *Obeying Christ in a Changing World: The Changing World* (vol. 3) (London: Collins, 1977).
Lloyd, Roger, *The Church of England 1900–1965* (London: SCM, 1966).
Loane, M., *These Happy Warriors: Friends and Contemporaries* (South Australia: New Creation, 1988).
Manwaring, Randle, *From Controversy to Co-existence: Evangelicals in the Church of England 1914–1980* (Cambridge: Cambridge University Press, 1985).
Marrin, Albert, *The Last Crusade: The Church of England in the First World War* (Durham, NC: Duke University Press, 1974).
Martin, William, *The Billy Graham Story* (London: Hutchinson, 1991).
Masterman, C.F.G., *The Condition of England* (London: Methuen, 1909).
McGrath, Alister, *To Know and Serve God: A Biography of James I. Packer* (London: Hodder & Stoughton, 1997).
McLeod, Hugh, *Religion and Society in England 1850–1914* (London: Macmillan, 1996).
Melinsky, Hugh, *Patterns of Ministry* (London: Church Information Office, 1974 – GS 202).
Mohan, Talbot, *History of Oak Hill College* (unpublished manuscript, 1978).
More, Charles, *The Training of Teachers 1847–1947: A History of the Church Colleges at Cheltenham* (London: Hambledon Press, 1992).
Morpurgo, J.E., *Master of None* (Manchester: Carcanet, 1990).

Murray, I., *Evangelicalism Divided: A Record of Crucial Change in the Years 1950–2000* (Edinburgh: Banner of Truth, 2000).
Neill, Stephen, *Anglicanism* (Harmondsworth, Middlesex: Penguin, 1958).
Newsome, David, *The Victorian World Picture* (London: John Murray, 1997).
Norman, Edward R., *Church and Society in England 1770–1970: A Historical Study* (Oxford: Oxford University Press, 1976).
Packer, J.I., *Fundamentalism and the Word of God: Some Evangelical Principles* (London: IVF, 1958).
—, *Keep Yourselves from Idols* (London: Church Book Room Press, 1963).
—, (ed.), *Here We Stand* (London: Hodder & Stoughton, 1986).
Paul, L., *A Church by Daylight* (London: Geoffrey Chapman, 1973).
Paul, L., *The Deployment and Payment of the Clergy* (London: Church Information Office, 1964).
Peterson, D. (ed.), *Witness to the World* (Carlisle: Paternoster, 1999).
—, *Possessed by God* (Leicester: IVP, 1995).
Pevsner, N., *The Buildings of England: London 4 North* (London: Penguin, 1998).
Randall, Ian, *Educating Evangelicalism: The Origins, Development and Impact of London Bible College* (Carlisle: Paternoster, 2000).
—, *Evangelical Experiences: A Study in the Spirituality of English Evangelicalism 1918–1939* (Carlisle: Paternoster, 1999).
Robinson, John, *Honest to God* (London: SCM, 1963).
—, *The Human Face of God* (London: SCM, 1973).
Schlossberg, Herbert, *The Silent Revolution and the Making of Victorian England* (Columbus, OH: Ohio State University Press, 2000)
Soards, M., *Scripture and Homosexuality: Biblical Authority and the Church Today* (Louisville, KY: Westminster John Knox Press, 1995).
Steer, Roger, *Church on Fire: The Story of Anglican Evangelicalism* (London: Hodder & Stoughton, 1998).
Stibbs, Alan, *The Church: Universal and Local* (London: Church Book Room Press, 1950).
—, *Expounding God's Word* (London: IVF, 1960)
—, *Obeying God's Word* (London: IVF, 1955)
—, *Sacrament, Sacrifice and Eucharist: The Meaning, Function and Use of the Lord's Supper* (London: Tyndale Press, 1961).
— (ed.), *Search the Scriptures* (London: IVF, 1949).
—, *Understanding God's Word* (London: IVF, 1950).

Stott, J.R.W., *Fundamentalism and Evangelism* (London: Crusade, 1957).
—, (ed.), *Obeying Christ in a Changing World: The Lord Christ* (vol. 1) (London: Collins, 1977).
Taylor, A.J.P., *English History 1914–1945* (Oxford: Clarendon Press, 1986).
Thiselton, A., *The Two Horizons* (Exeter: Paternoster, 1980).
Thompson, David, *England in the Twentieth Century* (Harmondsworth, Middlesex: Penguin, 1963).
Towler, R., & Coxton, A.P.M., *The Fate of the Anglican Clergy: A Sociological Study* (London: Macmillan, 1979).
Vidler, Alec, *The Church in an Age of Revolution* (London: Penguin, 1961).
—, *Soundings: Essays Concerning Human Understanding* (Cambridge: Cambridge University Press, 1962).
Welsby, Paul A., *The History of the Church of England 1945–1980* (Oxford: Oxford University Press, 1984).
Wiles, M., *The Remaking of Christian Doctrine* (London: SCM, 1974).
Wilkinson, Alan, *Dissent or Conform: War, Peace and the English Churches 1900–1945* (London: SCM, 1986).
Wolffe, John, *God and Greater Britain: Religion and National Life in Britain and Ireland 1843–1945* (London: Routledge, 1994).
Wood, M.A.P., *Like a Mighty Army* (London: Marshall, Morgan and Scott, 1957).
—, *Your Suffering* (London: Hodder & Stoughton, 1958).
— et al., in Peter Morgan (ed.), *The Anglican—Methodist Conversations* (London: SPCK, 1964).
Yates, T.E., *A College Remembered: St. John's College, Durham 1909–1979* (Spennymoor, County Durham: Macdonald Press, 1982).
Young, C.E.B. (ed.), *Hymns of Prayer and Praise with Tunes* (London: Oxford University Press, 1921).

ACCM/General Synod Reports (in chronological order)

Theological Colleges for Tomorrow, 1968 (the de Bunsen report).
Second Report on the Reorganisation of the Theological Colleges, 1969, CA1766.
Reorganisation of Theological Colleges: Capital Expenditure, 1972, GS 74.
Alternative Patterns of Training, 1975, GS 265.

Theological Training: A Policy for the Future (A Report by the House of Bishops) GS 303.
Theological Training: A Policy for the Future, 1977, GS Misc 57 (the Guildford report).
The Theology of Ordination: A Report by the Faith and Order Group of the Board for Mission and Unity, GS 281.
The First Report of the Working Party on Courses, 1977, GS Misc 62.
The Second Report of the Working Party on Courses, 1977, GS 359.
Theological Training: A Way Ahead, 1992 (the Lincoln report).
Theological Colleges: The Next Steps (London: Church House, 1993).

Author Index

Name Index